JESUS' JUSTICE

JESUS'
JUSTICE

JESUS' JUSTICE

A CRITICAL ANALYSIS OF THE "SOCIAL JUSTICE" MOVEMENT
IN VIEW OF THE MAJESTY, DIGNITY, AND POWER
OF THE LORD JESUS CHRIST

MICHAEL JOHN BEASLEY

Published by:

The
Armoury
Ministries
www.thearmouryministries.org

Jesus' Justice
A Critical Analysis of the "Social Justice" Movement in view of the Majesty, Dignity, and Power of the Lord Jesus Christ
Paperback, ISBN: 978-1-935358-19-0
Hardback, ISBN: 978-1-935358-20-6

Copyright © 9/29/2021 by Michael John Beasley:
Library of Congress Cataloging-in-Publication Data
Copyright Registration Number: TX 9-020-327
by Michael John Beasley
Includes text, artwork, bibliographic references, and index

For more information go to: www.thearmouryministries.org.

Dedicated to
Mr. Granville Sharp, Esq.
a.k.a. G#
1735-1813

Psalm 110

1 A Psalm of David.

THE LORD says to my Lord: "Sit at My right hand,

Until I make Thine enemies a footstool for Thy feet."

2 The LORD will stretch forth Thy strong scepter from Zion,

saying, "Rule in the midst of Thine enemies."

3 Thy people will volunteer freely in the day of Thy power; In

holy array, from the womb of the dawn,

Thy youth are to Thee as the dew.

4 The LORD has sworn and will not change His mind,

"Thou art a priest forever

According to the order of Melchizedek."

5 The Lord is at Thy right hand;

He will shatter kings in the day of His wrath.

6 He will judge among the nations,

He will fill them with corpses,

He will shatter the chief men over a broad country.

7 He will drink from the brook by the wayside;

Therefore He will lift up His head.

JESUS'
JUSTICE

TABLE OF CONTENTS

JESUS'
JUSTICE

Psalm 2:1–6:

*1 Why do the nations rage, And the people plot a vain thing?
2 The kings of the earth set themselves, And the rulers take
counsel together, Against the LORD and against His Anointed,
saying, 3 "Let us break Their bonds in pieces And cast away
Their cords from us." 4 He who sits in the heavens shall laugh;
The LORD shall hold them in derision. 5 Then He shall speak to
them in His wrath, And distress them in His deep displeasure:
6 "Yet I have set My King On My holy hill of Zion."*

INTRODUCTION
WHY DO THE NATIONS RAGE?

There is perhaps no other way to begin this introduction than by saying that *this book is about the longest war in human history*. No, this is not an exaggeration nor is it a cheap effort to garner the reader's attention. The fact is that our entry into the subject of *justice* brings us to the heart of a spiritual conflict that has raged throughout the ages, and is clearly described in the above text of Psalm 2:1-2: "WHY do the nations rage, And the peoples devising a vain thing? 2 The kings of the earth take their stand, and the rulers take counsel together Against the LORD and against His Anointed."

This scene of vehement rage and hostility reveals the tremendous enmity that has existed between humanity and the Creator throughout time. It also exposes what the human race produces as a result of this rage: "vain" things, or *emptiness*.

Remarkably, the psalmist's introductory question, *why do the nations rage?*, is never really answered within the psalm itself. Instead, we are shown the great *object* of humanity's rage: the Lord and His *Anointed* (מָשִׁיחַ > *māśiaḥ, Messiah*). In response to all this the Almighty laughs at His enemies while peacefully sitting on His majestic throne in Heaven. And why is this so? Because the men of the world, even in the full force of their rage, cannot touch divine Omnipotence, nor can they sully His eternal glory. After all, *the inhabitants of the earth are like grasshoppers*[1] and *the nations are like a drop from a bucket*[2] when compared to His eternal majesty. Yet despite humanity's tremendous finitudes, the nations continue in their impotent rage against the very Lord who restrains His wrathful *justice* by means of a patience that is more expansive than the universe itself.

Nevertheless, we must not ignore this unanswered question in Psalm 2 (*why do the nations rage?*) because the Bible is utterly saturated with its answer. They rage because of indwelling sin (Romans 3:1-18). They rage because they refuse to bow the knee to the sovereign Lord and His Anointed King (Psalm 2, Romans 1:18-32). And they rage because they refuse the Almighty's wisdom and justice, doing so out of the vain presumption that their own sense of wisdom and justice is better than His (1 Corinthians 1:18-25).

In the modern day we see evidence of this conflict whenever the masses cry for Social Justice as they deny the Lord's perfect justice as revealed in His Word. This reality isn't always apparent to those who try to understand the contemporary subject of Social Justice because the core tenets of this ideology are hidden beneath a cloud of sophistic rhetoric,

---

[1] Isaiah 40:22: It is He who sits above the vault of the earth, And its inhabitants are like grasshoppers, Who stretches out the heavens like a curtain And spreads them out like a tent to dwell in.

[2] Isaiah 40:15: Behold, the nations are like a drop from a bucket, And are regarded as a speck of dust on the scales; Behold, He lifts up the islands like fine dust.

making it difficult for the average observer to discern its philosophical roots. The only way to burn away this obscuring haze is by shining the light of God's truth on the "wisdom" of Social Justice ideology. By doing so we will find that what is foundational to this seemingly new and popular form of thinking is the very old ideology of Marxism, *but in the modified form of Neo-Marxism.* Upon writing this sentence, I am reminded of the common retorts that typically follow such a charge. For example, Jemar Tisby, a contemporary advocate for Social Justice ideology, attempted to dissociate himself from the Marxist label in his New York Times bestselling book, *The Color of Compromise:*

> Critics will assert that the ideas in The Color of Compromise should be disregarded because they are too "liberal." They will claim that a Marxist Communist ideology underlies all the talk about racial equality.[3]

Tisby has become a popular advocate for the Social Justice movement, especially within the professing church, and therefore his disclaimer is worth noting. Perhaps there are some who actually argue that *classic Marxism* comprises the movement's sole foundation, however, most critics understand that this movement is founded upon a composite structure of Neo-Marxism and Postmodernism (which will be discussed in greater detail in chapter one). Such a composite foundation is especially evident in the teachings of many Social Justice advocates, like Ibram X. Kendi, who has become a prominent and ubiquitous representative of the movement. Kendi has written 5 books on what he calls *antiracism* and serves as the director of the Center for Antiracist Research at Boston University. He also serves as the Frances B. Cashin Fellow at the Radcliffe Institute for Advanced Study at Harvard University and was included in Time Magazine's 100 Most Influential People of 2020. Kendi's Neo-Marxist teachings are quite evident in his books, but

---

[3] Jemar Tisby, *The Color of Compromise* (Zondervan: Kindle Edition), 21.

he too is aware of the concerns that come with such labels. For this reason, he admittedly avoids words like socialist and communist, but instead uses the word *anticapitalist* as a substitute. In his popular book, *How to be an Antiracist,* Kendi describes his own formulation of *antiracist anticapitalism* in view of the contributions of W.E.B. Du Bois' work:

> In the 1920s, W.E.B. Du Bois started binge-reading Karl Marx. By the time the Great Depression depressed the Black poor worse than the White poor, and he saw in the New Deal the same old deal of government racism for Black workers, Du Bois conceived of an antiracist anticapitalism. Howard University economist Abram Harris, steeped in a post-racial Marxism that ignores the color line as stubbornly as any color-blind racist, pleaded with Du Bois to reconsider his intersecting of anticapitalism and antiracism. But the reality of what scholars now call racial capitalism—the singular name of the conjoined twins—made up Du Bois's mind.[4]

Kendi is, to a significant degree, the product of Du Bois' version of *antiracist anticapitalism;* however, he is much more than this. His version of thinking is especially rooted in the more overtly religious form of the Social Justice movement consistent with James Cone, the "scholarly father of Black Liberation Theology"[5] who sought to "revolutionize society"[6] with his Neo-Marxist creed. In many respects, Kendi has become the most prominent torch bearer for Cone's Liberation Theology

---

[4] Ibram X. Kendi, *How to Be an Antiracist* (Random House Publishing Group), 159, Kindle.

[5] In his popular book, *How to be an Antiracist,* Kendi gives significant attribution to James Cone, whom he calls "the scholarly father of Black Liberation Theology." Kendi, *How to Be an Antiracist,* 16.

[6] Ibram Kendi, Presentation on How to Be an Antiracist, Judson Memorial Church in Manhattan, in August 2019.

in the modern day,[7] and this is why the subject of Marxism and Neo-Marxism must be addressed in this book. In a small work titled, *The Black church and Marxism*, Cone strongly advocated for the black church to "take a stand against capitalism and for democratic socialism, for Karl Marx"[8] in order to seek social justice. Cone should be given credit for his openness and honesty in proposing a composite foundation that is built upon religion and "Marxist philosophy":

> Perhaps what we need today is to return to that "good old-time religion" of our grandparents and combine with it a marxist critique of society. Together black religion and marxist philosophy may show us the way to build a completely new society.[9]

In a sense, Cone's baton of a cultural and religious Marxist revolution has been passed on to many in the modern day, and Kendi is currently leading the pack in this race to "justice." But unlike Cone, many who run in this race attempt to cloak their adherence to Neo-Marxist thinking. This is why Tisby's personal disclaimer against Marxism is somewhat of a sleight of hand procedure, especially since he was recently hired as the Deputy Director of Narrative and Advocacy for the Center for Antiracist Research, of which Ibram X. Kendi is the Director and Founder. Such a pairing of these two men is entirely unsurprising.

---

[7] When Cone died in 2018, Kendi wrote of his earlier correspondence with his distant mentor, saying, "He told me he appreciated my work, leaving me in the utter shock of happiness, allowing my life to come full circle...I will always be grateful for the life and work of James Cone." Jamal Watson, "Architect of Black Liberation Theology Dies at 79":
April 29, 2018 https://diverseeducation.com/article/115390/
[8] Cone, James H., *The Black church and Marxism: what do they have to say to each other* (New York: Institute for Democratic Socialism), 205-207, Kindle.
[9] Cone, *The Black church and Marxism*, 237-239, Kindle.

Like Kendi and Tisby, many today have joined forces and are advancing a form of Social Justice ideology consistent with Cone's vision of "religion and marxist philosophy." And this rapidly expanding form of thinking constitutes a Trojan horse that is quickly gaining entrance into the contemporary church. Because of this looming danger to Christ's body, the following subjects will be reviewed throughout the course of this book:

Chapter One: The Ancient Plague of the Muck-Rake Salesmen: In this chapter we will further investigate why the philosophies of Marxism and Neo-Marxism are so diametrically opposed to the wisdom of God. Such ideologies promote a form of justice that is entirely corrupt and hostile to the Gospel. And, as a religious ideology, these philosophies present themselves as a substitute for the Almighty Himself.

Chapter Two: Social Justice Ideology versus Jesus' Justice: Here we will consider how humanity's version of justice falls desperately short of the Lord's perfect and holy justice. Ultimately, any discussion concerning justice must recognize that Jesus' justice is perfect, eternal, and prevails over all.

Chapter Three: The Injustice of Intersectionality and Meritorious Oppression. Various ideologies and traditions have been formulated throughout history in order to address the reality of suffering and oppression. Within Neo-Marxist thinking, oppression establishes a presumption of personal merit and justification for retributive justice. However, God's Word reveals that all such assumptions are a dangerous and corrupting falsehood.

Chapter Four: The Injustice, Ignorance, and Idolatry of Racism. In this section, we consider the severe and dangerous ignorance that exists in the modern day concerning the concept of race and racism. In Scripture, the term race is extremely important and even formulates much of what is foundational to the Gospel itself. History clearly reveals that, without a proper understanding of this term, we all will enter into the dangerous territory of ignorance, idolatry, and gross injustice in our treatment of other members of the human *race*.

Chapter Five: Social Justice Ideology and the Doctrine of Self-Atonement. Cone's amalgamation of "religion and marxist philosophy" should remind us that Social Justice ideology bears the form of a new religion itself. As such, it operates in a similar manner to many other man-made religions that promote faulty systems of penance, absolution, and self-atonement; and the historic atrocities that have come from such invented religions serve as a clear warning to us in the present day.

Chapter Six: Social Justice Ideology and the Tale of Two Kingdoms. According to Scripture, humanity is not distinguished by superficial distinctions such as skin color or ethnicity. Instead, the only division of humanity that the Bible recognizes is this particular binary: the children of God and the lost of this world. This reality underscores why Christians have a form of conduct and culture[10] that is different than the world's. However, the *collectivist* philosophies that lie at the heart of Social Justice ideology pose a direct threat against Christians and even society as a whole. Therefore, this chapter exposes the dangerous aspects of Neo-Marxist *collectivism* that is inherent in this movement.

Chapter Seven: What the Bible Says about Slavery and Man-Stealing. Social Justice advocates repeatedly seek to place the blame of the historic injustices of slavery upon the backs of "white people" of the modern day. In view of this repeated procedure, we will explore the historic concepts and definitions of slavery, what Scripture has to say about slavery, and the Gospel's historic impact on slavery. Taken together, these lessons will aid us in understanding how we should view the history of racial bigotry while examining the Bible's prescriptions against this corrupting disease.

---

[10] The word culture originally referred to worship or reverential homage, but this specific connotation is obsolete and rarely used. Oxford English Dictionary (OED) Second Edition on CD-ROM (v. 4.0) © Oxford University Press 2009.

Chapter Eight: Judgment Begins with the Household of God. In this chapter we will consider the great contrast that exists whenever the Gospel is rightly heralded or grossly obscured in this world, especially where it relates to the foremost commandment of loving God and loving one's neighbor. Sadly, many who have named the name of Christ have fallen short of the Gospel's glorious standard and this has only served to mar the reputation of Christ and His church. Honesty demands a right reckoning of such issues because Judgment begins with the household of God.

Chapter Nine: God's Sovereignty over this World of Systemic Evil. One of the great dangers of Social Justice ideology is that it repeatedly undermines the reality of *systemic evil* and *God's sovereignty over all.* Those who imagine that only a portion of the human race is complicit with the evil of this world, while the rest are not, are engaging in a wild and dangerous fantasy. As well, those who resist the reality of God's sovereign providence will eventually spiral into a downgrade of ingratitude, bitterness, and hopelessness. Without the Gospel, all these dangerous trends are inevitable.

Also within the ninth chapter there is a brief mention of Phillis Wheatley, a slave who was sadly ripped from her country and family in 1761 at the tender age of eight. She came to saving faith in Christ and became a remarkably gifted poet of world renown, even capturing the attention of individuals like Thomas Paine, John Newton, and George Washington. In many of her works she gave glory to God for her salvation, devoid of a spirit of bitterness that is so commonly seen today by those who cry for justice. In fact, Wheatley's poems clearly reveal the contrast between the power of the Gospel versus the destructive influences of Social Justice, as in the case of Chanequa Walker-Barnes, whose recently published poem, *Prayer of a Weary Black Woman*, issues nothing but disdain and vitriol against "white people" even though she claims to be a Christian. The profound difference of spirit and attitude between Walker-Barnes (a highly privileged citizen of the United States) and Wheatley (a slave) could not be more extreme. Walker-Barnes, who petitioned that God would help her to "hate white people" is the clear antithesis to Wheatley who called for others to see "Jesus' blood for your redemption flow, see him with hands out-stretcht upon the cross; immense compassion in his bosom glows." When we compare the words and conduct of these two women we are reminded of the important lesson supplied in 1 John 3:10: "By this the children of God and the children of the devil are obvious: anyone who does not practice righteousness is not of God, nor the one who does not love his brother." Disturbingly, there are many today who claim to be Christians but are instead doing the Devil's bidding in the name of *Social Justice;* and as a result of this, the modern church is being over-run by a new wave of false teachers and spiritual charlatans.

One of the reasons why the modern church is being over-run in this manner is because many church leaders have forsaken Christ's supreme authority over *His church.* By seeking out worldly definitions and standards of justice, these leaders have abandoned the true source of all justice: the Lord Himself. An exchange such as this does far more than generate an abundance of societal chaos; it blasphemes the Lord and corrupts the professing church's Gospel witness.

However, when we consider the Lord's justice, as revealed in Scripture, we find several key terms like *righteousness* (ṣedeq),[11] *perfection* (śālăm), and even *judgment* (miśpāṭ).[12] Such terms and concepts point to

---

[11] Within the semantic domain of the English word justice, Wilson presents צֶדֶק, ṣedeq as the primary term in addition to יָשָׁר (yāśār, straight), שָׁלֹם (śālăm, perfect) and מִשְׁפָּט (miśpāṭ, judgment). William Wilson, *Wilson's Old Testament Word Studies,* (MA: Hendrickson Publishers), 235-36.

[12] "Sovereignty, the legal foundation of government in the sense of ultimate authority or right. Men today are accustomed to finding this in constitutions and the nature of man ("natural rights") but in the Hebrew Scriptures (a) all authority is God's and it is this authority which is denominated mišpāṭ." "The mišpāṭ is God's" (Deut 1:17); Robert D. Culver, "2443 שָׁפַט," ed. R. Laird Harris, Gleason L.

the idea of an *inviolable* and *holy standard* by which all things are to be measured (see appendix I).

This point is crucial to our study because these same terms and concepts are central to the person and work of the Lord Jesus Christ Himself. In fact, before the greatest injustice in all of human history (the crucifixion), Christ quoted from a psalm that clearly reveals His ministry as the *priestly King of Righteousness/Justice* (מַלְכִּי־צֶדֶק, *mǎlkiy-ṣeḏeq*). According to this psalm (Psalm 110),[13] Jesus redeems His people by His *righteousness/justice* (Psalm 110:3-4)[14] and will judge the world in His *righteousness/justice* (Psalm 110:1, 5-6).[15] Clearly, without an apprehension Jesus' eternal justice (Psalm 2; 110; Mark 12:36-37, 14:53-65; Hebrews 1:5; 5:5), there is no sense in which we could rightly adjudicate any discussion of justice, *societal* or otherwise. Those who try to define justice apart from the One who is *holy*, *righteous*, and *eternally just* may as well try to build a sky-scraper without a blueprint or engineer. Thus, seeing that His perfect justice prevails over all, now and forevermore, it is crucial that we pursue the Lord's infallible wisdom as that which will govern our study from beginning to end. To go by any other standard would be an utter waste of time seeing that He is the One who will bring *justice to the nations* (Matthew 12:18)[16] and lead *justice to victory* (Matthew 12:20) with all holiness, power, and perfection.

Archer Jr., and Bruce K. Waltke, *Theological Wordbook of the Old Testament* (Chicago: Moody Press, 1999), 949.

[13] For the N.T. teaching regarding Psalm 110:4, in which the Messiah is identified as "a priest forever according to the order of Melchizedek" (מַלְכִּי־צֶדֶק, *mǎlkiy-ṣeḏeq*), see Hebrews 5:5-10; 6:20; 7:1-28.

[14] See also Hebrews 1:3, 1 John 2:1.

[15] See also Psalm 2:8-12; Hebrews 1:8-9, 13; 10:13; Acts 17:31.

[16] Isaiah 42:1: 1 "BEHOLD, My Servant, whom I uphold; My chosen one in whom My soul delights. I have put My Spirit upon Him; He will bring forth justice (מִשְׁפָּט, *mišpāṭ*) to the nations."

In the end, all of human history resolves to the simple binary of *God's truth* versus *human "wisdom"*; *God's justice* versus *manmade justice*; those who *take refuge in the Lord and His perfect wisdom* (Psalm 2:12) versus *those who rebelliously rage against Him* (Psalm 2:1). Despite all of the complexities and details that one can observe regarding human society, past and present, it all boils down to a simple examination of the *longest war in human history*. And the contest over Social Justice ideology is just another battle within that longstanding war.

JESUS'
JUSTICE

James 3:14–16:

14 ...if you have bitter jealousy and selfish ambition in your heart, do not be arrogant and so lie against the truth.15 This wisdom is not that which comes down from above, but is earthly, natural, demonic.16 For where jealousy and selfish ambition exist, there is disorder and every evil thing..

CHAPTER 1

THE ANCIENT PLAGUE
OF THE MUCK-RAKE SALESMEN

We will begin our examination of Social Justice by taking a brief tour through London's historic Highgate Cemetery. As we walk along a winding path, amidst the Victorian era statues and headstones, we come to discover two memorials which mark a very significant segment of history. One such memorial is the tombstone of Herbert Spencer, the English philosopher and Darwinist who coined the popular phrase, *survival of the fittest.* In his book, *Social Statics,* he criticized the concept of social charity by arguing that such beneficence constituted an *injustice* by preventing "imbeciles" from being withdrawn from society "by death."[17] His work became foundational to the ideologies of *social Darwinism* and *scientific racism.*

---

[17] "Who, indeed, after pulling off the coloured glasses of prejudice, and thrusting out of sight his pet projects, can help seeing the folly of these endeavours to protect men against themselves? A sad population of imbeciles would our

Directly opposite from Spencer's gravesite is the towering bronze bust and granite tomb of Karl Marx. When Marx was buried in 1883, his longtime friend and co-author of The Communist Manifesto, Friedrich Engels, presented a eulogy in which he invoked, not the name of God, but the name of Charles Darwin[18] in his praise of the deceased: "Just as Darwin discovered the law of development of organic nature, so Marx discovered the law of development of human history."[19] His tribute brings to mind the fact that both Marx and Engels had a strong affinity for Darwin, believing that "socialism is indeed the logical outcome of

---

schemers fill the world with, could their plans last. A sorry kind of human constitution would they make for us—a constitution lacking the power to uphold itself, and requiring to be kept alive by superintendence from without—a constitution continually going wrong, and needing to be set right again—a constitution even tending to self-destruction. Why the whole effort of nature is to get rid of such—to clear the world of them, and make room for better. Nature demands that every being shall be self-sufficing. All that are not so, nature is perpetually withdrawing by death." Herbert Spencer, *Social Statics: or, The Conditions essential to Happiness specified, and the First of them Developed,* (London: John Chapman, 1851). https://oll.libertyfund.org/title/spencer-social-statics-1851#Spencer_0331_774.

[18] Engels' mention of Darwin isn't at all surprising. Engels also issued a similar comparison between Marx and Darwin in his preface to the 1888 publication of The Communist Manifesto. "This proposition [the evolution of class struggle], which, in my opinion, is destined to do for history what Darwin's theory has done for biology, we, both of us, had been gradually approaching for some years before 1845." Karl Marx, *The Greatest Works of Karl Marx: Capital, Communist Manifesto, Wage Labor and Capital, Critique of the Gotha Program, Wages, Price and Profit, Theses on Feuerbach* (Musaicum Books: Kindle), 93-94.

[19] Ian Angus, "Marx and Engels...and Darwin? The essential connection between historical materialism and natural selection," *International Socialist Review* (Issue #65, 2 May 2019). https://isreview.org/issue/65.

evolution and that its strongest scientific support is derived from the teaching of Darwin."[20]

It seems quite impossible for any student of history to stand between these two memorials without considering the secularist[21] trifecta they represent: Spencer, Marx, and, by ideological extension, Darwin. All three men were contemporaries of one another who possessed striking similarities and dissimilarities in their beliefs. Concerning their similarities, they were agnostic and philosophically *secular* in their convictions, believing that *morality should be based solely in regard to the well-being of mankind in the present life, to the exclusion of all considerations drawn from belief in God or in a future state.*[22] All three men held to the ideology of *naturalism*, thus excluding any consideration of spiritual or supernatural dimensions of reality.

As for Spencer and Marx, both men saw themselves as champions of *social justice.* In the case of Spencer, he wrote a great deal on the subject of societal justice, advocating a principle he called *equal freedom* in his book, *The Principles of Ethics.*[23] Marx tried to achieve social justice

---

[20] Edward Aveling, "Charles Darwin and Karl Marx: A Comparison" *The New Century Review*, (March-April 1897); Source: Pamphlet published by Twentieth Century Press; Transcribed: by Eric Egerton.

[21] As a point of detail, Marx's tomb was originally placed in another part of the cemetery and was later relocated to its current position, across from Spencer. As well, Marx and Spencer were buried in a section of the cemetery that was reserved for "dissenters" (those who were not members of the Church of England).

[22] secularism (ˈsɛkjʊlərɪz(ə)m) [f. secular a. + -ism.] 1.1 The doctrine that morality should be based solely on regard to the well-being of mankind in the present life, to the exclusion of all considerations drawn from belief in God or in a future state. OED.

[23] Gray, T.S., "Herbert Spencer's Theory of Social Justice – Desert or Entitlement?" History of Political Thought 2, no. 1 (1981): 161-86. Accessed June 7, 2021. http://www.jstor.org/stable/26211771.

through a revolutionary and forceful overthrow of the bourgeois class, requiring the abolition of private property and rights of inheritance while necessitating a governmental control of credit, communication, and the means of production; all of which was to yield a just and harmonious society through the elimination of "class antagonisms."[24]

The legacies these men left behind are only hidden from those who refuse to face history. Spencer's teachings propelled the eugenics movement that took the world by storm, leading to remarkable brutality and death. Marx's vilifying message of bourgeois oppression led to several bloody revolutions and *millions of deaths*: USSR (20 million dead), China (65 million), Vietnam (1 million), North Korea (2 million), Cambodia (2 million), Eastern Europe (1 million), Latin America (150,000), Africa (1.7 million), and Afghanistan (1.5 million).[25] Overall, the ironic and disturbing reality is that neither of these men achieved actual justice, but instead became the founders of incalculable suffering, pain, and death.

By pondering the lives of Marx and Spencer, along with the juxtaposition of their graves, we find a rather stark metaphor lying before us. Just as their tombs diametrically oppose each other, so did their views of justice. Yet despite this opposition, they shared the same secular and godless pathway; a winding trail which leads to nothing but decay and corruption. The reader should know that our visitation to Highgate Cemetery is not an irrelevant detour from our subject at hand, but is instead a crucial reminder that *many* throughout history have sought out justice in this world, fully believing that they were being faithful to their mission. However, this same span of history also reveals an abundance of confusion when it comes to discerning what justice is. Additionally, our

---

[24] In place of the old bourgeois society, with its classes and class antagonisms, we shall have an association, in which the free development of each is the condition for the free development of all. Karl Marx, *The Communist Manifesto* (Sanage Publishing: Kindle), 50.

[25] Stephane Courtois, et al, *The Black Book of Communism* (Harvard University Press, 1999), 3-4.

funerary metaphor should remind us that without *true wisdom there can be no true justice*. In many respects no one should be surprised that the pathway chosen by Marx and Spencer led to such pain and destruction. According to the Word of God, the outcome of these men's lives was entirely predictable for two key reasons:

1. The Wisdom of Man versus the Wisdom of God: Despite their philosophical differences regarding the subject of justice, Marx and Spencer travelled along the same pathway of secularism, resulting in a very predictable outcome. Both men heralded the "wisdom" of man over the eternal wisdom of God, which is a contest that no mere mortal can win. According to God's Word, man's wisdom is *earthly, natural, demonic,* and leads to nothing but *arrogance, jealousy, selfish ambition, disorder, and every evil thing.*[26] On the other hand, God's wisdom reflects His own nature and is therefore perfect,[27] eternal,[28] pure, peaceable, gentle, reasonable, full of mercy and good fruits, unwavering, and without hypocrisy.[29]

As well, since we will be discussing the subject of justice, it is important to note that God's wisdom is *just* by virtue of the fact that He is *just* by nature. Unlike mere mortals, God doesn't merely speak about that which is *just;* instead, He is by nature *just.* This is an important theme found throughout Scripture: the Lord *is a God of justice* (Isaiah 30:18); *righteousness and justice*

---

[26] James 3:14–16: 14 But if you have bitter jealousy and selfish ambition in your heart, do not be arrogant and so lie against the truth.15 This wisdom is not that which comes down from above, but is earthly, natural, demonic.16 For where jealousy and selfish ambition exist, there is disorder and every evil thing.

[27] Psalm 19:8–10: 8 The precepts of the LORD are right, rejoicing the heart; The commandment of the LORD is pure, enlightening the eyes. 9 The fear of the LORD is clean, enduring forever; The judgments of the LORD are true; they are righteous altogether. 10 They are more desirable than gold, yes, than much fine gold; Sweeter also than honey and the drippings of the honeycomb.

[28] Isaiah 40:8: 8 The grass withers, the flower fades, But the word of our God stands forever.

[29] James 3:17.

are the foundation of His throne (Psalm 89:14); and therefore, He is a God of faithfulness and without iniquity, *just and upright is He* (Deuteronomy 32:4). As a result of this essential nature of His we also understand that His character is just such that His is a kingdom of *justice and righteousness* and He reigns with true wisdom. The Lord *loves righteousness and justice* (Psalm 33:5); He condemns all expressions of injustice (Micah 2:1-3); He curses the unjust (Deut. 27:17) calls injustice an abomination (Proverbs 17:15) and promises judgment upon all who commit injustice (Proverbs 19:5). Unlike mere mortals, *there is no contradiction in God's nature and message of justice.*

This is why we began with a brief visit to Highgate Cemetery, traversing the pathway which led us to the graves of Marx and Spencer. As we consider this important subject of *justice,* we must face a very crucial fork in the road, leading either to God's wisdom and life while the other leads to human "wisdom," death, *and every evil thing.* The choice is quite simple, but it must be made with much solemnity and careful consideration.

2. There is Nothing New Under the Sun: There is another reason why the pathway traversed by Marx and Spencer had a predictable outcome and it is rooted in the truth of *Ecclesiastes 1:9-10: 9 "That which has been is that which will be, and that which has been done is that which will be done. So, there is nothing new under the sun. 10 Is there anything of which one might say, 'See this, it is new?' Already it has existed for ages which were before us."* This particular text is remarkably important to grasp because it reminds us that history serves as a faithful tutor for those who are willing to receive its pedagogy. This is why those who fail to learn from history are often doomed to repeat it.

As we examine the tutelage of history we see that countless ideologies of justice have been surmised, claiming to offer a new understanding of the human condition, but in the end they aren't new at all. All such human reason and knowledge is to be found along the same, well-trodden pathway of secularism, leading its followers away from the wisdom of God. Thus, Ecclesiastes 1:9-10 offers an important anchor to the modern mind.

Every generation has claimed to have discovered a new ideology or technology that will usher the world into Utopian bliss, but humanity's well-worn pathway has led to heartache, pain, agony, and death throughout time, being generationally repeated with haunting precision. In an age of spaceflight, bio-engineering, satellite communications, and countless electronic devices in our homes and hands, it is tempting to think that mankind is somehow changed by these innovations. But nothing could be further from the truth. If you could give Pol Pot access to all of the aforementioned technology, his essential being would not be improved at all. Instead of having a *new man* you would have the same murderous dictator who is now armed with a *new technology* which offers a greater capacity for death and destruction. The point is simply this: our social, material, and technological environment changes all the time, but human nature never changes.

These crucial principles will guide us throughout the course of this book, especially as we consider how the ideologies of Marxism, Neo-Marxism, and Social Justice are overtaking contemporary society *and the professing church*. Anyone who has taken the time to read books dealing with the Social Justice movement will notice several surviving strands of Marxist thinking in their writings, especially with authors like W.E.B. Dubois, Theodore W. Allen, James Cone, and, more recently, Ibram X. Kendi (among others). All such authors advocate a form of a modified *Neo-Marxism*, but with a *Postmodern* bent. Two such influences must be considered for the sake of our study:

1. From Marxism to Neo-Marxism: A central tenet found within the Social Justice movement has to do with the *oppressor* and *oppressed* binary view of society. In classical Marxism, we find this division (by economic distinction) in the opening words of the Communist Manifesto: "I. Bourgeois and Proletarians: The history of all hitherto existing society† is the history of class struggles. Freeman and slave, patrician and plebeian, lord and serf, guild-master‡ and journeyman, in a word, *oppressor and oppressed*, stood in constant opposition to one another, carried on an uninterrupted, now hidden, now open fight, a fight that each time ended, either in a revolutionary reconstitution of society at large, or in the common ruin of the contending classes."[30] Marx's strict emphasis on materialism led him to this division on the basis of economic factors. However, within the Social Justice movement, with its Neo-Marxist and Postmodern influences, society is still seen as consisting of this *oppressor* and *oppressed* binary, but now this distinction is principally established by social and cultural factors. Within this new framework, the Social Justice movement presents the oppressor class as consisting of "white supremacy" and the oppressed as consisting of "people of color."

As James Cone wrote in his work, *The Black Church and Marxsim:* "The development of a world capitalist economy utterly dominated by, and structured in the interest of, Western Capitalism made the white European civilization (which includes the United States) lord of the earth."[31] Through the teachings of Cone and many others, the Social Justice movement sustains the Marxist binary narrative of *oppressor and oppressed*, but with *white systemic racism* as being the foundation of nearly all discernable inequities within society.

2. From Collectivism to Neo-Collectivism: Another important distinctive of the Social Justice movement has to do with *Neo-Collectivism*. As already reviewed, Marx laid great stress on the *oppressor* and *oppressed* classes within society. He was persuaded that this simplistic division of society was reasonable, partly in view of his belief in materialistic determinism: "It is not the consciousness of men that determines their existence, but, on the contrary, their social existence determines their consciousness."[32] Such reasoning as this established the key building block for his collectivist thinking whereby people were classified based upon their *societal and material conditions in life,* effectively abolishing any notions of *individualism.*[33] This same building block

---

[30] Karl Marx, *The Communist Manifesto* (Sanage Publishing), 26-27, Kindle, italics mine.

[31] Cone, *The Black church and Marxism*, 332-333.

[32] Karl Marx, *A Contribution to The Critique Of The Political Economy* (Chicago: Charles H. Kerr & Co.), 92, Kindle.

[33] The word *individualism* is utilized in this book in view of its secondary connotation of *free agency* and *personal responsibility*: "The social theory which advocates the free and independent action of the individual, as opposed to

of thinking also laid the foundation for stressing *communal cooperation* between individuals for the greater good of all. In Friedrich Engels' *Draft of a Communist Confession of Faith*,[34] he asserts that "the happiness of the individual is inseparable from the happiness of all."[35]

For Marx and Engels, there was only one pathway to such communal happiness (as already mentioned): the abolition of private property and inheritance rights along with the requirement of a governmental control of credit, communication, and means of production. Of course, this led to a loss of individual freedom, and, with it, *individualism.* Those who failed to comply with this "pathway to happiness" were deemed enemies of the people. Today, such elements of collectivist thinking are similarly found within the Social Justice movement, but with a modified binary: *allies* and *enemies* of Social Justice. Anyone who bothers to view the news in the current day is likely aware of what can happen to those who dare to question or critique the tenets of Social Justice teaching: too often they are silenced from various internet platforms, receive societal vilification, and some even lose their employment. Like its ideological predecessor, Neo-Collectivism has little room for nuanced debate, nor does it offer special consideration of the individual's personal beliefs or character. Conformity or nonconformity with the dictates of Social Justice determines an individual's standing as an *ally* or *enemy.*

Ibram Kendi offers such a binary mandate in his popular book, *How to be an Antiracist*: "Antiracist policies cannot eliminate class racism without

---

communistic methods of organization and state interference. Opposed to collectivism and socialism." OED.

[34] Prior to the completion of the Communist Manifesto, Engels and Marx interacted frequently with one another about the development of several founding documents. In June 1847, Engels had written a *Draft of a Communist Confession of Faith* in catechetical form containing 22 questions and answers. In November of that year, Engels advised Marx against the use of the expression, confession of faith: "Give a little thought to the Confession of Faith. I think we would do best to abandon the catechetical form and call the thing Communist Manifesto." Eventually, the substance of the *Draft of a Communist Confession of Faith* would provide the core substance of the *Principles of Communism*.

[35] Marx, *Communist Manifesto*, 70.

anticapitalist policies...To love capitalism is to end up loving racism. To love racism is to end up loving capitalism. The conjoined twins are two sides of the same destructive body...Capitalism is essentially racist; racism is essentially capitalist. They were birthed together from the same unnatural causes, and they shall one day die together from unnatural causes."[36] Kendi then adds this binary ultimatum a few chapters later: "We cannot be antiracist if we are homophobic or transphobic."[37] For Kendi, such is the new pathway to harmony and happiness, and all must decide if they are allies or enemies to his particular version of justice.

The subjects of Marxism and Neo-Marxism often provoke a variety of responses among scholars today. Some wholly embrace their Marxist or Neo-Marxist connections while others, in an effort to avoid such labels, will twist and contort themselves in what appears to be an impressive game of sophistic-dodgeball. Especially when it comes to those manifestations of Social Justice teaching that have entered into the church, significant effort is frequently made to veil the Neo-Marxism that is inherent to this new movement. This is especially apparent in the writings of Ibram X. Kendi: "I keep using the term 'anticapitalist' as opposed to socialist or communist to include the people who publicly or privately question or loathe capitalism but do not identify as socialist or communist."[38]

As well, James Cone criticized himself for his early failures to unveil his Marxist convictions. According to him, this was due to his struggles with being identified with the Marxist community, as he describes in *The Black church and Marxism:*

"It was an intellectual failure on my part that I did not deal with marxism and socialism when I wrote Black Theology and Black Power which was published in 1969. Neither did the issue of socialism appear in my A Black Theology of

---

[36] Kendi, *How to Be an Antiracist,* 159-63.

[37] Ibid., 197.

[38] Ibid., 160.

Liberation (1970) and God of the Oppressed (1975). But…I have been convinced that the black church cannot remain silent regarding socialism, because such silence will be interpreted by our Third World brothers and sisters as support for the capitalistic system which exploits the poor all over this earth.[39]

Perhaps more than anyone else, Cone has been instrumental in introducing the Marxian *oppressor* and *oppressed* binary into the professing church with many of his followers preaching the message of "white European [capitalist]" oppression. In his writings, Cone frequently vilifies "whites" as being *inherently incapable* of making "any valid judgment about human existence,"[40] while insisting that such thinking is not evidence of racial bigotry. In one example, Cone cites James Baldwin who wrote in, *Letter from a Region in My Mind*: "it is not hard for him ("the Negro") to think of white people as devils." Baldwin's justification for such suspicion was that "most Negroes cannot risk assuming that the humanity of white people is more real to them than their color." It is in this context that Cone defended Baldwin, insisting that such presumption and vilification is not an example of racial bigotry:

"This feeling should not be identified as black racism. Black racism is a myth created by whites to ease their guilt feelings. As long as whites can be assured that blacks are racists, they can find reasons to justify their own oppression of black people."[41]

---

[39] Cone, *The Black church and Marxism*, 100-106.

[40] "If there is one brutal fact that the centuries of white oppression have taught blacks, it is that whites are incapable of making any valid judgment about human existence. The goal of black theology is the destruction of everything white, so that blacks can be liberated from alien gods." James Cone, James H., *A Black Theology of Liberation - Fortieth Anniversary Edition* (Orbis Books), Kindle.

[41] James Cone, *Black Theology and Black Power* (Orbis), 17, Kindle.

31

It is disturbingly ironic that both secular and religious manifestations of Social Justice ideology claim to be against *racial bigotry*, when in reality the movement repeatedly advances *racial bigotry*.[42] The illogical nature of such thinking seems to know no bounds, and this movement appears to permeate every sector of society; even that of the medical community.

Writing for the Journal of the American Psychoanalytic Association, NYU Psychoanalytic Institute faculty member, Donald Moss insists that "Whiteness is a condition one first acquires and then one has—a malignant, parasitic-like condition [for which there is] not yet a permanent cure."[43] It should be quite evident that such thinking is highly reflective of Marx's *materialistic determinism*, but with a Neo-Marxist

---

[42] It should be noted that Kendi is not as blatant as Cone when discussing the "white community." In his book, *How to be an Antiracist*, Kendi makes an effort to distance himself from some of the overtly racist comments given by some advocates of Social Justice, however, he still maintains a rigid oppressor versus oppressed – "white" versus "black" narrative of society which ultimately belies such efforts.

[43] "Whiteness is a condition one first acquires and then one has—a malignant, parasitic-like condition to which "white" people have a particular susceptibility. The condition is foundational, generating characteristic ways of being in one's body, in one's mind, and in one's world. Parasitic Whiteness renders its hosts' appetites voracious, insatiable, and perverse. These deformed appetites particularly target nonwhite peoples. Once established, these appetites are nearly impossible to eliminate. Effective treatment consists of a combination of psychic and social-historical interventions. Such interventions can reasonably aim only to reshape Whiteness's infiltrated appetites—to reduce their intensity, redistribute their aims, and occasionally turn those aims toward the work of reparation. When remembered and represented, the ravages wreaked by the chronic condition can function either as warning ("never again") or as temptation ("great again"). Memorialization alone, therefore, is no guarantee against regression. There is not yet a permanent cure." Donald Moss, "On Having Whiteness," *Journal of the American Psychoanalytic Association (JAPA)*, Volume: 69 issue: 2, page(s): 355-371.

and Postmodern twist. Instead of an *economic determination* of one's class, a person's epidermis becomes *determinative* of their class as either *oppressor* or *oppressed* within a world that is presumed to be ruled by "white supremacy." Within such reasoning, having a light epidermis automatically corresponds to a classification of *oppressor*. This is why many within the Social Justice community constantly engage in public denunciations and self-loathing confessionals renouncing "whiteness." For example, Jessica Bridges, an Oklahoma State University teaching assistant, openly repented before her peers concerning her sin of being a "white" Spanish teacher:

> "Racism originates with and is perpetuated by white people. Learning Spanish from a white woman - I wish I could go back and tell my students not to learn power or correctness from this white woman. I would tell them to stand in their own power. White isn't right. I'm holding myself accountable to this journey. Part of my accountability is to continue the struggle and grapple my internalized white supremacy. Dismantling white supremacy in society looks like dismantling white in my heart first. It means that I am not going to teach Spanish. Accountability is ongoing because there is no end to the process."[44]

Unfortunately, none of Jessica's colleagues participating in the zoom call had the wherewithal to remind her that the Spanish language originated from the *European* nation of Spain, the native population of which consists of a broad spectrum of skin colors, including the now dreaded "white" skin. Yet such facts, details, and nuanced historical consideration have no place in the world of Social Justice. It would appear that Jessica wants everyone to know that she is an *ally of justice*, and her public self-denigration should prove the point. Within the binary, Neo-Collectivist

---

[44] Oklahoma State teaching assistant says she can't teach Spanish because she's White. (Southern Connecticut State University's 2021 Virtual Women's and Gender Studies Conference) https://www.foxnews.com/us/oklahoma-state-teaching-assistant-spanish-white.

world of Social Justice, Jessica will likely spend her days seeking ally-ship out of the sheer dread of being labelled an "enemy of justice." All of this constitutes a remarkably confusing and sad display of intellectual and spiritual bankruptcy. We could easily go on, *ad nauseam*, reviewing similar examples, but this is not the point and focus of this book.

Returning to our analogy of the fork in the road, leading either to the wisdom of God or of man, we are reminded that our focus must be set on the better pathway of the two. If we were to employ our time and energy cataloguing all that can be found along the pathway of Social Justice, this book would transform into a multivolume series and would prove to be an exhausting waste of time. While I certainly salute those who expend much energy discerning the nuanced details of *Social Justice,* to include some of its related categories of *Racial Justice, Economic Justice, Environmental Justice, Critical Theory, Critical Race Theory,* and *Intersectionality (just to name a few)*; I certainly have no intention of replicating such efforts.

The good news is that it is not necessary to become a degreed member of this movement in order to see whether it is promoting truth or error, just as it isn't necessary to have an engineering degree in order to comprehend that pigs don't fly. Yet it is important to compare and contrast some of the central tenets of Social Justice ideology to that of God's Word. To do this we will focus on three key reasons why the Social Justice movement is a dangerous philosophy:

1. Social Justice Collectivism vs. God's Wisdom: As already reviewed, Neo-Collectivism is inherently problematic in view of its diminished valuation of the individual. When overly simplistic classifications of humanity are established, *by human judgment,* this often leads to the *careless* abuse of others. For centuries history has broadcasted this lesson and yet the advocates of Social Justice are persuaded that their new version of collectivistic thinking will work this time in their pursuit of genuine justice and peace.

However, when we go to God's Word we find that the Lord Himself does not judge humanity in this manner. He instead judges on the basis of His holy justice and sees each person *individually,* no matter what their social or material circumstances may be (this will be our primary focus in chapter 2). Whenever we classify and treat others in a manner that contradicts God's ways and wisdom, *it is an affront to the Creator.*

2. Social Justice Racialism vs. God's Wisdom: One of the core problems with Social Justice ideology has to do with the transformation of language. When reading the related materials of this movement, one will find deeply sophistic efforts to retool and redefine the meaning of various words. Unsurprisingly, several lexicons have been developed in order to track and discern such linguistic contrivances.

One key word that has been dramatically retooled is the word *race.* As delineated by Social Justice advocates, the very concept of "race" was *invented as a ruling-class social control*[45] mechanism that is designed to preserve the power and privileges of the "white" population.[46] Interestingly, Social Justice teachers correctly identify that this use of the word *race* is a faulty contrivance, and yet they repeatedly employ it anyway. Kendi acknowledges this contradiction, calling such an approach *ironic* yet *necessary.*[47]

What is actually ironic about this methodology is that the Social Justice movement resultantly promotes the very same forms of ignorant discrimination they claim to oppose. Such a procedure of utilizing contrived and faulty language yields a great deal of confusion and sets an unsettling precedent. The thought of employing the tools of ignorance and evil (whether real or perceived) should be repulsive to anyone with a modicum of moral sense. In view of this, many have charged that the Social Justice movement is in fact *racist* in view of its binary "white" vs. "black" narrative. I would modify this charge by saying that it actually promotes *racial bigotry.* By adding the

---

[45] Jeffrey Perry, Introduction to *The Invention of the White Race,* Part 1, by Theodore Allen (Veso Books), 119, Kindle.

[46] Ibid.

[47] "It is one of the *ironies* of antiracism that *we must identify racially* in order to identify...racial privileges and dangers [italics mine]." Kendi, *How to Be an Antiracist,* 38.

substantive word *bigotry* I seek to preserve the meaning of the word race while exposing the unreasonable and faulty nature of how the term is used and serially abused. When we employ the word bigotry, we are speaking of someone who has an unreasonable devotion to a developed ideology or opinion. This is what we find with the advocates of Social Justice: an unreasonable devotion to a contrived connotation of race which bears the destructive result of casting human beings into the sorting bins of "white" and "black," oppressor and oppressed, without any significant consideration of the individual. Clearly, such racial bigotry is ignorant, hateful, divisive, and utterly destructive to society.

However, while we could expend an abundance of ink and paper discussing just how destructive this is to society as a whole we must remember that there are far greater issues that extend beyond the temporal cares of this life and reach into eternity itself. Ultimately, we must understand that *all racial bigotry is a blasphemous affront to Christ's majesty, dignity, and power.* Because of this, our primary focus will be set upon what God's Word has to say about this very important term, *race.* For us to understand the value of the *human race*, we must look to the One who created all of humanity for His manifest glory.

3. Social Justice Religion vs. God's Wisdom: Karl Marx wrote that religion "...is the opium of the people. The abolition of religion as the illusory happiness of the people is required for their real happiness."[48] This is why both Marx and Engels envisioned a world in which Communism would *supersede* and *replace* religion, resulting in true freedom and joy. Friederick Engels wrote in his draft of the *Communist Confession of Faith* that "...communism is that stage of historical development which makes all existing religions superfluous and supersedes them."[49] Actual history reveals that such *supersession* has led to the vilification and persecution of religion, resulting in the exaltation of the state as its replacement.

When we consider the Neo-Marxist strands of influence within the Social Justice movement we find that even its most secular expressions bear a striking resemblance to organized religion. In many respects, Social Justice

---

[48] Karl Marx, Friedrich Engels, *On Religion* (Dover Publications), 42, Kindle.
[49] Marx, *Communist Manifesto*, 76.

ideology has its own doctrinal creed, prescribed confessions, and its "gospel" message of freedom through societal justice. Its disciples are called woke, an obsolete past tense form of wake – related to the word *awakening* which is often used in reference to spiritual revival. The movement continually seeks new converts (allies) and repeatedly enjoins its followers to grow in their commitment to the cause of liberation from oppression.

Liberation Theology, which is embraced by James Cone and Ibram X. Kendi, is the *overtly religious* branch of the Social Justice movement and includes a complex infusion of various allegorical interpretations from the Bible. In both its secular and overtly religions forms, this movement presents its own Neo-Gospel which proselytizes others to become committed allies for the hope of creating a world that will be *forever free* from the oppression of white supremacy. As such, both versions of this movement present a message of freedom which supersedes humanity's true need for freedom from the slavery to sin. As Jesus said, "Truly, truly, I say to you, everyone who commits sin is the slave of sin…If therefore the Son shall make you free, you shall be free indeed" (John 8:34, 36).

Unlike the message of Social Justice, the biblical Gospel reveals that humanity's true need does not center upon deliverance from earthly oppression, but rather deliverance from the wrath of the One who will someday judge the world in righteousness/justice.[50]

Remarkably, the Social Justice movement is being pushed on modern society with the fervor of a religious cult and most of its representative messiahs will not take no for an answer. As such, it presents itself as a modern day savior even though it has no power to redeem our broken humanity. Because of its veil of religion, many within the professing church have come to believe that this movement is an ally to the message of the Gospel when in fact it only introduces the dross of secularism. But of course, this is not the first time that the professing church has allowed

---

[50] Acts 17:31: because He has fixed a day in which He will judge the world in righteousness through a Man whom He has appointed, having furnished proof to all men by raising Him from the dead."

the tadpole of error into its ranks.[51] Still, this movement, as armed with its Neo-Collectivism, corrupted views of race, and its veil of religion, has nothing to offer whatsoever when it comes to the subject of the true and eternal freedom that only Jesus Christ can give. Overall, this movement elevates itself as *the true pathway of wisdom and freedom*, and is therefore *an idolatrous and blasphemous affront to the majesty, dignity, and power of the Lord Jesus Christ.*

Because of this movement's deeply flawed views of justice, I will utilize the label *Social Justice Ideology* (SJI) from this point forward. In addition to simplifying the text of this book, such a label should remind us that this movement is just another debatable *ideology.*[52] In free societies, all *ideologies* must be subject to critical analysis in order to determine their validity or the lack thereof. However, whenever such critical analysis is shunned or prohibited, untested ideologies can be transformed into something that is very destructive: mandated dogmas. Sadly, in more and more states throughout the nation, SJI has become *a mandated, canonical standard.*

Despite this, as long as America remains a free society, SJI must be subject to critical evaluation in the public square even though many of its advocates seek to silence any and all dissent. Whatever freedoms are retained or lost in this nation, the greatest question that still remains for

---

[51] "If anyone wishes to know where the tadpole of Darwinism was hatched, we could point him to the pew of the old chapel in High Street, Shrewsbury, where Mr. Darwin, his father, and we believe his father's father, received their religious training. The chapel was built for Mr. Talents, an ejected minister; but for very many years full-blown Socinianism has been taught there, as also in the old chapel at Chester, where Matthew Henry used to minister, and where a copy of his Commentary, of the original edition, is kept for public use, the only witness, we fear, to the truths he taught there." Charles Spurgeon, *The Down-Grade Controversy*, (Sword and Trowel: April, 1887) 262, Kindle.

[52] The substantive, *ideology*, will be an important reminder that this ubiquitous movement is nothing more than a systematic collection of interpretations and ideas about the world in which we live which must be scrutinized and debated.

every individual is this: "am *I* walking on the pathway of *truth* or of *error?*" This particular *binary division* constitutes the fork in the road leading either to *manmade justice* or *Jesus' justice.* Ultimately, the eternal state of our souls depends on which of the two paths we take.

Finally, before proceeding to the next chapter, I would like to offer a simple yet powerful image derived from John Bunyan's classic allegory, *The Pilgrim's Progress;* one which supplies a striking picture for our overall study. In part II of *The Pilgrim's Progress,* we find that the lead character, Christiana, was taken by the one who was called The Interpreter to a room where she was shown a very interesting scene where a man is found with a muck-rake in hand:

"The Interpreter took them aside again and led them first into a room where there was a man who could look no way but downwards and who had a muck-rake in his hand. Another individual stood over his head with a celestial crown in his hand and offered to trade him the crown for his muckrake, but the man neither looked up nor regarded it, but raked to himself the straw, the small sticks, and dust of the floor. Then Christiana said, 'I'm persuaded that I know something of the meaning of this, for this is a figure of a man of this world, is it not, Good Sir?' 'You've said it rightly,' said the Interpreter, 'and his muckrake shows his sinful mind. And in that you see him rather paying attention to raking up straw, sticks, and the dust of the floor rather than to what He who calls to him from above says, it is to show that Heaven is only like a fable to some and that things here are accounted the only things substantial. Now, in that it was also showed you that the man could look no way but downwards, it is to let you know that when they are with power upon men's minds, earthly things quite carry their hearts away from God.'"[53]

What is so remarkable about this portion of Bunyan's allegory is that it encapsulates so much of what the entire Bible teaches. The Muck-Raker

---

[53] John Bunyan; Hazelbaker, L. Edward, *The Modern English Edition of Pilgrim's Progress* (Bridge-Logos), 5969-5979, Kindle.

is nothing more than a portrait of a person who is a slave of his own making, believing that the cares of this temporal world (sticks, straw, and the dust of the floor) constitute the most important focus in life. He is therefore incapable of looking up to the riches of Christ (the celestial crown). Because of his preoccupation over earthly things, *his heart is carried away from God.*

Such an image as this encapsulates a great deal of my concern over SJI. There is within this Neo-Marxist and Postmodern movement a constant drive to secure power and wealth from those who are deemed the *oppressor class.* Thus, according to the Communist Manifesto, the "oppressed" who seek such revolution "have a world to win."[54] And so one must wonder what would happen if the advocates of SJI succeed in their *Neo-Marxist revolution.* What if this movement could secure all that the world has to offer in terms of wealth and power, seizing it all from the "white oppressors"? According to Jesus, it would still amount to nothing *without Him*:

Matthew 16:26: 26 "For what will a man be profited, if he gains the whole world, *and forfeits his soul?*"[55] (italics mine)

We all must guard against the grave danger of being drawn away from Jesus and His saving grace for a *faux* justice which cannot save. Thus, my challenge; my encouragement; my *warning* to you is simply this: Anyone who comes to you with a message of "justice," devoid of the truth of Jesus'

---

[54] Marx, *Communist Manifesto*, 63.

[55] Matthew 16:24–27: 24 Then Jesus said to His disciples, "If anyone wishes to come after Me, let him deny himself, and take up his cross, and follow Me.25 "For whoever wishes to save his life shall lose it; but whoever loses his life for My sake shall find it. 26 "For what will a man be profited, if he gains the whole world, and forfeits his soul? Or what will a man give in exchange for his soul? 27 "For the Son of Man is going to come in the glory of His Father with His angels; and WILL THEN RECOMPENSE EVERY MAN ACCORDING TO HIS DEEDS.

justice, is nothing more than a *professional muck-rake salesman*. What they are offering is a dangerous distraction from Christ and His eternal kingdom, and it is a *blasphemous plague.*

Dear reader, my simple appeal to you is that you would forsake their wares and flee to the King of Righteousness who no longer remains in the tomb, but has risen from the dead and will come again in glory to judge the living and the dead *with perfect justice.* Flee to Christ and to the celestial crown of life that only He can give, for only He can give you true freedom and eternal joy.

JESUS'
JUSTICE

CHAPTER 2

SOCIAL JUSTICE IDEOLOGY
VERSUS JESUS' JUSTICE

Without God's wisdom, mankind's understanding of justice is deeply flawed and tremendously dangerous. And when we distill the particular version of justice found within Marxism and Neo-Marxism, we discover a disturbing system of thought that is rooted in *societal retribution*.[56] This is evident in light of the fact that, for Marx, the Proletariat had been robbed of their fair share throughout history and the only *just* response was to take back what had *presumably* been taken from them. The construct of such thought is simple enough: the injustice of *past thievery* can only be corrected by *present thievery*. Of course, Marx died before he could witness what his monstrous imaginations would produce in the real world: the history of his brainchild, Communism, speaks for itself.

When people are led to believe that they are justified in stealing the property and rights of others they will predictably commit horrific

---

[56] "to give in return; to repay; to retaliate." OED.

acts *in the name of justice.* When it comes to the Neo-Marxism of SJI, we find the disturbing recapitulation of this same form of thinking in advocates like Ibram X. Kendi:

> "The only remedy to past discrimination is present discrimination. The only remedy to present discrimination is future discrimination."[57]

This simple postulate regarding prejudicial discrimination formulates the centerpiece of Kendi's *anti-racist* agenda and it clearly advances a Neo-Marxist agenda. When reading this for the first time, I was struck by its plainness and honesty. To his credit, this clear declaration of his well distills much of the logic of SJI, doing so in a manner that is transparent, though disturbing. To suggest that present discrimination can serve as a remedy for past discrimination is an inherent contradiction even based upon Kendi's own definitions. In his book, *Stamped from the Beginning*, Kendi clearly expressed his disgust over prejudicial discrimination. When mentioning the O. J. Simpson trial, he made this sweeping judgment of America as a whole, saying: "...discrimination was everywhere in 1995 for people who cared enough to open their eyes and look at the policies, disparities, and rhetoric all around them."

    Throughout his writings, he makes it quite evident that he understands *prejudicial discrimination* to be *unjust,* yet he seems to imagine that an *unjust means* can lead to a *just end.* Such is Kendi's fundamental fallacy. What Kendi and others like him are advocating is the promotion of *unjust retributive discrimination* under the pretext of Social Justice. In short, this is a philosophy of *vindication* on the basis of an individual's epidermis. But rather than solving the problems of past and present discrimination, such thinking obliterates the best achievements of the civil rights movement here in America. Most importantly, it blasphemes the God of all true justice.

---

[57] Kendi, *How to Be an Antiracist,* 19.

One of the ways in which we learn about SJI's twisted version of justice is by examining how its advocates interpret and utilize highly publicized and controversial court cases. A favorite among SJI authors is that of the O. J. Simpson trial. That particular case was unique since it dominated the news cycle, 24/7, in a manner not before experienced in American society. Media outlets were busy pumping out updates around the clock and most stations had no hesitation to make prejudgments long before the jury reached its conclusion. During this same time I recall preaching a message on the text of Deuteronomy 19:15-21, which deals with the principles of biblical jurisprudence. In this message I issued solemn warnings regarding the sin of presumption, the need for evidence on the basis of witnesses, and the dangers of pre-judging issues before facts can be known. Not once did I mention the O. J. Simpson trial. I didn't have to. All of us at that time were so drenched in the ether of media conjecture that the relevancy of Deuteronomy 19 was *self-evident.*

What became clear during that time is that certain court cases have the potential of being forged into juridical tools to be used by activists within the media and society at large; and these tools can be weaponized, before, during, *and long after a case's conclusion* in order to advance certain narratives about justice. For example, in the fifth chapter of *How to Be an Antiracist,* Kendi recalls his childhood memory of hearing that O.J. Simpson was pronounced not guilty for the murders of Nicole Brown Simpson and Ron Goldman:

"When 'not guilty' sliced the silence like a cleaver, we leapt from behind our desks, shouting, hugging each other, wanting to call our friends and parents to celebrate...Over in Manhattan, my father assembled with his accounting co-workers in a stuffed, stiff, and silent conference room to watch the verdict on television. After the not-guilty verdict was read, my father and his Black co-workers migrated out of the room with grins under their frowns, leaving their baffled White co-workers behind. Back in my classroom, amid the hugging happiness, I glanced over at my White eighth-grade teacher. Her red face shook as she held back tears…I smiled at her—I didn't really care. I wanted O. J. to run free. I had been listening to what the Black adults around me had been lecturing about for months in 1995. *They did not think O. J. was innocent of murder any more than they thought he was innocent of selling out his people. But they knew the criminal-justice system was guilty, too.*"[58]

What is so striking about this passage is the manner in which Kendi objectifies O. J. Simpson and the murder victims, reducing them to mere puzzle pieces within his broader schematic of "racial" and social justice. Thus, the details of this case essentially vanish amidst his *neo-collectivist* agenda in which he divides America into the oppressor and oppressed classifications as promoted by SJI.

Popular author, Baptist minister, and television host, Michael Eric Dyson, expressed similar sentiments in a 2005 interview for the PBS/Frontline program, *The O. J. Verdict*.[59] When asked if African Americans who were "rejoicing" over Simpson's acquittal believed that he was innocent of murder, Dyson responded, "Absolutely not. I don't think we should make the mistake of believing that black people who celebrated a) thought O. J. was innocent, or b) were even concerned most about O. J. as opposed to their Uncle Charlie or Bubba or their sister Shanaynay or their Aunt Jackie, who had been screwed by a system that never paid attention to them." In this same interview, Dyson repeatedly paralleled Kendi's objectification of Simpson saying, "O. J. was a term that represented every black person that got beat up by the criminal justice system, and now we have found some vindication, and guess what, white America? It was with a black man that you loved." Similar to other SJI advocates, Kendi and Dyson have no timidity when presuming to speak for "white" and "black America."

---

[58] Kendi, *How to be an Antiracist*, 19.

[59] Michael Eric Dyson, "The O. J. Verdict" (PBS/Frontline, 10/4/2005). https://www.pbs.org/wgbh/pages/frontline/oj/interviews/.

In the end, their overall judgment of an entire nation remains the same: America is condemned as "discriminatory" and "racist" and deserves the retribution of having a presumed murderer set free.

One must wonder how such "justice" will impact the United States and other nations throughout the world, especially when *skin color formulates the basis of such compensatory retribution*. If we fail to learn from history regarding the dangers of such thinking, then there is little hope for a course reversal in the present day.

Whatever the expositors of SJI may say about the importance of Simpson's acquittal, there is nothing just or righteous about a *presumed* murderer escaping condemnation. Whenever mere mortals presume the right to adjudicate their own standards of justice, chaos is the guaranteed outcome. One act of evil is never cancelled by more evil; sin is never nullified by more sin, and for this reason we must "never pay back evil for evil to anyone." (Romans 12:17). But when it comes to the question of justice for the act of murder, the command of God is quite clear and *truly unimpeachable*:

Genesis 9:6: "Whoever sheds man's blood, by man his blood shall be shed, for in the image of God He made man."

This brief passage reveals much about the differences between the Lord's justice and the "justice" proffered by SJI. The valuation of a single human life is not found in some tabulation of discriminatory sins found within any given society. Instead, the valuation of a single human life is found, exclusively, *in the Creator Himself*: "in the image of God He made man." Though an entire book could easily be generated from this statement alone, we should at least note the crucial nature of this lesson: The value of a single human life is inestimable by virtue of the inestimable value of the Creator. The depth and breadth of this consideration is tremendous. Should any one of us ever nullify the value of a single human life, whether by superficial classifications (skin color, ethnicity, social status), or by

47

some contrived *ideology*, one that ignores the value of the individual for other causes, *this is nothing other than an affront to the Creator.* The thought of anyone *of any skin color* rejoicing over a *presumed* murderer's release is plainly disturbing *in view of God's perfect justice.*

The reader should know that what Kendi and Dyson promote is consistent with the thinking and reasoning of the *ideology* of Social Justice overall. Common among SJI advocates is a broad emphasis placed on societal policies and institutions, yielding nothing more than a loss of individualism and, with it, a corruption of genuine justice:

1. **Neo-Collectivism and the Loss of Individualism:** Kendi and Dyson's treatment of Simpson reveals how *collectivism,* along with its emphasis on *societal systems,* destroys the individual's importance and personal responsibility. By using Simpson as a mere tool within their SJI arguments they make light of questions regarding his "individual traits like character or merit,"[60] or even his guilt. For them, the trial was about *the system* versus *the black community*, and O.J. Simpson was only a tool within this contest.

2. **Neo-Collectivism and the loss of Genuine Justice:** By making Simpson nothing more than a sacrificial pawn for the cause of Social Justice, all questions regarding his guilt or innocence were rendered irrelevant. If Simpson was guilty, those who used him as a tool had no regard for the *injustice* of his release. This is a corruption of genuine justice at every level. According to the logic of SJI, Simpson was a carrier of "all the righteous anger that black people had,"[61] such that his presumably undeserved acquittal, though unjust, was beneficial because it sent a *"wakeup call to white America."*[62] Within the world of SJI, this is "justice."

---

[60] James Lindsey, Critical Race Theory, New Discourses
https://newdiscourses.com/2021/04/critical-race-theory-two-page-overview/.
[61] Dyson, "The O.J. Verdict."
[62] Ibid.

How does all this square with Jesus' justice? In short, SJI's version of justice is utterly condemned by the Lord's standard. With Jesus' justice, everything falls beneath His holy and righteous judgment, not only in His adjudication of societal systems, *but especially in view of His judgment of the individual.*

In Scripture we find a powerful display of this reality just prior to the greatest injustice ever committed in human history: the brutal crucifixion of the Lord Jesus Christ. In His final days, during what is commonly called Passion Week, Christ was received in the city of Jerusalem with great praise and fanfare from the people. They heralded Him as the *son of David*[63] while crying out: "Blessed is the coming kingdom of our father David; Hosanna in the highest!"[64] Yet this festive moment was quickly disrupted when Christ entered the Temple and, in His just and righteous indignation, cast out all who were buying and selling, overturning the moneychangers' tables, and condemned them for making the Temple of God a "robbers' den." In the days leading up to His arrest, Jesus taught the people in parables while the religious leaders questioned His authority to do so. As Christ taught in the Temple, He delivered several stern rebukes against the unrighteous acts of Israel's religious leaders, thereby provoking a remarkable public contest.

In the synoptic Gospels we find that the Pharisees, along with some of Herod's representatives,[65] sought to trap Christ with a question about paying taxes to Caesar. Then some Sadducees asked Him a question about the resurrection of the dead,[66] followed by a scribe's question regarding which commandment is the foremost of all, wherein Christ responded by heralding the commandment of love for God and

---

[63] Matthew 21:9.

[64] Mark 11:10.

[65] Mark 12:13.

[66] Matthew 22:23-33; Mark 12:18-27; Luke 20:27-38.

49

man.[67] Because of the remarkable teachings of Christ, all in attendance became quiet. It was then that Jesus pierced through the silence with a question of His own about Psalm 110:

> Matthew 22:42–46: 42 "What do you think about the Christ, whose son is He?" They *said to Him, "The son of David." 43 He *said to them, "Then how does David in the Spirit call Him 'Lord,' saying, 44 'THE LORD SAID TO MY LORD, "SIT AT MY RIGHT HAND, UNTIL I PUT THINE ENEMIES BENEATH THY FEET" '? 45 "If David then calls Him 'Lord,' how is He his son?" 46 And no one was able to answer Him a word, nor did anyone dare from that day on to ask Him another question.

Christ's audience was stumped because of this important query: why would David call his descendent, *Lord*? The inferred answer is that David called Him Lord because "the Christ" (the Messiah) *was his superior*. By introducing Psalm 110 in this manner (a psalm that would become the most quoted Old Testament text in all of the New Testament),[68] Christ was revealing the crucial reality of His eternal Lordship and supremacy as the King of Righteousness. To a society that was steeped in systemic unrighteous, Christ's pedagogy was crucial. The masses who cried out, "Hosanna to the son of David...*the coming kingdom of our father David*," demonstrated that their focus was more *earthly and temporal*,[69] with a

---

[67] Matthew 22:34-40; Mark 12:28-34; Luke 20:39-40.

[68] (Psalm 110:1-2: Matthew 22:44, 26:62; Mark 12:36, 14:62; Luke 20:42-43; 22:69; Acts 2:34-35; 1 Corinthians 15:25; Ephesians 1:20; Colossians 3:1; 1 Peter 3:22; Hebrews 1:3, 13; 8:1; 10:12-13; 12:2. Also, Psalm 110:3: Hebrews 5:6; 6:20; 7:17, 21).

[69] "The concept of a kingdom 'coming' is familiar from Mark 1:15 and Mark 9:1, but that was the kingdom of God announced by Jesus. The kingdom of David has an altogether more political and nationalistic ring." R. T. France, *The Gospel of Mark*, A Commentary on the Greek Text, New International Greek Testament Commentary (Grand Rapids, MI; Carlisle: W.B. Eerdmans; Paternoster Press, 2002), 434.

view to political reforms rather than the eternal reforms promised in the *Messiah's kingdom*. However, texts like Psalm 110 make it clear that the Lord's kingdom will not be a *temporal kingdom of David*, but the *eternal kingdom of the Messiah, who serves in the order of Melchizedek – the King of Righteousness*:

> Psalm 110: 1 A Psalm of David. THE LORD says to my Lord: "Sit at My right hand, until I make Thine enemies a footstool for Thy feet." 2 The LORD will stretch forth Thy strong scepter from Zion, saying, "Rule in the midst of Thine enemies." 3 Thy people will volunteer freely in the day of Thy power; In holy array, from the womb of the dawn, Thy youth are to Thee as the dew. 4 The LORD has sworn and will not change His mind, "Thou art a priest forever According to the order of Melchizedek (מַלְכִּי־צֶדֶק, *mălkiy-ṣedeq*)." 5 The Lord is at Thy right hand; He will shatter kings in the day of His wrath. 6 He will judge among the nations, He will fill them with corpses, He will shatter the chief men over a broad country. 7 He will drink from the brook by the wayside; Therefore He will lift up His head.

Because of the importance and gravity of this Psalm, I would encourage the reader to consult Appendix I, *Psalm 110 – Jesus, The King of Righteousness*, for further consideration of its message. But for the sake of our brief study in this section we will review why it is that Christ questioned His hearers about the meaning of this psalm, and how it relates to His teaching just prior to His crucifixion.

Psalm 110 is often referred to as a *royal* and *messianic* psalm in view of its description of the promised Messiah's *monarchial reign* and *priestly labors* as the *King of Righteousness/Justice (Melchizedek, mălkiy-ṣedeq)*. Uniquely, this Priest-King is Himself eternal, just as the office He holds is eternal (Psalm 110:4, Hebrews 7), and He exercises His dominion over just two categories of people: *1. His enemies who rebel against His monarchial authority (Psalm 110:1-2, 5-6); and 2. His redeemed people who "volunteer freely" as willing servants (Psalm 110:3)*.

51

Christ's mention of Psalm 110 exposed much of the confusion that prevailed among the people concerning the Messiah. At the time, the people believed that the Messiah would be a descendant of David *in the flesh* and nothing more. They did not understand that He was also David's Lord as the exalted King of kings.[70] Different rabbinic traditions abounded during this time, with some speculating that King Hezekiah would return as the Messiah.[71]

Overall, the people's expectation about the coming kingdom of God remained focused on earthly, temporal solutions. We especially see this when, after Jesus fed the 5,000 in the sixth chapter of John, many came to believe that He was the promised Prophet of Deuteronomy 18:18-19 and sought to "take Him by force to make Him king" (John 6:15). In light of their desire for earthly reforms and freedom from Roman rule, they "wanted someone to rule them who would feed them and guarantee their security."[72] However, the fact that the people believed they could take this King of kings by force[73] and make Him a monarch by their own will[74] clearly reveals their ignorance regarding the majesty, dignity, and power of the Son of God. All this confusion over who the Messiah would

---

[70] "Naturally speculation was rife as to who the Messiah would be, and Scriptural texts were studied for enlightenment. On one point the Rabbis were unanimous, viz. he would be just a human being divinely appointed to carry out an allotted task. The Talmud nowhere indicates a belief in a superhuman Deliverer as the Messiah." Abraham Cohen, *Everyman's Talmud*, (BN Publishing), 458, Kindle.

[71] Ibid.

[72] Frank R. Gaebelein, ed., *The Expositor's Bible Commentary*, Vol 9 (MI: Zondervan Publishing, 1981), 72.

[73] ἁρπάζειν: "to grab or seize by force, with the purpose of removing and/or controlling." Johannes P. Louw and Eugene Albert Nida, *Greek-English Lexicon of the New Testament: Based on Semantic Domains* (New York: United Bible Societies, 1996), 220.

[74] ποιήσωσιν [>ποιέω] βασιλέα: There is no sense of an appeal for cooperation in what is presented in the text. The verb employed here speaks of the agency of one prevailing over that of another.

be, and what His kingdom would be like, is why Jesus' mention of Psalm 110 was so crucial. By citing this important psalm, Jesus was reminding all who heard Him that the coming kingdom was *His kingdom* and it would be established in *His righteousness/justice* (צֶדֶק, *ṣeḏeq*), *forever*. Moreover, when the nations are judged by the Lord and His anointed King (Psalm 110:1-2, 5-6; 2:8-12) the hearts, minds, intentions, and actions of *all*[75] will be adjudicated with holy perfection. As a result of such judgment the Lord will clearly disclose those who are His *willing servants* versus those who are His *enemies among the nations*.

With the introduction of this psalm the Lord was giving His audience a foretaste of His coming justice, especially as He issued a series of verbal rebukes against those who were practicing evil.[76] In Matthew's gospel, we find 7 pronouncements of judgment against the scribes and the Pharisees, whereby Christ called them hypocrites, blind guides, whitewashed tombs full of dead men's bodies, murderers, and serpents who are worthy of hell. In Mark's Gospel, we are taught that these false leaders sought to cloak their corruption with "long robes," "respectful greetings in the market places," "chief seats in the synagogues," and "places of honor at banquets."[77] This they did while committing the treacherous act of stealing widows' houses while offering long prayers for appearance' sake. Christ offered no justification for such conduct, nor did He excuse any sin because of the centuries of oppression and injustice endured by the Jewish people. Yet, amidst Christ's rebukes against all this systemic corruption, a remarkable event took place which should draw our attention:

Mark 12:41-44: 41 And He sat down opposite the treasury, and began observing how the multitude were putting money into the treasury; and many

---

[75] Matthew 25:31-46.

[76] Matthew 23:1-36, Mark 12:38-40, Luke 20:45-51.

[77] Mark 12:38-40.

rich people were putting in large sums. 42 And a poor widow came and put in two small copper coins, which amount to a cent. 43 And calling His disciples to Him, He said to them, "Truly I say to you, this poor widow put in more than all the contributors to the treasury; 44 for they all put in out of their surplus, but she, out of her poverty, put in all she owned, all she had to live on."

Mark's description of the tithes offered by the multitudes, along with the widow, tells us much about the nature of Judaism in the 1st century. At this time the Temple in Jerusalem had become a busy and bustling center of religious activity, and yet much of it consisted of the mere appearance of devotion. The priesthood itself, along with the organized system of tithing, had become grossly corrupt. The Jewish historian Josephus described such corruption by calling the High Priest Annas (also known as Ananias[78]) "a great hoarder of money;" his servants were known to take the tithes "by violence" and he often used these temple offerings to secure "presents" for others in order to curry political favor.[79] Such a context as

---

[78] This Ananias was not the son of Nebedeus, as I take it, but he who was called Annas or Annanus the Elder, the 9th in the catalogue, and who had been esteemed high priest for a long time; and besides, Caiaphas his son-in-law had five of his own sons high priests after him, who were those of numbers 11, 14, 15, 17, 24, in the foregoing catalogue. Nor ought we to pass slightly over what Josephus here says of this Annas or Ananias, that he was high priest a long time before his children were so, he was the son of Seth, and is set down first for high priest in the foregoing catalogue, under number 9. He was made by Quirinus, and continued till Ismael, the 10th in number, for about twenty-three years; which long duration of his high priesthood, joined to the successions of his son-in-law, and five children of his own, made him a sort of perpetual high priest, and was perhaps the occasion that former high priests kept their titles ever afterwards; for I believe it is hardly met with before him. Flavius Josephus and William Whiston, *The Works of Josephus: Complete and Unabridged* (Peabody: Hendrickson, 1987), 538.

[79] "...as for the high priest Ananias, he increased in glory every day, and this to a great degree, and had obtained the favor and esteem of the citizens in a signal manner; for he was a great hoarder up of money; he therefore cultivated the

this helps us to understand, in part, why Jesus sternly rebuked those who had turned the Temple into a "den of thieves."

Not only was there corruption among the priests, but many of those who served as the teachers of Israel (scribes and Pharisees) were repeatedly rebuked by Christ for their false piety, hypocrisy, and corruption of God's authority. Instead of being the faithful stewards of God's Word, they had exalted an entire system of oral traditions which empowered themselves, abused the people, and nullified the Scriptures, as Jesus said: "Neglecting the commandment of God, you hold to the tradition of men...You nicely set aside the commandment of God in order to keep your tradition."[80] So great was the exaltation of their oral traditions that, salvation (they taught) could only be obtained by those who equated such oral traditions with the authority of God's Word.[81] This made the authority of these false leaders *appear* to be inviolable. Clearly, *systemic corruption* covered Jerusalem like a thick cloud, and yet the poor widow's sacrificial gift was, "in Christ's eyes, worth more than all the

---

friendship of Albinus, and of the high priest, by making them presents; (206) he also had servants who were very wicked, who joined themselves to the boldest sort of the people, and went to the threshing floors, and took away the tithes that belonged to the priests by violence, and did not refrain from beating such as would not give these tithes to them. (207) So the other high priests acted in the like manner, as did those his servants without anyone being able to prohibit them; so that [some of the] priests, that of old were wont to be supported with those tithes, died for want of food." Ibid.

[80] Mark 7:8-9.

[81] "The Halacha or traditional law, as developed and settled by the labours of the scribes, was declared to be as legally binding as the written Thorah. R. Eleasar of Modein said: He who interprets Scripture in opposition to tradition has no part in the world to come." Emil Schürer, *A History of the Jewish People in the Time of Jesus Christ* (Capella Press), 9988, Kindle.

other money cast into the treasury."[82] By the assessment of mere mortals, her gift was small, but the Lord knew that "she put in all that she owned" whereby He adjudged her offering as consisting of "more (πλεῖον, *pleion*) than all the contributors."

By this brief example we are reminded that Lord not only sees the broader realities of systemic evil in this world, but He also sees and adjudicates the actions, thoughts, and motives of every single individual, *for better or for worse*:

> "I, the LORD, search the heart, I test the mind, Even to give to each man according to his ways, according to the results of his deeds." (Jeremiah 17:10).[83]

In all of this we can easily see the gargantuan difference between SJI and the Lord Himself. The former renders its broad and sweeping judgement of everything based upon faulty collectivist presumptions; but the Lord issues *true justice* in view of His perfect, holy, *and Omniscient judgment of everything and everyone*. In the case of the widow, we are not told what happened to her two small copper coins. We don't know if they went towards the service of the Temple or if they were confiscated by Annas and his henchmen only to be used for treacherous purposes. All that we know is that her singular act was a distinguishable rebuke of the systemic

---

[82] "Our gifts are not to be measured by the amount we contribute, but by the surplus kept in our own hand. The two mites of the widow were, in Christ's eyes, worth more than all the other money cast into the treasury, for 'she of her want did cast in all that she had, even all her living." Charles Spurgeon, "The Best Donation" (Sermon #2234, Metropolitan Tabernacle, 1891).

[83] In Jeremiah 17, the Lord rebukes those who *trust [חֹטֵ, bāṭaḥ] in mankind* (v. 5-6) versus those who *trust [חֹטֵ, bāṭaḥ] in the Lord* (vs. 7-8). The former is like a bush in the desert (v. 6), but the latter is like a *tree planted by the water* (v. 8). God not only sees the external fruit of all, but He sees the hearts and minds of all. Though men may be confused when evaluating the life and doctrine of others (Matthew 13:24-30), the all-knowing, all-seeing God is never confused with such matters.

evil all around her. In the end, we must remember that the things unseen, ignored, or misunderstood by mere mortals are never unseen, ignored, or misunderstood by the all-knowing Lord, for "no creature is hidden from His sight, but all things are open and laid bare to the eyes of Him with whom we have to do" (Hebrews 4:13).

Alternately, sinful mortals repeatedly render their judgments of others on the basis of ignorance and prideful presumption (Proverbs 13:10). This predictably leads to an unjust adjudication of others on the basis of superficial classifications such as ethnicity, social status, or physical appearance. All such presumptions are wholly corrupt and contradict the One who renders His perfect judgment *of everything* with a righteous adjudication of the individual's heart, mind, ways, and deeds no matter what their ethnicity, social status, or physical appearance may be. Clearly, there is no comparison between mankind's "justice" versus that of the King of justice/righteousness.

And so it is that, throughout this time of Passion Week (Matthew 21:1-26:16; Mark 11:1-14:11; Luke 19:29-22:6), Jesus taught the multitudes about the nature of His coming kingdom. Before He was finally betrayed, arrested, falsely accused in a sham trial, mocked, brutalized, and crucified, Jesus taught the people about the coming days of tribulation, the nature of His second coming, and the reality of His final judgment of the nations of mankind in which He will condemn some to eternal punishment, but others, His willing servants, will enter into eternal life (Matthew 25:31-46). As such, His work would not result in a reformed Roman Empire, or yield any other temporal, earthly kingdom;[84] nor would Christ seek to establish justice by means of *injustice*. Instead, the Messiah's great work would bring about a holy, just, and eternal kingdom that is comprised of those who know, trust, love, and follow Him.

---

[84] John 18:33-38.

Jesus' teaching regarding His kingdom reflects a crucial truth that is found throughout Scripture. From Genesis to Revelation, we repeatedly find this simple, twofold categorization of humanity: *Those who believe in the Lord and serve Him, versus those who rebelliously rage against the Lord and His Messiah (Psalm 2).* Such a twofold categorization as this reveals the Lord's particular focus on every member of the human race *as individuals.* This reality pierces through the aforementioned classifications of humanity often cherished in secular society: ethnicity, societal rank, gender, professional status, wealth, and physical appearance (whether skin color or anything else). Such classifications as these, no matter how much they are exalted in any given society, cannot augment or diminish an individual's status in the eyes of God; after all, *God is not a respecter of persons.*[85]

In the end, no matter what can be said about a person's background, genealogy, or social status, the only thing that matters is this aforementioned, God-ordained binary: those who pay homage to King Jesus and those who don't. This important principle is clearly disclosed in Psalm 2, as previously reviewed within the introduction:

Psalm 2:7–12: 7 "I will surely tell of the decree of the LORD: He said to Me, 'Thou art My Son, Today I have begotten Thee. 8 'Ask of Me, and I will surely give the nations as Thine inheritance, And the very ends of the earth as Thy possession. 9 'Thou shalt break them with a rod of iron, Thou shalt shatter them like earthenware.'" 10 Now therefore, O kings, show discernment; Take warning, O judges of the earth. 11 Worship the LORD with reverence, And rejoice with trembling. 12 Do homage to the Son, lest He become angry, and you perish in the way, For His wrath may soon be kindled. How blessed are all who take refuge in Him!

With striking similarity to Psalm 110, this popular messianic text promises certain judgment for those who refuse to bow before the

---

[85] Acts 10:34.

Messiah in all his monarchial glory: "Do homage to the Son, lest He become angry." However, glorious blessings are promised to all those who *"take refuge in Him."* We must take special note of this idea of taking refuge in the Messiah. The Hebrew word translated as *take refuge* (חָסָה, *ḥāsâ*) speaks of the trust one has in a place of safety, like someone who hides in a shelter from a rainstorm.[86] When it is used figuratively, it can speak of someone who vainly trusts in the power and protection of a nation,[87] or in false gods.[88] But in Psalm 2:12, it clearly speaks of the genuine faith and trust one places in the Son of God and in the protection and salvation He alone can provide. Such trust and genuine faith is known by the Lord (Jeremiah 17:7), *who sees the heart and tests the mind (Jeremiah 17:10).*

Knowing this important truth helps us to understand what we have reviewed concerning Passion Week. During this time Jesus issued many judgments against religious *groups* and *individuals* alike for their corruption; clearly, the *system* of Judaic religion during this time was fraught with sin. However, such corruption could never impede the genuine faith and devotion of those *individuals* who sought out Christ in faith: like the scribe who was "not far from the kingdom of God"[89]; like the Roman Centurion who witnessed Christ's death, saying "truly this was the Son of God";[90] like Joseph of Arimathea, who was a "respected member of the council [of the Sanhedrin]" but was looking for the kingdom of God in his ministry to Christ;[91] and like the believing thief on the cross who asked Christ to remember him when He entered into His kingdom.[92] Examples

---

[86] Isaiah 4:6; 25:4; Job 24:8.

[87] Isaiah 30:2.

[88] Deuteronomy 32:37.

[89] Mark 12:28-34.

[90] Luke 23:47-49.

[91] Mark 15:43.

[92] Luke 23:39-43.

such as these reveal a timeless lesson for all generations: in this world of systemic evil, those who take refuge in the Son find a true haven of eternal peace, rest, and *true justice*; but those who supplant His authority and justice *resultantly blaspheme His name and thereby stand condemned.*

By mentioning this serious matter of *blaspheming the Son of God,* I would like to draw the reader's attention to some important, concluding thoughts, especially since I have already asserted that the "Social Justice" movement is a *blasphemous affront* to the majesty, dignity, and power of the Lord Jesus Christ. By asserting this charge of *blasphemy,* I realize that this may confuse, disturb, or even shock some. It is often the case that words like this are seen as petty pejoratives containing little substance or meaning, but in the case of the word *blasphemy* (G. βλασφημία, *blasphēmia*), we find an abundance of important meaning. It generally refers to abusive or derisive speech and is frequently used in the New Testament to describe those who attempt to mock God and His authority.

A term such as this should remind us that many individuals and ideologies stand as a blasphemous affront to the Almighty. This is especially evident with respect to the *faux* trial of Christ. When the Savior was being tried by the Council of the Sanhedrin, just before His crucifixion, Caiaphas, the high priest, demanded that He answer this question: "tell us whether You are the Christ the Son of God." Jesus first answered in the affirmative, saying, "I am," and then quoted, *once again,* Psalm 110:1 in addition to Daniel 7:13: "...and you shall see THE SON OF MAN SITTING AT THE RIGHT HAND OF POWER, and COMING WITH THE CLOUDS OF HEAVEN." Those who heard Him that day had no difficulty understanding what was said. Jesus' overall response affirmed that He was *the* Son of God possessing magisterial authority over all the nations (Psalm 110:1), and His allusion to Daniel 7:13 revealed that He was the promised Messiah whose kingdom is eternal, *never to be destroyed.*[93] Upon hearing this, Caiaphas tore his robe and said to the

---

[93] Daniel 7:13–14: 13 "I kept looking in the night visions, And behold, with the clouds of heaven One like a Son of Man was coming, And He came up to the

Council, "what further need do we have of witnesses? You have heard *the blasphemy*" (Mark 14:53-65, italics mine). Such an accusation is both *ironic* and *horrific.*

Ironically, Caiaphas and the Council believed that they were upholding *true justice* through their verdict. However, by rendering such an accusation, *they themselves were guilty of blasphemy against the Lord Jesus Christ.*

Horrifically, having called the King of *Righteousness* a practitioner of *unrighteousness,* they were replicating the wickedness of those who rage against the Lord and His Anointed (the Messiah). The very image of Caiaphas (a frail and sinful priest of the temporal order of Aaron)[94] reviling *the Great High Priest,*[95] whose priesthood is rooted in divine Omnipotence, monarchial righteousness, and eternal efficacy (Psalm 110:4, Hebrews 5:7-10, 7:11-8:2), truly strains the bounds of credulity.

Jesus' repeated use of Psalm 110, this time in the presence of Israel's most revered authorities, clearly exposed the longstanding antithesis that exists between human concepts of justice and the Lord Himself. By falsely accusing Jesus in this manner, these Jewish leaders were blaspheming the majesty, dignity, and power of Jesus Christ. I say the *majesty of Christ* because they were denying His kingly rule and authority; I say *His dignity* because they were denying His divine dignity and worthiness to be glorified as *the* righteous and just Son of God; and I say *His power* because they had rejected the fact that, in Him, all the fullness of deity dwells (Colossians 2:9).[96] And this blasphemy of theirs led

---

Ancient of Days And was presented before Him. 14 "And to Him was given dominion, Glory and a kingdom, That all the peoples, nations, and men of every language Might serve Him. His dominion is an everlasting dominion Which will not pass away; And His kingdom is one Which will not be destroyed.

[94] Hebrews 5:1-3, 7:23-28.

[95] Hebrews 4:14.

[96] Colossians 2:9: For in Him all the fullness of Deity dwells in bodily form,

to the greatest injustice in all of human history when their rebellion led to the crucifixion of the *King of Righteousness*.

How stunning it is that the One who could have turned His accusers into an ash heap instead restrained Himself in His infinite mercy and patience. It is also stunning that Jesus' accusers believed they were *serving the cause of justice* even though their blasphemous denial of Christ made them the promoters of *profound injustice*. This isn't just ironic, *it is horrifically demonic*, and it stands as a solemn lesson for us all.

Sometimes those who profess to be the advocates of justice are instead doing the very opposite, and this is true in any generation. And though we live in a day where the reigning chorus of many is that *the only remedy to past discrimination is present discrimination*, this is nothing more than a well-polished, well-published, and well-promoted machination of gross injustice. Above all, it is a blasphemous affront to Jesus and His holy justice.

J E S U S'
J U S T I C E

Matthew 11:28–30:
28 "Come to Me, all who are weary and heavy-laden, and I will give
you rest. 29 "Take My yoke upon you, and learn from Me, for I am
gentle and humble in heart; and YOU SHALL FIND REST FOR YOUR
SOULS. 30 "For My yoke is easy, and My load is light."

CHAPTER 3

THE INJUSTICE OF INTERSECTIONALITY
AND MERITORIOUS OPPRESSION

When we examine the life and teaching of Christ we find that He faithfully rebuked, rather than ignored, the injustices of His day. Clearly, He did not see the injustices of the past as offering an excuse for injustice in the present. Today, however, we are surrounded by a renewed system of thought which subverts the wisdom of Christ. When we view society with a contrived binary classification of *oppressor and oppressed,* we tend to view the world in oversimplified terms as consisting of *villains and innocents,* as if *oppression* automatically generates such *innocence.*

As a pastor, I often encounter such thinking at funerals where people will say: "I just know [the deceased] is in heaven right now *because they went through hell on earth."* There is within this statement a form of calculation which assumes that *personal suffering is meritorious* and *redemptive* in nature. How people quantify these valuations of suffering, innocence, and merit will likely vary from person to person, but it is a ubiquitous form of reasoning. Unfortunately, it is profoundly wrong, dangerous, and has a remarkably sordid history.

A similar form of this teaching is found in the rabbinic oral traditions[97] which Jesus hotly rebuked. In one example, a person who suffered from the plague was to regard their suffering as "an altar of atonement."[98] Similar to this, another rabbinic tradition taught that, in addition to physical infirmity, *poverty* and *governmental oppression* could achieve a form of personal merit sufficient to keep a soul out of hell:

> "Three classes of persons will not behold the face of Gehinnom: they who have suffered the *afflictions of poverty*, disease of the bowels, and the *tyranny of Roman rule*" (Erub. 41b, italics mine).[99]

In both of these examples, we find a faulty connection between *suffering* and *personal merit.* Though such thinking saturated rabbinic dogma for centuries, it is entirely alien to Scripture.

In the modern day, there is a variant form of this thinking being promoted in SJI, but with a socio-political and material orientation. In this version of things, a person's experiences of oppression and suffering are seen as establishing *societal merit*, rather than *salvific merit.* Despite this difference, both viewpoints deal in the currency of *false and irrational expectations* based upon an individual's real or perceived experience of *suffering and oppression.*

SJI's own version of this kind of thinking is called *Intersectionality.* With Intersectionality, special consideration is given to an individual's claimed experience of oppression due to their skin color, gender, class or other categorizations. Central to this system of thought is

---

[97] Many of the ancient Jewish oral traditions were preserved in the written record of the Talmud, giving us a better understanding of the fog of theological confusion that existed in the 1st century.

[98] Cohen, *Everyman's Talmud*, 165, Kindle.

[99] Ibid.

the *quantification* of one's oppression. When an individual possesses several identities (intersections) that are deemed as *marginalized within society*, that individual's *quantified* oppression increases. The more oppression and marginalization a person can claim, the more societal leverage is accrued. It is this mechanism of quantified oppression that results in a kind of societal point system of merits or demerits, depending on one's intersectional standing. All such reasoning is rooted in our now familiar *oppressor/oppressed* binary of humanity. While Intersectionality places its primary focus on those who claim to be oppressed, it also recognizes the oppressor class as well. Thus, a white, heterosexual, conservative male is readily placed in the *oppressor* column of this scheme. As a result, every member of the human race is tossed into one of two societal sorting bins according to the stipulations of SJI.

Perhaps the best way to conceptualize this is by looking at a situation where the ideology of Intersectionality was clearly applied. We find one such example in the 2017 protests at Evergreen State College (ESC), Olympia Washington. When white students and staff were asked to leave campus, voluntarily, for the daylong event called Day of Presence, professor Bret Weinstein declined to do so, saying: "On a college campus, one's right to speak — or to be — must never be based on skin color."[100] What appeared to be an entirely reasonable defense of equal rights from the professor, consistent with our nation's defense of civil rights, was instantly denounced as racial bigotry. Weinstein's stand for freedom sparked a deluge of protests with claims that he was a "racist." Students began to seize control of public meetings with profanity laced demands for Weinstein's resignation. In one such meeting, the president of the college (George Bridges) met with students in a small conference room. The students then locked the doors, made their list of demands, and told

---

[100] Hartocollis, Anemona (June 16, 2017). "A Campus Argument Goes Viral. Now the College Is Under Siege," (The New York Times, July 25, 2020).

him that he could only go to the bathroom with an escort.[101] One black student, who repeated the unproven accusation that Weinstein was a racist, said: "I'm so sorry...your free speech is not more important than the lives of, like, black trans, fems, and students on this campus."[102] In a sense, this student's denunciation of Weinstein's right of free speech well summarizes the very real impact that Intersectionality has on our world. The student who denounced Weinstein's freedom to speak was also part of President Bridges' involuntary internment. In both situations, the student had a *twofold intersectional standing of marginalization (black and "transgender"),* establishing a form of *double merit.* Within the calculus of Intersectionality, this gave the student significant power among peers and over faculty. As of the writing of this book, multiple videos remain available online showing several ESC students promoting their claims of oppression in order to exert greater power and influence in their quest for systemic change within the institution. Many of their demands were eventually met.

All of this reveals the simple mechanics of Intersectionality: claims of oppression translate into greater societal power and control. As for Bridges and Weinstein, they received a triple portion of demerits for being white, male, and in positions of authority at the school. This trifecta of demerits was sufficient to warrant their being treated as societal vermin. That was 2017. Now, with the explosion of SJI in government, media, education, and even healthcare, it would seem that Evergreen State College has come to the rest of America. Yet, how should we respond to this new world in which we live?

---

[101] Jon Miltimore, "Evergreen Insanity: Students Forced College Pres. To Pee Under Escort," (Intellectual Takeout: June 19, 2017): https://www.intellectualtakeout.org/article/evergreen-insanity-students-forced-college-pres-pee-under-escort/.

[102] Nikita Vladimirov, "Evergreen students: 'F*** free speech' that 'validates' hate" (Campus Reform: June 20, 2017), https://www.campusreform.org/?ID=9333.

By critiquing the ideology of Intersectionality, my agenda is not to deny the presence of injustice and oppression in this world, both past and present. Far from it. Instead, the point of this chapter is to come to a deeper understanding about what God's Word has to say to those who have been oppressed under the weighty systems of injustice in this world. This must be our pursuit if we wish to increase our understanding of how SJI compares with the important message of Jesus' justice.[103]

In order to do so I would like to introduce the reader to a tribal[104] community of people from many centuries ago who not only were the objects of disdain and oppression by governmental leaders but were also dejected as villains by most within their own familial/tribal community. Moreover, many of their ancestors endured compulsory servitude and slavery, and some of those same conditions of oppression continued in their own day. The people of whom I speak were the 1st century Jews who professed faith in Christ, particularly those who are addressed in the New Testament book of Hebrews. The counsel that they were given in Hebrews, especially in view of the severity of their mistreatment within the Roman Empire, is deeply instructive to all oppressed peoples of any generation.

But before we summarize the biblical counsel that they received in their day, we should further consider the details of their oppression, remembering that their isolation and mistreatment came from multiple sources: government, society, and even their own familial/tribal community:

---

[103] James 3:17–18: 17 But the wisdom from above is first pure, then peaceable, gentle, reasonable, full of mercy and good fruits, unwavering, without hypocrisy.18 And the seed whose fruit is righteousness is sown in peace by those who make peace.

[104] "Tribe: 1. a.1.a A group of persons forming a community and claiming descent from a common ancestor; spec. each of the twelve divisions of the people of Israel, claiming descent from the twelve sons of Jacob." OED.

1. Governmental Oppression: While it is impossible to do justice to the breadth and depth of this subject, a brief summary of Jewish oppression under the tyranny of Roman rule is needful in order understand the peculiar circumstances of the 1st century Jewish-Christian. Overall, the 1st century Jewish community was immersed in the regular reminder of Rome's broad and penetrating control over the region. Even the Jerusalem Temple was overshadowed by a military citadel called the Antonia Fortress, named after the famous general and politician, Mark Antony. Jews living at this time were not far removed from Judea's subjugation to Roman authority. In fact, they were only a few generations removed from Pompey's decisive siege of Jerusalem and subsequent desecration of the temple in 63 B.C.; and they were merely one generation removed from Governor Varus'[105] suppression of a rebellion in 4 B.C. in which 2,000 Jews were publicly crucified in Jerusalem. Haunting events like these further magnified tensions such that by 70 A.D. a Jewish revolt was crushed by Rome with as many as 1 million Jews killed and 70,000 sold into slavery.

As long as Judea remained a client state under Rome many Jews were sold into slavery, but this was not uncommon in a world where the slave market was a ubiquitous reality.[106] Though historians continue to debate the issue, it is believed that Rome's slave population may have ranged from one third to one half overall.[107] Unsurprisingly, many Jews had experienced the harsh realities of slavery during this time, whether directly or indirectly.[108]

---

[105] "Varus then led his troops up and down through the country, apprehending the rebels who were now lurking here and there in small parties. He had two thousand of them crucified, while he granted pardon to the mass of the people." Schürer, *A History of the Jewish People*, 3246, Kindle.

[106] Milton Meltzerz, *Slavery I (Volumes I & II), A World History*, (DA Capo Press, 1993), 106.

[107] Ibid., 128.

[108] "As the wars became less frequent, the supply of slavery from this source fell off. People in the Roman provinces who rebelled were sold, such as the Jews whom Titus threw on the slave market by the thousands when he took Jerusalem in 70 A.D. Piracy, even after Pompey's suppression, still supplied some slaves and

Additionally, as Rome transitioned from a republic to that of imperial rule, the development of the Imperial Cult made toleration of religious freedom rather *intolerable*. Jews and Christians, because of their monotheistic convictions, were often indistinguishable from the viewpoint of Roman officials, resulting in various degrees of oppression for both groups.[109] In one such case, devotees of the Roman Imperial Cult of Caligula assaulted a Jewish community; many were publicly scourged, arrested, and had their property confiscated.[110]

2. Societal Oppression: Similar to the aforementioned example of Caligula's Imperial Cult, religious sacrifices to the pagan deities of the Graeco-Roman world were not seen as optional, but absolutely essential *for the good of Roman society as a whole*. The reason for this is that all such sacrifices were believed to be necessary for the support and strengthening of the gods who in turn supplied favorable seasons and circumstances for the worshipper.[111] Since the

---

some of the poor still sold themselves or their children into slavery. But most slaves now came from birth – children born of slave mothers. Slaves were bred for sale. It was legal to sell foundlings or newborn babies, and the demand was heavy." Ibid., 132.

[109] Harold Mattingly, *Christianity in the Roman Empire*, (W.W. Norton Company, New York), 25-26.

[110] "In A.D. 38 a mob of Greeks invaded the synagogues and insisted on placing in each of them a statue of Caligula as a god. The Roman prefect, Avillius Flaccus, annulled the Alexandrian citizenship of the Jews and ordered those of them who lived outside the original Jewish section to return to it within a few days. When these had elapsed the Greek populace burned down 400 Jewish homes, and killed or clubbed Jews, outside the ghetto; and thirty-eight members of the Jewish gerousia or senate were arrested and publicly scourged in a theater. Thousands of Jews lost their homes, their businesses, or their savings." Will Durant, *Caesar and Christ: The Story of Civilization*, Volume III (Simon & Schuster: Kindle), 11399.

[111] Robert Maxwell Ogilvie, *The Romans and Their Gods*, (WW Norton & Company, New York, 1969), 42. "The gods were essentially gods of activity-they did things, such as controlling childbirth or repelling disease-and activity requires vitality. If the god's vitality was not sustained and renewed, that activity

deities of their world were seen as needy and dependent in this manner, great pressure was often placed on all citizens within the empire to partake in such offerings.[112]

Unsurprisingly, Christians could not, in good conscience, participate in such pagan worship, and their lack of participation led others to believe that the followers of Christ were the source of all economic and environmental calamities. Their conduct was considered to be *dangerously antisocial*,[113] leading to further religious oppression and culminating in the first official persecution of Christians under Nero. Though the book of Hebrews may predate the Neronian persecution in 64 A.D., the book was most likely written while the vilification of the Christian community was reaching a critical point.

3. Tribal Oppression: In this third layer of oppression we observe, in particular, how the Jewish-*Christian* community was ostracized, not only by a pagan government and society, but even by their own Jewish brethren. Jews who rejected Jesus as the Messiah saw Christianity as a heretical cult and therefore sought to extinguish its influence far and wide. A key example of this phenomena is found in the case of a man named Saul (later converted and known as Paul, an Apostle of Jesus Christ), who sought to crush the Christian message along with its messengers. Being commissioned by the chief priests, he

---

would be weakened and they would no longer be able to function efficiently. Crops would fail or disease would spread because the relevant gods did not have enough vigour to perform their tasks even if they wanted to."

[112] "...The existence of the gods depends to an appreciable extent on man's devotion to them. Varro puts this quite simply when he writes: 'I am afraid that some gods may perish simply from neglect.'" Ibid.

[113] Minucius Felix, *Octavius* 8.4, 5; 9.2, 4-7; 10.2, 5; 12:5. "You apprehensive and anxiety-ridden Christians abstain from innocent pleasures. You don't watch the public spectacles, you don't take part in the processions, you absent yourselves from the public banquets, you shrink away from sacred games, sacrificial meat, and altar libations. That's how frightened you are of the gods whose existence you deny!"

sought out believers in synagogues in order to have them either thrown in jail or killed.[114]

One of the earliest examples of this is clearly seen in the martyrdom of Stephen, as recorded in the seventh chapter of the book of Acts. Being accused of blasphemy, Stephen was dragged before the Jewish Sanhedrin in order to have his views scrutinized. After giving evidence that Jesus was the Messiah he was driven out of Jerusalem and stoned to death while Saul stood by giving hearty approval to the brutality.[115] Saul offered such approval because he was filled with "furious rage" over the message of the Gospel. Though many of these Christians were his brethren in the flesh (as Jews), Saul sought to extinguish their life, message, and influence one way or the other.

When we try to grasp these layers of persecution, it is admittedly an impossible task. Not only was the combined oppression from a pagan government and society extremely weighty for the 1st century Jewish-Christian, but the additional factor of persecution from fellow Jews heaped a burden of hardship upon them that transcends the experiences of most in the modern day, especially here in America. This is why I have introduced the reader to this ancient people. All who seek justice in the present day have much to learn from the biblical counsel that these oppressed people received centuries ago.

The author of Hebrews was very focused on this matter of delivering a needful message to his much afflicted readers. He understood their plight and expressed great compassion for them in view of the "great

---

[114] Acts 26:9–11: 9 "So then, I thought to myself that I had to do many things hostile to the name of Jesus of Nazareth. 10 "And this is just what I did in Jerusalem; not only did I lock up many of the saints in prisons, having received authority from the chief priests, but also when they were being put to death I cast my vote against them. 11 "And as I punished them often in all the synagogues, I tried to force them to blaspheme; and being furiously enraged at them, I kept pursuing them even to foreign cities.

[115] Acts 8:1.

conflict of sufferings" that they endured.[116] He knew that they were made a public spectacle, being mocked, ridiculed, reproached, and persecuted for their belief in Jesus Christ.[117] He also knew that they had suffered the grave injustice of having their property seized for no other reason than being followers of Jesus.

When we consider the totality of oppression and affliction endured by these 1st century Jewish Christians, one must wonder what kind of counsel they would be given by the modern day advocates of Social Justice. If we were to perform a side by side analysis between the two, would we discover *any* fundamental correlations between the teachings of SJI and the commands and exhortations in Hebrews? In a word, *no*.

At no time does the author of Hebrews exhort his readers to do anything remotely reflective of modern day SJI. For example, he doesn't exhort them to chronologue the inequities of Roman jurisprudence, or to seek out allies who would protest the *structures, policies, practices, and norms[118]* of institutional injustice within the empire. Nor were they encouraged to promote *present discrimination,* in their own favor, in order to undo Rome's *past discrimination.*[119] Neither were they told that their suffering under Roman rule established a kind of redeeming merit in the eyes of God according to the aforementioned rabbinic traditions. Instead, the book of Hebrews begins with something vastly different. It begins with a spectacular disclosure of the majesty, dignity, and power of Jesus and His justice, followed by a solemn *exhortation and warning.* The nature of his exhortation and warning is crucial for our study, but we must first unpack his remarkable presentation of Jesus' glory.

---

[116] Hebrews 10:32.

[117] Hebrews 10:33.

[118] Camara Phyllis Jones, "Confronting Institutionalized Racism," Vol. 50, No ½ (Clark Atlanta University: 2002), 7-22.

[119] Kendi, *How to Be an Antiracist,* 19.

Though Hebrews chapter 1 contains only 14 verses it is saturated with 10 references from the OT, including our familiar texts of Psalms 2 and 110. As we already observed, Psalm 2 establishes the Messiah's crucial identity as *the Son of God*. To understand the significance of this unique title, we must remember that the Jewish understanding of the prominence of the firstborn son is that he was the principal inheritor of the father's possessions and power.[120] As *the only* Son of God, the Messiah's monadic identity reveals that He is the Father's singular heir and equal in everything. Thus, when the Jews came to understand that Jesus was "calling God His *own*[121] Father" and therefore "making Himself equal with God," they sought to kill Him.[122] They responded in this manner because they saw His declarations of deity (equality with the Father) as being heretical. After all, the common expectation among rabbinic teachers at the time was that the Messiah would only be a divinely appointed mortal,[123] not deity incarnate (Romans 1:3; Galatians 4:4; Philippians 2:4; Colossians 1:13-19; 1 John 1:1; 4:2; John 1:1-18, c.f. Revelation 19:13).

Not only did the Jewish rabbis have a diminished view of the Messiah, but they had an elaborate system of teaching which exalted the angels far above their station. Some even elevated a mythological angel,

---

[120] Deuteronomy 21:17.

[121] G. ἴδιον, *idion*: This term denotes an exclusive relationship with another, like the relationship of a wife with *her own* husband (Ephesians 5:22). Jesus spoke in terms of such exclusivity by referring to God the Father as *His Father* rather than *our Father*.

[122] John 5:18.

[123] "Naturally speculation was rife as to who the Messiah would be, and Scriptural texts were studied for enlightenment. On one point the Rabbis were unanimous, viz. he would be just a human being divinely appointed to carry out an allotted task. The Talmud nowhere indicates a belief in a superhuman Deliverer as the Messiah." Cohen, *Everyman's Talmud*, 457, Kindle.

Metatron, to a status of equality with God Himself.[124] It is for this reason that the author of Hebrews issued a *heavy refutation of these errors* while revealing the Messiah's supremacy over the angels and every created thing, all within the first chapter of the book. His readers had been sorely oppressed and afflicted and for this reason they needed to behold the Omnipotent strength of their Redeemer and true King, Jesus Christ the Son of God:

1. Jesus is *the Eternal Son and Exalted Redeemer*: He is the heir of all (Hebrews 1:2), the sustainer of all (Hebrews 1:3a), the eternal Son (Hebrews 1:5, Psalm 2), and exalted Redeemer *who is at the right hand of the Majesty on high* (Hebrews 1:3, Psalm 110:1). Because of this, He is the worthy object of worship and adoration (Hebrews 1:6, c.f. Psalm 97:1-7).

2. Jesus is *the Lord of Hosts*: As the sovereign sustainer of all creation He is exalted above the angelic host and dispatches them for His own righteous purposes (Hebrews 1:7, c.f. Psalm 104).

3. Jesus is *the King of Righteousness*: Jesus possesses all the fullness of deity, and His eternal, monarchial rule is perfectly just (Psalm 45:6). He "loves righteousness" and "hates lawlessness," therefore His is a kingdom of true justice, eternal joy, and gladness (Hebrews 1:8-9, c.f. Psalm 45:7).

4. Jesus is *the Creator of a New Heavens and a New Earth*: Like the changing of a garment, the Lord will bring this present creation to an end, establishing a new heavens and a new earth; yet He Himself remains the same without end (Hebrews 1:10-12, c.f. Psalm 102:25-26).

---

[124] This heretical identification of Metatron with God is hinted at elsewhere. Of the apostate Acher it is related that when he ascended to Paradise, "He saw Metatron, to whom permission was given to remain seated while he recorded the merits of Israel. Acher said, 'It has been taught that in heaven there is no sitting, contention, back, or weariness. Are there then two Powers!'" Ibid., 102.

5. Jesus is *the Returning Lord and Judge*: Jesus, the eternal Son of God, reigns at the right hand of the Majesty on high and will someday judge His subdued enemies with perfect and holy justice (Hebrews 1:13, c.f. Psalm 110:1, 5-6).

The first chapter of Hebrews reads like a mini systematic theology concerning the promised Messiah, Jesus Christ. It begins and ends with references to Psalm 110, starting with a description of Jesus the Messiah as the exalted Redeemer (Hebrews 1:3; Psalm 110:1, 4) and concluding with a solemn reminder of the Lord's coming judgment (Hebrews 1:13; Psalm 110:1, 5-6). Along with these core truths from Psalm 110 is the indispensable reality of His identity as the *priestly King of Righteousness* (*mălkiy-ṣeḏeq*: Psalm 110:4, Hebrews 1:3, 7:2) whereby He entered into this world and shared the same flesh and blood as every other member of the human race (Hebrews 2:14a); He suffered and died on a cross for our sin (Hebrews 2:14b) and thereby *made purification for sins* (Hebrews 1:3). This work of His is a priestly one, a sinless and righteous one which secures eternal salvation for all those who believe in Him (Hebrews 5:6; 6:20; 7:17, 21).[125] Because of His perfect *righteousness/justice* (*ṣeḏeq*), His suffering and death can deliver anyone from the coming day of wrath: a wrath that is *justly due to all* because *all have sinned and fall short of the glory of God (Romans 3:23)*. Thus, when this priestly King of Righteousness died on the cross, He did so as the sinner's substitute so that God may be *just* and the *justifier* of the one who has faith in Jesus (Romans 3:26).

Those believers in the 1st century who had experienced such severe trials by means of governmental, societal, and tribal oppression,

---

[125] Unlike the Old Testament priests who repeatedly offered temporary, ineffectual, and imperfect sacrifices with blood not their own, the Son of God was manifested in the flesh to put away sin by the righteous sacrifice of Himself, not offering the blood of goats and calves, but offering the sacrifice of His own blood, thereby obtaining eternal redemption for His people. Hebrews 9:11-14.

and who cried out for justice, needed to know that *God's justice was satisfied through the sacrifice of Christ.* Without this sacrifice for sin, all that is left is the *terrifying*[126] *expectation of judgment* (Hebrews 10:27). In view of this reality, the first chapter of Hebrews is followed with a warning to those who were drifting away from God's Word:

> For this reason *we* must pay much closer attention to what we have heard, lest we drift away from it...how shall *we* escape if *we* neglect so great a salvation? (Hebrews 2:1, 3, italics mine).

We must note the author of Hebrew's use of the first common plural pronoun, "we," when qualifying his statement, *how shall we escape if we neglect so great a salvation?* This form of expression is designed to present a universal principle for *anyone,* that is, it includes the author as well as all his readers. It is as if he had said: "If I or *anyone* were to drift from God's Word and ultimately neglect His provision of salvation, how could we hope to *escape?*"

But this raises yet another question: *escape from what?* The answer to this question is clearly repeated in our already reviewed texts of Psalm 2 and 110, where we learned that there is *no escaping from the wrath of the Son of God (Psalm 2:12 "for His wrath may soon be kindled")* whereby the Lord will *"judge among the nations" (Psalm 110:6) and "shatter kings in the day of His wrath" (Psalm 110:5).* Clearly, the author is not picking out any particular sector of society, *per se,* but is presenting a universal warning about the danger of rejecting *the knowledge of the truth* regarding God's provision of *a sacrifice for sins.* In fact, grave warnings such as these run throughout the entire book of Hebrews (Hebrews 2:1-3; 3:12-18; 4:7-13; 5:11-14;, 6:1-8; 10:26-31, 12:15-17).

By now the reader may be wondering why a book that is filled with such an *encouraging* presentation of Christ's exalted nature is also

---

[126] "...it is a terrifying thing to fall into the hands of the living God." Hebrews 10:31.

saturated with so many *solemn warnings*. If you are thinking this, it is likely that you are not alone with such thoughts. But also understand that such a query proves just how alien and unknown the message of Scripture is to so many. The justification for his repeated warning is at least twofold:

First, the author of Hebrews repeatedly confronts the problem of religious self-deception. Just as it was then, there are many today who have placed their faith and trust in some philosophy or religious ideology but have rejected the person and work of Jesus Christ to their own peril, and this damning reality is exactly what Satan seeks in this world of systemic evil.[127] In the end, the book of Hebrews (like any other book of the Bible) is dealing with matters that have eternal consequences. Those who lived in a haze of their own religious self-deception needed to be shaken out of their stupor so that they might understand that the consequences of their choices would result in either Heaven or Hell.

Second, the beauty and wonder of the Gospel's rich promises often justify *warnings of commensurate magnitude* for those who deny its message. If you were to hand over an antique Stradivarius violin of great worth to a young child, you would likely do so with many words of warning and caution. Their inability to comprehend the value of what they hold justifies such words of warning, lest they be tempted to cast it to the ground as an irrelevance. Yet this frail analogy falls short of what the author of Hebrews was doing with his readers. The solemnity and repetition of his warnings were justified in view of the matchless worth of Christ and His redemptive work, a subject which constituted the very centerpiece of his letter: "NOW the main point (Κεφάλαιον, *kephalaion*[128]) in what has been said is this: we have such a high priest,

---

[127] The subject of systemic evil is further addressed in chapter 9.

[128] Κεφάλαιον, *kephalaion*: From κεφαλή (*kephalē*), head, superior. Here the author of Hebrews is letting us know that *the chief or greatest point* that he is

who has taken His seat *at the right hand of the throne of the Majesty in the heavens[129]...*" (Hebrews 8:1, italics mine). Such a *main point* as this directs us to the matchless worth of Jesus Christ who is "such a high priest, holy, innocent, undefiled, separated from sinners and exalted above the heavens" (Hebrews 7:26) and whose redemptive blessings and riches are incalculable, beyond human comprehension. Therefore, rejection of this *King of Righteousness* will result in an incalculable loss and eternal suffering that is also beyond human comprehension.

Yet, the centerpiece of the book of Hebrews is not found in its warnings, but in the *main point* of Christ's glory as the exalted Redeemer and returning King of kings. Sadly, a great number of pulpits today have so elevated the earthly and temporal cares of this life that they resultantly trample underfoot the immeasurable riches Christ. As well, pastors who have fallen beneath the sway of SJI reasoning are typically found chasing after earthly justice to the point of obscuring any and all discussions about Jesus' justice. And those pastors who only emphasize the Gospel message's words of encouragement and hope, betray their people by hiding the Gospel's severe pleadings and warnings *if rejected.*

However, unlike such modern-day preachers, the author of Hebrews faithfully delivered the very message that his oppressed audience needed: the message of Gospel *hope and warning.* He wrote out of a serious concern that some in their midst had become so caught up with the afflictions and cares of this life that they were *growing weary and losing heart*[130] and thereby losing sight of what matters most. Like a person who sees a fellow traveler wandering towards a dangerous precipice, the author of Hebrews wasted no time in calling out to his

---

making is that Jesus, the King of Righteousness, is exalted to the right hand of the throne of the Majesty in the heavens as our high priest.

[129] Psalm 110:1 is here cited in Hebrews 8:1 and constitutes the 3rd of five citations of this passage throughout the book: Hebrews 1:3, 13; 8:1; 10:12-13; 12:2.

[130] Hebrews 12:3.

wayward companions with repeated and forceful pleadings and warnings in the Gospel. Overall, the entire book of Hebrews repeatedly points to the beauty and efficacy of Christ's sacrifice for sin, underscored with the repeated exhortation to trust in no one but Him for deliverance. He began his letter with a high and holy vision of the Son of God's beauty, matchless worth, and glory in order to give his hurting readers the world-transcending vision that they needed. In all of this it is crucial that we understand that *no matter how much suffering and societal oppression one may experience in this life, there is no other provision of atonement, no other sacrifice needed, and no other Savior who can deliver us completely and eternally. Alternately, anyone who attempts to ignore or reject this Savior will not be able to escape Him when He returns; for apart from His saving grace there is no hope.* The profound contrast between the pleadings and encouragements from Hebrews (as just one example from Scripture) versus the vacuous tenets of SJI is simply immeasurable.

Overall, the reader must understand that I am not promoting an attitude of *indifference* towards the matters of this life. The foremost commandment of love[131] forbids such indifference by calling all believers to do "no wrong to a neighbor,"[132] thus compelling the disciples of Christ to seek truth and justice in all their relations. No, like any other book in the Bible, the Christ-centered focus found in the book of Hebrews *is a preservative against the danger of exalting the affairs of this world above Christ and His kingdom.* Moreover, this is the very teaching of Christ Himself who instructs us to *seek first His kingdom and His righteousness* as the highest of all priorities.[133] Consistent with this principle, the book of Hebrews exhorts its readers to invest themselves in God's eternal kingdom rather than in this world which is passing away. They were to *fix*

---

[131] Mark 12:28-31.

[132] Romans 13:8-10.

[133] Matthew 6:33.

their eyes on Jesus (Hebrews 12:2), the author and perfecter of faith,[134] by imitating those faithful believers throughout history who suffered unspeakable affliction and yet looked well beyond this fallen and unjust world to that of a better kingdom: the eternal kingdom ruled by the very One who has "prepared a city for them" in Heaven (Hebrews 11:13-16; John 14:1-6). They were to be like Moses who, by faith, "refused to be called the son of Pharaoh's daughter; choosing rather to endure ill-treatment with the people of God, than to enjoy the passing pleasures of sin; considering the reproach of Christ greater riches than the treasures of Egypt; for he was looking to the reward." (Hebrews 11:24-26).

Ultimately, like the book of Hebrews, the whole message of Scripture is that we must look above to the *celestial crown*, that is, the *greater riches* of Christ and His kingdom. We must understand that His sacrifice is the only one offered that makes *purification of sins* on our behalf. Our suffering and affliction in this life can neither substitute nor augment the *merit* of His suffering and sacrifice. Ultimately, Jesus really is the only hope of mankind.

---

[134] Hebrews 12:1-2.

JESUS' JUSTICE

Acts 17:29:
29 Being then the offspring of God, we ought not to think that the
Divine Nature is like gold or silver or stone, an image formed by the art
and thought of man.

CHAPTER 4

THE INJUSTICE, IGNORANCE,
AND IDOLATRY OF RACIAL BIGOTRY

In a Newsweek article dated 5/5/2021,[135] Julia Marnin described an unsettling moment that occurred on *The ReidOut* show, hosted by Joy Reid, in which video was played of an obviously distraught mother who expressed concern that Critical Race Theory was being taught to her children in school. Addressing the board of her school district (Rockwood School District) she made this solemn and tearful assertion: "Just because I do not want critical race theory taught to my children in school does not mean I am a racist, damn it!" As the video clip faded, a jovial Reid came back into view and laughingly retorted: "Actually, it does." Marnin well summarized Reid's response: "[according to Joy Reid] parents who don't want critical race theory (CRT) taught in schools are in fact racist."

---

[135] Julia Marnin, "MSNBC Host Joy Reid Says Parents Who Don't Want Critical Race Theory Taught in Schools Are Racists" (Newsweek: May 5, 2021), https://www.newsweek.com/msnbc-host-joy-reid-says-parents-who-dont-want-critical-race-theory-taught-schools-are-racists-1588967

It is important to note that Reid's public mockery of a tearful parent, though disturbing, isn't particularly surprising to anyone who understands the mindset commonly fostered by SJI. Reid's lack of hesitancy to judge a stranger falls in line with what we have learned about the reasoning of SJI thus far: *1. SJI's diminishment of the individual logically leads to such a dismissive attitude. This mother's personal life experiences, motives, attitudes, beliefs, guilt or lack thereof, do not matter. By disagreeing with a mandated ideology, which claims to be at odds with systemic racism, that mother haplessly fell into the "racist" sorting bin as defined by SJI. 2. In terms of Intersectionality, a "white" person who criticizes SJI is automatically deplatformed from any assumed place of authority. Joy Reid, however, by virtue of her Intersectional status (black, female), is afforded a voice and granted an authority not possessed by the concerned mother.*

Overall, within the demerit/merit system of Intersectionality, there is no actual debate to be had, just a declaration of condemnation from Joy Reid over a "white person" who is a privileged member of a "white supremacist" society. Reid's charge of "racism," which we will clarify further within this chapter, represents a very stark and degrading accusation. It infers a deep and abiding corruption within a person's mind and soul. Though the concerned mother's tearful plea is understandable, Reid's jovial mockery of another human being is *incredible*.

What our concerned parent expressed to her school board is now becoming a common experience throughout America. Despite the efforts of some, K-12 public schools continue to fall under the influence of SJI indoctrination with insufficient resistance. As this influence continues to spread, more and more parents are reporting similar experiences. They all are finding that anyone who dares to question SJI, or any of its subordinate tenets, *is a "racist."* Much of this is evident in the overwhelming majority of SJI authors who consistently advance two fundamental premises amidst their advocacy of "anti-racism":

1. Systemic Racism in America: America was originally rooted in racism and is therefore inexorably racist, in the present day, in all its policies, institutions, and societal construct.

2. Systemic Racism among "White People": All people with white skin are racist, by default, because of their implicit biases and complicity with the white supremacy and institutional racism which is "baked into the foundation of the nation."[136]

This first premise is heavily emphasized by nearly every SJI author, but most notably by the NY Times 1619 Project creator, Nikole Hannah-Jones. The arguments universally presented in such works are that America was established in large part for the purpose of preserving slavery. Of course, in these same works no substantial analysis is ever given regarding: *1. The historical and worldwide reality of slavery that existed when America was founded; 2. The profound impact that the Gospel had on the dissolution of the slave trade and the advancement of civil rights; and 3. The continued progress towards freedom experienced in this nation such that it has become a beacon of liberty throughout the world (these three observations are further addressed in chapters 7, 8, and 9).*

I should remind the reader that it is not the point of this book to argue that America is devoid of problems. No nation on earth is, however, if white-supremacy and systemic racism really do plague this land to the extent argued by the advocates of SJI, then one must wonder why it is that so many from around the globe are willing to risk life and limb to come here. If broader questions and analyses like these could be addressed for

---

[136] Shannon R. Waite Ed.D., "Your Discomfort is Killing Us," (Education Week: June 7, 2020), https://www.edweek.org/teaching-learning/opinion-four-ways-schools-can-support-teachers-to-become-actively-anti-racist/2020/06.

the sake of further understanding, then a more productive dialogue could be pursued over this subject. But SJI does not seek such two-way dialogue. Instead, as already observed, the advocates of SJI do not present their viewpoint as a *debatable ideology*, but instead as a *mandated indoctrination;* and this religious dogma continues to spread throughout every institution in America, including that of education. As one educator has asserted, failure to agree and comply with SJI isn't just *racist*, it is complicity with *murder*:

> "If you as a teacher have not committed to doing the work of understanding your internal racism, implicit bias, and prejudice, *you* are complicit in the deaths of Black people, and people of color broadly, across the nation. If you are not committed to the work of being actively anti-racist, *you* are complicit in validating the physical and spiritual murders of Black men, women, and children daily. If you espouse the ideology of colorblindness and champion the myth of meritocracy, *you* are complicit in the vilification and denigration of Black people in this country."[137]

Such tortured efforts to convert and garner followers for the SJI movement strain the bounds of credulity, but they are fairly common. While it's bad enough to tell SJI opponents they are racial bigots, the thought of raising an accusation of complicity with *murder* mutilates all standards of logic. Yet, this form of twisted reasoning, replete with its guilt assertions, accusations, and vilification, is quite normative among SJI speakers and writers. And for a person with a certain epidermis ("white"), there is no escaping the inexorable guilt that comes with that flesh tone, as Robin DiAngelo surmises:

> "There are many approaches to antiracist work; one of them is to try to develop a positive white identity. Those who promote this approach often suggest we develop this positive identity by reclaiming the cultural heritage that was lost during assimilation into whiteness for European ethnics. However, a positive

---

[137] Ibid.

white identity is an impossible goal. *White identity is inherently racist; white people do not exist outside the system of white supremacy.* This does not mean that we should stop identifying as white and start claiming only to be Italian or Irish. To do so is to deny the reality of racism in the here and now, and this denial would simply be color-blind racism. Rather, I strive to be 'less white.' To be less white is to be less racially oppressive."[138]

It is likely that the reader is familiar with expressions like *white privilege* and *systemic white supremacy*. These are normally employed in order to establish an unimpeachable *guilt by association* link between a person's "white" skin and these vilified "systems of whiteness." As DiAngelo admits, there is no escape; no possibility of dissociating oneself from such guilt. The only proposed solution that she offers is to "be less white," with this lexical qualification: *To be less white is to be less racially oppressive.* In DiAngelo's world of reasoning, "white" people simply can't help themselves from being oppressive. Such a self-derogating maze as this is something like a version of the board game Monopoly, where players with *white tokens* are sent to jail *on every turn*. But this is no game at all. The promotion of such self-loathing for any person is quite disturbing, but the fact that children are now being subject to this indoctrination is especially despicable.

There should be no surprise that many parents are enraged and in tears over how American schools are being ravaged by SJI. For parents and children to be slurred as racists, haters, and oppressors because of their skin color and their failure to submit to the mandates of SJI, defies every point of progress ever made since the civil rights era. Amidst it all, we must again return to our central question: What do the Scriptures have to say about all this?

When it comes to the subject of *race*, the Bible actually says a great deal, much of which is central to the Gospel itself. Contrary to the

---

[138] Robin DiAngelo, *White Fragility* (Beacon Press), 150, Kindle.

confused connotations of this term as used and applied in secular society, the Bible employs the word race in a very specific, important, and linguistically precise manner. Simply put, the term race refers to a person's *genealogical lineage*.[139] In the New Testament, the Greek term γένος, *genos* is often translated as *race* and speaks of the *generation* of life from one source to another, as in the case of parents begetting or *generating* children.[140] Modern connotations of the word *race* typically deviate from this historic denotation and repeatedly yield much unwarranted confusion and dissension in the world today. In fact, Ibram X. Kendi manages to flip this important word's meaning entirely when he writes: "there is no such thing as *racial ancestry*" (italics mine).[141]

However, when we consult Scripture, we gain clarity on how we should think of the subject of race. For the sake of our study of race, and the related Greek term *genos*, we will examine a tremendously important passage of Scripture where the Apostle Paul preached the Gospel in the city of Athens where the subject of *race* was particularly significant. A careful examination of how Paul used this term, and the context in which he used it, will help us to sort through the ignorance and idolatry of racism as seen in the modern day.

In the seventeenth chapter of the book of Acts we find that the Apostle Paul entered the city of Athens after preaching the Gospel at

---

[139] race, n.2 (reis) [a. F. race, earlier also rasse (1512), a. It. razza = Sp. raza, Pg. raça, of obscure origin.] I.I A group of persons, animals, or plants, connected by common descent or origin. In the widest sense the term includes all descendants from the original stock, but may also be limited to a single line of descent or to the group as it exists at a particular period. 1. a.I.1.a The offspring or posterity of a person; a set of children or descendants. OED.

[140] This idea normally extends beyond the simple reality of parents generating children, but extends itself to multiple generations: γένοςα, ους n: a non-immediate descendant (possibly involving a gap of several generations), either male or female—'descendant, offspring.' Louw & Nida, Greek-English Lexicon, 115.

[141] Kendi, *How to Be an Antiracist*, 53.

Thessalonica and Berea. As he walked about the city, we read that Paul's "spirit was being provoked within him as he was beholding the city full of idols." Paul responded to such idolatry by doing what he always did: he preached the good news about the Lord Jesus Christ. As he did this, many curious listeners wanted to evaluate his teaching further, and so they brought him to the Areopagus. Paul began his message by describing the idols he saw in their city and the *nature* of their worship:

> Acts 17:22–23: 22 And Paul stood in the midst of the Areopagus and said, "Men of Athens, I observe that you are very religious in all respects. 23 "For while I was passing through and examining the objects of your worship, I also found an altar with this inscription, 'TO AN UNKNOWN GOD.' What therefore you worship in ignorance, this I proclaim to you.

Before we evaluate the bulk of Paul's message, we must consider his profound and piercing introduction. His initial mention of their *altar to an unknown god* reveals much about their religious state of affairs at this time. The Graeco-Roman world had become a melting pot of customs and religions, and the cities of Greece were no exception.[142] The convergence of Greek and Roman religion meant that there were as many as 200 recognized gods and deities at the time, with each deity being valued based on his or her functional influence over weather, agriculture, war, or even civilization overall.[143] This often led to confusion about which deity should be addressed or what name should be invoked whenever there was a particular need in society. Such ambiguity was evident when prayers were concluded with nameless addresses such as, "to the responsible deity;"[144] or "...whatever name you please, be

---

[142] Robert Turcan, *The Cults of the Roman Empire*, (Blackwell Publishing, MA: 1992), 2.

[143] Ogilvie, *The Romans and Their Gods*, 10-11.

[144] Ibid., 27.

hallowed."[145] By including an altar to an unknown god, the Athenians were seeking to cover all their bases amidst such a pantheon. Paul's mention of this altar underscored the massive confusion and ignorance that existed among the Athenians; yet this same altar provided a *tabula rasa* upon which Paul would teach them about the true God and Creator whom they did not know. Paul then proceeded with a primitive lesson regarding the true God's actual nature:

> Acts 17:24–25: 24 "The God who made the world and all things in it, since He is Lord of heaven and earth, does not dwell in temples made with hands; 25 neither is He served by human hands, as though He needed anything, since He Himself gives to all life and breath and all things;

Remarkably, Paul's initial description concerning the nature of God was completely antithetical to everything his audience believed. Within the mindset of his audience, the gods *required temples and sacrifices* for their subsistence and function.[146] As already mentioned in the third chapter, the gods required sacrifices so that favorable seasons and circumstances would result for the worshipper. But, *"if the god's vitality was not sustained and renewed [via sacrifices], that activity would be weakened and they would no longer be able to function efficiently."*[147] Such a "relationship" with the gods was no more than a contractual business agreement: *"do ut des,* 'I give that you may give too.'"[148]

The massive contrast between God's true nature and the Athenians' ignorance was clearly exposed by Paul up to this point, but this was only the beginning. Paul's continued message was about to strike at the heart of Athenian religion: a religion that was rooted in *racialist worship*. In order to understand such racialist worship, and Paul's

---

[145] Ibid., 26.

[146] Mattingly, *Christianity in the Roman Empire*, 20.

[147] Ogilvie, *The Romans and Their Gods*, 42.

[148] Mattingly, *Christianity in the Roman Empire*, 20.

refutation of it, we must first consider the venue in which Paul was speaking.

As already mentioned, Paul was preaching on the Areopagus, which means Hill of Ares (G. *Areios Pagos*). This historically significant hill was named after the god Ares who was one of the Twelve Olympians: the principal deities of the Greek pantheon. This *Hill of Ares* had a profound and austere purpose throughout Athenian history as being the place in which trials were held for those accused of the most severe crimes, particularly homicide, arson, and tyranny.[149] By the time Paul came to Athens, the Areopagus was only utilized for philosophical debate; however, as one of the last remaining landmarks of a city ravaged by war, it represented a memorable period of Athenian independence that was lost to Rome after the Achaean War in 146 B.C. Some of the most important temples that still remained were readily visible from the Areopagus. Less than 200 meters to the S.E., dwarfing the Areopagus, was the prominent hill of the Acropolis featuring the gigantic *Athena Promachos:* a massive thirty foot tall bronze statue of Athens' tutelary deity, Athena. Surrounding this colossal statue stood three temples: The Parthenon (Temple of Athena), the Temple of Athena Nike (dedicated to Athena & Nike), and the Erechtheion (Temple of Erichthonios). In addition to this prominent backdrop, less than a half a Kilometer N.W. of the Areopagus, was the Hephaisteion (Temple of Hephaestus).[150]

While such details may seem like a heap of irrelevance, they loudly broadcast the Athenian belief system that was rooted in autochthony[151] and genealogical supremacy. Taken together, the names,

---

[149] Douglas M. MacDowell, *The Law in Classical Athens,* (Ithaca, New York: 1978), 27-28.

[150] Ἥφαιστος, Héphaistos.

[151] Gr. αὐτόχθων "sprung from that land itself." An *autochthon* was an individual who claimed to be an indigenous inhabitant of the land in which he lived. Such a claim as this was rooted in a mythological claim of being begotten out of the land

Athena, Hephaestus, and Erichthonius[152] formulate the tawdry mythology of such worship:

> Hephaistos (god of fire, craftsmen, and metalworking) tried to make love to Athena, but she repelled him in such circumstances that he emitted some semen on to the ground, causing it to become fertilized [with Gaia, goddess of earth].[153]

The resultant progeny of this mythical union was Erichthonius,[154] who was raised on the Parthenon by the goddess Athena and became *the autochthonous ancestor of the Athenian people*. Their view of the world was rooted in a mythical notion of *polygenesis* such that all humans came from multiple, diverging sources. Because of this the Athenians cherished their deified genealogy as that which distinguished them among other nations.[155] Of course, it is not as though the Athenians were alone in advancing a polygenetic view of humanity *via* divine genealogy and autochthony, however, the fact that their claims established a genealogical connection with two of the 12 Olympian gods (Hephaestus by lineage and Athena by tutelage) did make their religious claims quite unique. If any one nation wanted to claim to be the master race, it would hard to beat the elaborate religious claims of the Athenians. Taken

---

itself. Though the Athenians weren't the only society to make such a claim, the complexity and depth of their religious worship surrounding such a claim was somewhat uncommon among other autochthonous societies.

[152] While there is evidence that Erechtheus was the name of an ancient king of Athens, his identity became conflated with the mythical Erichthonius in later years: "It seems altogether probable in any case that the longer name was of later origin, especially in view of the fact that Erechthoneus/Erichthonius was known as Erechtheus in connection with his cult on the Acropolis." Robin Hard, *The Routledge Handbook of Greek Mythology*, (Routledge, NY), 184.

[153] Ibid.

[154] Ibid.

[155] Ibid., 364.

together, the fact that Paul was about to present the Gospel on the Areopagus is no small detail. Being surrounded by the elaborate vestiges of Athenian race-worship, Paul continued his message with a declaration that proved to be the death knell to these proud "descendants of the gods":

> Acts 17:26: And He has made from one blood every nation of men to dwell on all the face of the earth, and has determined their preappointed times and the boundaries of their dwellings.

When Paul asserted that God "...*made from one blood*, every nation of men to dwell on the face of the earth," he was decimating the Athenian belief in a distinct, *deified genealogy*: one which gave them a special claim of *racial supremacy*. We should keep in mind that Paul was not seeking to belittle his audience nor tear them down *as individuals*. As he asserted to the Corinthian church that this was never his goal.[156] But he was unashamedly about the business of *destroying speculations and every lofty thing raised up against the knowledge of God.*[157] Clearly, Paul's brief statement in Acts 17:26 was the veritable wrecking ball that laid waste to the Athenians' racialist religion. Paul was not at liberty to ignore core truths of the Gospel, even if this meant deeply offending his proud audience.

---

[156] In 2 Corinthians 10:8 Paul indicated that the authority given to him from the Lord was for building up the Corinthians and not *destroying (καθαίρεσιν - kathairesin)* them.

[157] Alternatively, Paul was about the business of *destroying* all thoughts and ideologies which contradicted God's wisdom: 2 Corinthians 10:5: We are *destroying (καθαιροῦντες - kathairountes)* speculations and every lofty thing raised up against the knowledge of God, and we are taking every thought captive to the obedience of Christ.

It should be noted that when we say that the Athenians' religion was racist, we are employing the aforementioned historic, denotative sense of the word which speaks of genealogy (G. γένος, *genos*). Paul's Athenian audience needed to understand that *the one true God* who created the heavens and the earth also created all the nations of mankind from *one blood*. Rather than the mythological notion of polygenesis (multiple races), every person on earth throughout history is a member of a single race (monogenesis) called *the human race.* It is this universal reality of human origin and value, established by the Creator Himself, which stands as the foundation of the Gospel's *universal call.*

Yet Paul was not finished with this crucial Gospel truth regarding the essential unity of the human race. Continuing his emphasis on mankind's universal need for the Gospel, he taught his audience that *every member of the human race*, without exception, has a divine obligation not to craft or fabricate ideas about God's nature on the basis of human reasoning:

Acts 17:29: "Being then the offspring of God, we ought not to think that the Divine Nature is like gold or silver or stone, an image formed by the art and thought of man."

What this text clearly teaches is that *no member of the human race* should entertain thoughts about God that He Himself has not revealed.[158] This

---

[158] "...that the Divine Nature is like gold or silver or stone, an image formed by the art and thought of man." This text reveals the other side of Paul's argument. On the one hand (as previously noted), men are not free to think of God as they wish; on the other hand, Paul reveals that men have this sinfully innate tendency to liken the infinite God to the finitudes of this fallen world. As Paul was surrounded with a full bevy of idols and temples, his references to gold, silver, and stone would have been extremely self-evident. His point of instruction is piercing: all members of the human race have this natural inclination to craft deities after the art and thought of man. What a deep and penetrating blow this must have been to his proud audience, teaming with an abundance of artisans

word, *ought (opheilōmen)*, speaks of one's debt to another, and, in the case of man's relationship with God, it refers to humanity's divine obligation towards the Creator of all.[159]

What Paul states in this passage is both crucial and powerful. His Athenian audience had developed an entire system of religion that was devised *out of the art and thought of man* which resulted in a system of religion that *dishonored God and man*. Though it was elaborate, highly developed, and adorned with much gold and silver it was entirely repugnant in the sight of the Almighty. But Paul's instructions about how we *ought not to* think about God were not just for the Athenians, but were for the whole human race, *without distinction*. This is clearly evident by virtue of his operative premise with which he begins verse 29: *"Being then the offspring* [γένος, *genos*] *of God."* This is now the second time that Paul employed the term *genos*[160] which affirms the unitary nature of the human race.

Taken together, verses 26 and 29 end all debate about race/genealogy in view of the fact that the whole human race is the *genos* of God. It is this repetition of emphasis regarding the singularity of the human race that is so crucial in understanding the Gospel itself:

---

and academics. Their highest achievements of hand and mind were quickly thrown into the trash heap of human depravity by this one statement.

[159] "We ought not to think that the Divine Nature is like...": Implicitly, Paul is indicating to us that it is Scripture, and Scripture alone (sola Scriptura), that must be embraced in order to have an explicit revelation of the One who is, Himself, the exegesis of the Father: Jesus Christ (John 1:18). Ultimately, man's lack of freedom to think of God as he wishes mirrors the principal commandments of the Decalogue.

[160] Paul's operative premise in verse 29 is connected with the prior verse (v. 28) in which he asserted that "we also are His *offspring* [γένος, *genos*]."

1. Humanity's Universal Nature: As discussed in chapter 1, it is essential that we assess human life according to God's valuation, as already observed: "Whoever sheds man's blood, by man his blood shall be shed, *for in the image of God He made man*" (Genesis 9:6, italics mine). When men degrade their understanding of the nature of God, *through the art and thought of man*, they resultantly corrupt their view of humanity: the former establishing the value of the latter. In the case of the Athenians, their destructive idolatry yielded nothing more than the exaltation of themselves which led to the degradation of all others. This is why Paul's emphasis on the singularity of the human race is so crucial. It is not that some members of the human race are created in God's image and others are not. This is true because the entire human race is the *genos* of God, being created in *His image and likeness* (*imago dei*). Ultimately, any dispute about so-called "races" of men, or distinctions made on the basis of eye color; hair color; skin color; societal class; personal experiences of oppression; tribal histories; or familial associations, have no distinguishing value whatsoever. In the end, all such divisive views of the human race are *a blasphemous affront to the Creator Himself.*

2. Humanity's Universal Need: Paul's description of the human race, as being the *genos* of God, also carries with it an implicit reminder regarding humanity's shared need for Jesus Christ the Messiah, *without distinction*. When writing to the church at Rome, Paul spoke of this very need. Though he came from the lineage of the Jewish people, through which the Messiah came into the world, his need for Christ was no different than anyone else's: "...Are we (the Jews) better than they (the Greeks)? Not at all; for we have already charged that *both Jews and Greeks are all under sin*; as it is written, 'THERE IS NONE RIGHTEOUS, NOT EVEN ONE'" (Romans 3:9-10, italics mine). Within the entire human race, all are created in God's image, yet all have fallen in sin and therefore face the coming wrath of God's judgment against sin. The good news is that Christ's sacrifice for sin is not for any one tribe or nation within the human race. Instead, those who are His by faith will be drawn from *every* tribe, tongue, people, and nation, and they will be members of *His kingdom* forevermore.[161]

It is this singularity of the human race that established Paul's premise in Acts 17:29: *all members of the human race* have a divine obligation before the Creator not to think of Him in earthly and degrading terms according to *the art and thought of man.* The language that Paul used in Acts 17:29 should remind us that whenever we stray from God's revelation of Himself in Scripture, we enter into spiritually lethal territory. When Paul spoke of the *art* and *thought* of man, he was speaking of that which comes from the intellect and emotions of the human mind and heart. The word *art* (τέχνης, *technēs*), from which we get the word technology, speaks of the specialized skill of a craftsman.[162] The word *thought* (ἐνθυμήσεως, *enthumeseōs*), rarely used in the N.T., comes from the root word *thumos* (passion) and is used to speak of the *hidden musings and imaginations* of men.[163] Taken together, these terms teach us that though our world is filled with an abundance of knowledge, skills, ideas, specialized training, and imagination, all such machinations of *art* and *thought* cannot replace God's revelation of Himself in His Word.

Those who engage in such substitution predictably yield great *ignorance* and *idolatry.* In the worst of all cases, this same substitution also yields *horrific violence* against the human race. Sadly, history is filled

---

[161] Revelation 5:9–10: 9 And they *sang a new song, saying, "Worthy art Thou to take the book, and to break its seals; for Thou wast slain, and didst purchase for God with Thy blood men from every tribe and tongue and people and nation. 10 "And Thou hast made them to be a kingdom and priests to our God; and they will reign upon the earth."

[162] "τέχνη, *techne* …an activity involving specialized training and skill—'craft, occupation.'" Louw & Nida, *Greek-English Lexicon*, 514.

[163] Matthew 9:4: And Jesus knowing their thoughts [*enthumeseis*] said, "Why are you thinking [*enthumeisei*] evil in your hearts?, Hebrews 4:12: For the word of God ...able to judge the thoughts [*enthumeseon*] and intentions of the heart.

with multiple examples of these corrupting elements, some of which has even been delivered in the name of *science*. Several such examples demand our consideration.

Under the pretext of *empirical scientific research*, the writings of Charles Darwin in the 19th century became the fertile breeding ground for several pseudo-sciences such as *craniometry* (the categorization of human "races" based upon brain size) and *anthropological typology* (the categorization of human "races" based upon superficial distinctions: head shape, skin color, hair, body shape etc.). These pseudo-sciences were placed under the broader category of thought called *scientific racism*. The implications of such hypotheses become quite evident when the writings of Darwin are objectively scrutinized. For example, Darwin clearly asserted the idea of racialism in view of what he considered to be the evolutionary ascendency of the race of "white Europeans" over "Melanian" and "savage races":

> At some future period, not very distant as measured by centuries, the civilised races of man will almost certainly exterminate, and replace, the savage races throughout the world. At the same time the anthropomorphous apes, as Professor Schaaffhausen has remarked (18. 'Anthropological Review,' April 1867, p. 236.), will no doubt be exterminated. The break between man and his nearest allies will then be wider, for it will intervene between man in a more civilised state, as we may hope, even than the Caucasian, and some ape as low as a baboon, instead of as now between the negro or Australian and the gorilla.[164]

On the basis of his *hypothesized* hierarchy of evolution, Darwin repeatedly made comparisons between the "races of man," with *white civilized Europeans* at the top of the scale and "negros or Australians," which he also refers to as *"Melanian" races*, at the bottom. Such *anthropological typology* ("white" versus "black") is particularly vacuous, especially since

---

[164] Charles Darwin, *On the Origin of Species*, Kindle, 1199.

all members of the human race possess the skin pigment called *melanin*; some having more and others less. Such efforts to distinguish humans were no better than the flawed thinking of craniometry. In the above example, Darwin's citation of Professor Schaaffhausen, from the 1867 Anthropological Review, reflects a hierarchic form of thinking on the basis of craniometry. In this cited article, Schaaffhausen argues that the brain size and intelligence of men and apes is greater than the comparative brain size and intelligence found between Europeans and Australians. The particular grouping in his comparison follows the hierarchic presumption of scientific racism and craniometry (gorilla-Australian, Australian-European):

> The brain of the Australian exceeds two or three times the volume of the brain of the gorilla, whilst the brain of a European exceeds that of the Australian only by one-fifth.[165]

Such pseudo-sciences as *craniometry* and *anthropological typology* continued to thrive throughout this time without any scientific basis, becoming part of the canonical record of popular literature and standard reference materials. For example, in the 1911 Encyclopaedia Britannica article on the "Races of Mankind," we find an argument for scientific racism *via* craniometry and anthropological typology:

> Races of Mankind – The classification of mankind into a number of permanent varieties or races, rests on grounds which are within limits not only obvious but definite. Whether from a popular or scientific point of view, it would be admitted that a Negro, a Chinese, and an Australian belong to three such permanent varieties of men, all plainly distinguishable from one another and from any European...among the best marked race-characters are the colour of the skin, eyes, and hair; and the structure and arrangement of the latter...*The*

---

[165] Hermann Schaaffhausen, "The Anthropological Review" (Paris Anthropological Society, Vol. 5, No. 17, Apr. 1867), 235-239.

capacity of the cranium is estimated in cubic measure by filling it with sand, &c., with the general result that the civilized white man is found to have a larger brain than the barbarian or savage.[166]

Similarly, though Darwin believed that "American aborigines, Negroes, and Europeans" had their similarities, to a degree, he saw far greater distinction between them in terms of their respective mental faculties: "The American aborigines, Negroes and Europeans are as different from each other in mind as any three races that can be named."[167] Similarly, his dehumanizing description of a tribe of "Fuegians" led him to admit his preference of being related to a "little monkey" or to an "old baboon," rather than to such "savages."[168] Such a viewpoint as this accounts for his

---

[166] Encyclopaedia Britannica, A Dictionary of Arts, Sciences, Literature and General Information (1911), 112-13, Italics mine.

[167] Charles Darwin: *On the Origin of Species, The Voyage of the Beagle, The Descent of Man, The Autobiography,* 1226, Kindle.

[168] "The main conclusion arrived at in this work, namely, that man is descended from some lowly organised form, will, I regret to think, be highly distasteful to many. But there can hardly be a doubt that we are descended from barbarians. The astonishment which I felt on first seeing a party of Fuegians on a wild and broken shore will never be forgotten by me, for the reflection at once rushed into my mind—such were our ancestors. These men were absolutely naked and bedaubed with paint, their long hair was tangled, their mouths frothed with excitement, and their expression was wild, startled, and distrustful. They possessed hardly any arts, and like wild animals lived on what they could catch; they had no government, and were merciless to every one not of their own small tribe. He who has seen a savage in his native land will not feel much shame, if forced to acknowledge that the blood of some more humble creature flows in his veins. For my own part I would as soon be descended from that heroic little monkey, who braved his dreaded enemy in order to save the life of his keeper, or from that old baboon, who descending from the mountains, carried away in triumph his young comrade from a crowd of astonished dogs—as from a savage who delights to torture his enemies, offers up bloody sacrifices, practices

belief in the ascendancy of the "civilized nations" such that "at the present day civilized nations are everywhere supplanting barbarous nations."[169] All such musings reflect a hierarchical, evolutionary view of humanity which was strongly aligned with Schaaffhausen: "In the present state of things, the distance between man and the animal increases under our own eye. *Not merely the human races standing lowest in the scale, and presenting in their organisation many resemblances to animal forms*, are gradually becoming extinct, but the superior apes approaching nearest to man become more rare from century to century; and will, perhaps, in a few centuries have entirely disappeared."[170] It is at this point that we must recognize that Darwin's evolutionary machinations placed him well within the reasoning found in eugenic ideology:

> We civilised men, on the other hand, do our utmost to check the process of elimination; we build asylums for the imbecile, the maimed, and the sick; we institute poor-laws; and our medical men exert their utmost skill to save the life of every one to the last moment....thus the weak members of civilised societies propagate their kind. No one who has attended to the breeding of domestic animals will doubt that this must be highly injurious to the race of man. It is surprising how soon a want of care, or care wrongly directed, leads to the degeneration of a domestic race; but excepting in the case of man himself, hardly any one is so ignorant as to allow his worst animals to breed.[171]

Though Darwin most often spoke of the supremacy and advantage of civilized societies, the above text reveals his mindset regarding how they

---

infanticide without remorse, treats his wives like slaves, knows no decency, and is haunted by the grossest superstitions." Ibid., 1735.

[169] Ibid., 1165.

[170] Schaaffhausen, *The Anthropological Review*, 235-239.

[171] Charles Darwin: *On the Origin of Species, The Voyage of the Beagle, The Descent of Man, The Autobiography*, 1171, Kindle.

might falter: by providing aid to the "weak members of society."[172] Employing the same form of reasoning, Darwin's half-cousin, Sir Francis Galton, asserted the following in his open advocacy of eugenic ideology:

> Man is gifted with pity and other kindly feelings; he has also the power of preventing many kinds of suffering. I conceive it to fall well within his province to replace Natural Selection by other processes that are more merciful and not less effective. This is precisely the aim of Eugenics.[173]

For Galton and others like him, the eugenicist sought to assist and accelerate natural selection by manipulating human procreation so that a "good generation" would be the result. This involved a sorting and sifting process of what might be deemed as either good or bad genetic traits. In view of the broader realm of eugenic thinking, this could require the sterilization or even death of someone deemed as genetically defective.

---

[172] Many have disputed any ideological connection between Darwinism and Social Darwinism, arguing that Darwin refuted the concept of eugenics; however, the arguments promoting this view fall short of any concrete evidence. Consider the contrast between Manuel Ruiz Rejon (Professor of Genetics at the University of Granada) and the words of Darwin himself: Granada: "Darwin did not support the movement "social Darwinism," born after the publication of 'Descent of Man', which defended that the action of natural selection and nature's fight for survival should be extended to human societies, going so far as to advocate drastic eugenic measures. On this matter, Darwin ended the last chapter of "Descent of Man" (1871, chapter 21) by saying that it was not necessary to employ any means to reduce the natural proportion in which the human species increases even if this increase brings a lot of suffering." Manuel Ruiz Rejon, Two Clashing Giants - Marxism and Darwinism (bbvaOpenMind.com 13 August 2018) Darwin, Descent of Man, chapter 21: "In general we can only say that the cause of each slight variation and of each monstrosity lies much more in the constitution of the organism, than in the nature of the surrounding conditions; though new and changed conditions certainly play an important part in exciting organic changes of many kinds." Ibid., 1722.

[173] Francis Galton, *Memories of my Life* (London: Methuen & Co, 1908), 323.

In addition to Galton, English philosopher Herbert Spencer also helped to advance the cause of eugenics. As noted in the first chapter, he was an agnostic with deep interest in the writings of Charles Darwin. As the progenitor of social Darwinism he coined the phrase, *survival of the fittest,* in keeping with Darwin's arguments. In his book, *Social Statics,* he argued that "imperfect" specimens of the human race are "nature's failures, and are recalled by her laws when found to be such. Along with the rest they are put upon trial. If they are sufficiently complete to live, they do live, and it is well they should live. If they are not sufficiently complete to live, they die, and it is best they should die."[174] Like Galton, Spencer was convinced that it was necessary to assist and accelerate the process of "Natural Selection," believing that it was an act of mercy to do so. It was this eugenic philosophy that quickly spread throughout England and would soon take America *and Germany* by storm.[175]

Advocates for eugenics quickly advanced their cause in America, beginning with the state of Indiana where forced sterilizations were performed on those who were considered to be the most dangerous within society (i.e., those in an "almshouse, insane asylum, institute for the feeble minded, reformatory or prison").[176] Individuals like Harry

---

[174] Spencer, Herbert. *Social Statics* (Illustrated, Kindle), 340.

[175] "Modern eugenics, which had emerged in England among followers of Charles Darwin, had crossed the Atlantic and become a full-fledged intellectual craze. The United States suddenly had a new enemy: bad "germplasm," and those who carried it. The 'unfit,' the eugenicists warned, threatened to bring down not only the nation but the whole human race." Adam Cohen, *Imbeciles* (Penguin Publishing Group), 2, Kindle.

[176] "So he (Dr. Harry Clay Sharp – physician at the Indiana Reformatory at Jeffersonville) urged his fellow institutional doctors to lobby for both restrictive marriage laws and legal authority for every institutional director in every state to "render every male sterile who passes its portals, whether it be an almshouse, insane asylum, institute for the feeble minded, reformatory or prison." Sharp declared that widespread sterilization was the only 'rational means of eradicating

Laughlin (sociologist, eugenicist), Charles Davenport (biologist, eugenicist), and Margaret Sanger became some of America's loudest advocates of this new philosophy. Sanger, a prominent eugenicist and founder of Planned Parenthood, openly derogated all forms of charity for the blind, deaf and mute, the mentally challenged, "imbeciles," and epileptics, calling them "human waste" and "weeds"[177] that should be exterminated.[178] For Sanger, abortion was the principal means for achieving what she called *racial health*.[179]

However, the philosophy of eugenics remained a fledgling movement in America until it was given remarkable legal credibility through the U.S. Supreme Court in the case of Buck v. Bell. Carrie Buck, a Virginia resident who had been deemed to be a "feeble minded" and "promiscuous imbecile," was forcibly sterilized in 1924. Her civil rights having been severely violated, she appealed this action under the Equal Protection Clause of the 14th Amendment. The U.S. Supreme court ruled against her with an overwhelming 8-1 majority. Justice Oliver Wendell Holmes Jr., writing a three page defense of the ruling, asserted the following:

"We have seen more than once that the public welfare may call upon the best citizens for their lives. It would be strange if it could not call upon those who

---

from our midst a most dangerous and hurtful class.... Radical methods are necessary.'" Edwin Black, *War Against the Weak: Eugenics and America's Campaign to Create a Master Race* (Dialog Press: 2012), 106, Kindle.

[177] Margaret Sanger, *The Pivot of Civilization*, (Project Gutenberg: 1922), 112, Kindle.

[178] Ibid., 109, 112, 116.

[179] "Birth control, which has been criticized as negative and destructive, is really the greatest and most truly eugenic method, and its adoption as part of the program of Eugenics would immediately give a concrete and realistic power to that science. As a matter of fact, Birth Control has been accepted by the most clear thinking and far seeing of the Eugenists themselves as the most constructive and necessary of the means to racial health." Ibid., 189.

already sap the strength of the State for these lesser sacrifices, often not felt to be such by those concerned, to prevent our being swamped with incompetence. It is better for all the world, if instead of waiting to execute degenerate offspring for crime, or to let them starve for their imbecility, society can prevent those who are manifestly unfit from continuing their kind. The principle that sustains compulsory vaccination is broad enough to cover cutting the Fallopian tubes."

Predictably, this disturbing precedent accelerated forced sterilizations in the U.S. By 1940, 35,878 men and women had been forcibly sterilized, with 30,000 of those having been performed after *Buck v. Bell*. Sadly, as many as 60,000 men and women were forcibly sterilized during the 20th century in the name of eugenic progress.[180]

The power that the eugenics movement amassed during this time was extensive and individuals who were on the wrong side of the equation of this pseudo-science had little hope of being freed from its grip, like Carrie Buck.[181] In the present day, the fact that Buck v. Bell has never

---

[180] Black, *War Against the Weak*, 18.

[181] "While many of the court's worst decisions are now central parts of American history, Buck v. Bell is little remembered today. Even in constitutional law courses, it is rarely discussed or is mentioned only in passing. The second edition of American Constitutional Law, by the Harvard law professor Laurence Tribe, which weighed in at 1,778 pages, devoted just half a sentence and a footnote to the case. A recent 953-page biography of Brandeis, written by another respected law professor and hailed by some critics as 'definitive,' did not try to explain why the legendary progressive joined the Buck v. Bell majority; it relegated the case to a single sentence in a footnote. Many of those who would airbrush Buck v. Bell from history offer a simple explanation: it is an anomaly. The Supreme Court, they argue, was briefly caught up in eugenics, but it was a short-lived, onetime mistake." Cohen, *Imbeciles*, 11.

been fully overturned[182] raises serious questions about what lessons the world has actually learned in the wake of scientific racism's atrocities.

When we consider the unique devotion that was garnered by the eugenics movement, we see that it had its own *doctrinal Creed of Social Darwinism, a priesthood of racialist zealots, and a system of atonement via racial hygiene*. Overall, Social Darwinism, Scientific Racism, and Eugenics constituted far more than extremely bad and ignorant pseudo-sciences; they were despicable, false, and deadly idols which eventually demanded human sacrifices. These pseudo-sciences became an inviolable *religion* to many, and some were quite open about their religious zeal. For example, Eugenicist, Albert Wiggam, argued in his book, *The New Decalogue of Science*, that heredity is the chief maker of man, the laboratory is the new Mount Sinai, and the "duty of eugenics" is *the first commandment*. In addition to this he added the following to his *faux-liturgy*:

> "...in our day, instead of using tables of stone, burning bushes, prophecies and dreams to reveal His will, He has given men the microscope, the spectroscope, the telescope, the chemist's test tube and the statistician's curve in order to enable men to make their own revelations. These instruments of divine revelation have not only added an enormous range of new commandments-an entirely new Decalogue-to man's moral codes, but they have supplied him with the technique for putting the old ones into effect."[183]

We should at least credit Wiggam for his honesty. The entire world of eugenics eventually developed a cult-like following with little dissent. At the time, it appeared that the leaders of this movement were forming and fashioning a brave new world, and for this reason those who disagreed

---

[182] "Another reason Buck v. Bell cannot be left in the past is that unlike so many of the Supreme Court's worst rulings it has never been overturned." Ibid., 12

[183] Albert Edward Wiggam, *The New Decalogue of Science*, (Bobbs-Merrill Company: 1923), 17.

with their canonized ideology were typically dismissed as either naïve or reckless. After all, the inclusion of intellectuals like Alexander Graham Bell, Winston Churchill, John Maynard Keynes, and Woodrow Wilson gave it a significant *appearance* of credibility.[184] Unsurprisingly, this dark precedent in American history provided a chilling blueprint for Hitler's Third Reich:[185]

"…American raceologists were intensely proud to have inspired the purely eugenic state the Nazis were constructing. In those early years of the Third Reich, Hitler and his race hygienists carefully crafted eugenic legislation modeled on laws already introduced across America, upheld by the Supreme Court and routinely enforced. Nazi doctors and even Hitler himself regularly communicated with American eugenicists from New York to California, ensuring that Germany would scrupulously follow the path blazed by the United States."[186]

Eventually, the lethal pathogen of this pseudo-science manifested itself in a most suitable host, Adolph Hitler, who wrote the following in *Mein Kampf*:

---

[184] Steven A. Farber, "U.S. Scientists' Role in the Eugenics Movement (1907–1939): A Contemporary Biologist's Perspective" (U.S. National Library of Medicine National Institutes of Health, PMID: 19133822, Dec 2008). https://www.ncbi.nlm.nih.gov/pmc/articles/PMC2757926/.

[185] "The reach of Buck v. Bell extended beyond the United States. The Nazi Party, which was on the rise in Germany, used America as a model for its own eugenic sterilization program. The Supreme Court's ruling influenced the *Erbgesundheitsgerichte*, the Hereditary Health Courts that decided who should be forcibly sterilized. And at the Nuremberg trials that followed World War II, Nazis who had carried out 375,000 forced eugenic sterilizations cited Buck v. Bell in defense of their actions. Cohen, *Imbeciles*, 10-11.

[186] Black, *War Against the Weak*, 391.

Historical experience offers countless proofs of this. It shows with terrifying clarity that in every mingling of Aryan blood with that of lower peoples the result was the end of the cultured people. North America, whose population consists in by far the largest part of Germanic elements who mixed but little with the lower colored peoples, shows a different humanity and culture from Central and South America, where the predominantly Latin immigrants often mixed with the aborigines on a large scale. By this one example, we can clearly and distinctly recognize the effect of racial mixture. The Germanic inhabitant of the American continent, who has remained racially pure and unmixed, rose to be master of the continent; he will remain the master as long as he does not fall a victim to defilement of the blood.[187]

It is this hellish descent of reasoning that ultimately led to The Holocaust: the horrific slaughter of six million Jewish men, women, and children. This dark legacy of "science" underscores for us, once again, that *the art and thought of man*, detached from the wisdom of God, has but one outcome: blasphemy against the Creator.

Our pursuit of this dark and disturbing trail of madness was necessary for our consideration of the Apostle Paul's crucial assertions in Acts 17. Not only were the Athenians guilty of gross ignorance and idolatry, but those who invented the ravenous monsters of social Darwinism and eugenics of the past century are guilty of the same. *Though the effects of such ignorance and idolatry vary, they all represent the severe danger that comes when God's Word is abandoned.* As Paul taught the Athenians, through *one blood* the Lord made *all the nations of men* (Acts 17:26) such that *all humans* are the *genos (generation/race) of God* (Acts 17:29). The rejection of this simple truth leads to *countless* forms of madness and violence. Because of this, it should be no surprise that those who reject such truth may even descend into the abyss of mass murder. The wisdom of James 3:13-16 is once again vindicated: *any departure from God's wisdom from above predictably leads to that which is earthly, natural, and even demonic.*

---

[187] Adolph Hitler, *Mein Kampf*, Chapter XI: Nation and Race.

As we come to the close of this chapter it is only fitting that we consider Paul's closing appeal in his message to the Athenians. Having twice propounded the singularity of the human race (Acts 17:26, 29), Paul concludes his message with God's universal call for *all everywhere* to repent and turn to Him:

> **Acts 17:30–31:** 30 "Therefore having overlooked the times of ignorance, God is now declaring to men that *all everywhere* should repent, 31 because He has fixed a day in which He will judge the world in righteousness through a Man whom He has appointed, having furnished proof to all men by raising Him from the dead."

When Paul concluded his message with God's universal appeal that *all everywhere should repent,* he was reminding his hearers, *for the third time,* of the *singularity of the human race.* There are no exceptions to the Gospel's call to humanity. Its call of repentance is not just for the Athenians or any other people group to the exclusion of others. It is for all, everywhere, in every generation, without distinction or exception. The need for every member of the human race to repent is evident because *a day has been appointed in which the whole world will be judged in righteousness by One who has been raised from the dead.* And that coming Judge is the risen Savior, the Lord Jesus Christ.

This mention of Christ's coming judgment is reflective of what we have already gleaned from Psalms 2 and 110. Though Paul's audience was unfamiliar with these Old Testament passages, the Athenians still needed such a message of warning and Gospel hope: *Do homage to the Son, lest He become angry, and you perish in the way, For His wrath may soon be kindled. How blessed are all who take refuge in Him! (Psalm 2:12).* Paul appealed for the repentance of his hearers so that they would be found *taking refuge in the Son of God* through faith in Him, rather than facing His wrath in the day of His judgment.

Every generation of humanity has crafted its own idols of *racialism via* the art and thought of man, resulting in massive division and destruction, and SJI's reformulation of this historic corruption presents a very real threat in the modern day. The contrast between SJI and the Gospel could not be clearer. The former proffers a destructive message of discrimination which divides humanity for the sake of political power, offering no reconciliation, no forgiveness, *and no hope;* while the latter offers redemption, forgiveness, and eternal joy to *all, everywhere, with absolutely no distinction.*

J E S U S'
J U S T I C E

Romans 1:25:
25 For they exchanged the truth of God for a lie, and worshiped and
served the creature rather than the Creator,
who is blessed forever. Amen.

CHAPTER 5

SOCIAL JUSTICE IDEOLOGY
AND THE DOCTRINE OF SELF-ATONEMENT

In the previous chapter we examined the importance of the word *race*,
especially in view of how this term has been dangerously misunderstood
and abused. God is the creator of the *single human race*. He made them
male and female, in His image and likeness, and those who reject this will
predictably enter into grave ignorance and idolatry. This, once again, calls
to mind the great fork in the road that we all must face, with one pathway
leading to secularism and the other leading to God's wisdom from above.
Sadly, the historic denials of the singularity of the human race are many
and varied, ranging from the aforementioned Athenian claim of racial
supremacy, to the pseudo-sciences of scientific racism and eugenics.

Not only do such faulty notions of race reflect a profound level of
ignorance, they also reveal the problem of *religious idolatry*. Of course,
this was most evident with the Athenians in view of their vast array of
temples, shrines, and altars dedicated to their genealogical mythology and
worship. But it is also the case that the pseudo-scientists who claimed
"white-European" supremacy over the "melanian races" were guilty of

idolatry because they were exalting their own sense of wisdom over God's true wisdom. It is in this sense that they were also practicing a form of religious worship, even though it was hidden beneath secular garb.

While I realize that this may seem like an odd statement to some, I issue the accusation on solid authority. Among the many implications which flow from our shared humanity is the fact that we all have a natural inclination to engage in idolatry. Though humanity was originally created to worship God, this has been corrupted by sin. The Apostle Paul described this very reality when he wrote about the extensive nature of humanity's sin:

> Romans 1:25: For they exchanged the truth of God for a lie, and worshiped and served the creature rather than the Creator, who is blessed forever. Amen.

Within this simple passage Paul presents two massive charges against the fallen human race. First, he states that sinful human beings have a natural inclination to *exchange* (μετήλλαξαν, *metēllaxan*) or *substitute* God's revealed truth for a lie. Second, this results in the creation of false religion in which the adoration of the Creator (κτίσαντα, *ktisanta*) is replaced with the worship of His creation (κτίσει, *ktisei*). Many crucial lessons flow from this, but we are principally reminded by this teaching that *all members of the human race* were created in order that we might know the Creator, worship Him, and have a personal relationship with Him.

It is this principle of *worship* which represents yet another important implication of what it means to be created *in God's image*: As image bearers, our capacities of intellect, communication, reasoning, and affection (among others) establish the means by which we can know and relate with the One who made us.

However, because of the universal reality of sin, this principal purpose for which we were created has been horribly marred and mangled. Though we still bear God's image, that image has been sullied by the reality of sin. Because of this, all men and women have the *natural inclination* to engage in worship: not the genuine worship of God, but rather the idolatrous act of substitution, as described in Romans 1:25. This important passage gives us a foundation for understanding my earlier charge that the Social Justice movement has several religious characteristics seeing that it has its own doctrinal creed, prescribed confessions, system of self-atonement, and a "gospel" message of *faux*-freedom through societal justice.

However, before we enter more directly into the subject of this chapter, *Social Justice and the Doctrine of Self-Atonement*, there are a few historical artifacts that we need to consider. Like many other movements in history, SJI represents the *threefold* convergence of *religious dogma*, *monetary wealth*, and *political power* making it an above average threat to society. History reveals that whenever such *trifectas* are achieved, great destruction often follows. Thus, for the sake of our study, we will draw from history's pedagogy once again by examining the *profit* and *power* that comes through the man-made religious dogma of *self-atonement*:

1. The *Profit* of the Doctrine of Self-Atonement: Whereas the biblical Gospel teaches us that only Christ can atone for our sins, the message of false religion teaches the very opposite through its claim that we must work and strive to achieve self-atonement. In Christ alone, atonement is final and certain; with false religion, the act of striving for self-atonement is never-ending and uncertain; the damaging effects of which are devastating.

In the years leading to the Reformation, Europe was engulfed in the darkness and superstition of Roman Catholicism. Robbed of the Gospel message the people lived in fear and dread for their souls beneath a religious system that offered no real hope. During this era Pope Leo X and Albert of Hohenzollern sought to fill Rome's coffers by selling indulgences that were said to offer the remission of sins. To this end, Albert drafted specific instructions (Summary Instructions) that were designed to help increase indulgence sales.[188]

---

[188] Hans J. Hillerbrand, *The Reformation – A narrative history related by contemporary observers and participants*, (New York: Harper & Row Publishers, 1964), 39.

These instructions promised absolution to the partakers of the indulgence, provided that there was *a confession of sin, a commitment of obeisance,*[189] *and the giving of money for the indulgence.*[190] Albert also developed a detailed fee schedule that was established for all members of society, from members of royalty all the way down to mere peasants. Those who sold these indulgences took with them the papal banner which signified the pope's claimed authority as *the father of princes and kings* and *the ruler of the world* who had sole authority to "release whatever souls he pleases from further suffering [in Purgatory]."[191] With superstitious dread and fear, people from all walks of life rushed to purchase these indulgences with the false hope of eradicating their sin and guilt.

The people were not told the truth of the Gospel (that eternal forgiveness is given *freely* to all who have faith in Christ); instead they were treated to abusive sermons that heralded a kind of self-atonement that was achieved through sufficient penance and indulgences paid to the Pope through his henchmen. Driving this monetary engine were the coercive and manipulative tactics employed by the indulgence salesmen. Johan Tetzel habitually scolded his audience with false claims of the Pope's power to forgive sin: "...why do you hesitate to convert yourself? Why don't you confess now to

---

[189] Albert of Hohenzollern, "Instructions for Selling Indulgences" (1517) "In the first place every one who is contrite in heart, and has made oral confession, or at all events has the intention of confessing at a suitable time, shall visit at least the seven churches indicated for this purpose, that is to say, those in which the papal arms are displayed, and in each church shall say devoutly five Paternosters and five Ave Marias in honor of the five wounds of our Lord Jesus Christ, whereby our salvation is won, or one Miserere [the prayer beginning "Lord have mercy"], which Psalm is particularly well adapted for obtaining forgiveness of sins."

[190] Four "principal graces" were said to go to the purchaser: 1. The grace of forgiveness; 2. A letter of indulgence confirming rightful ownership of the indulgence; 3. The bestowal of the church's righteous merit to the purchaser of the indulgence along with their deceased relatives; and 4. Pardon for the souls of those now suffering in Purgatory. Hillerbrand, The Reformation, 39.

[191] Loraine Boettner, *Roman Catholicism* (Phillipsburg: The Presbyterian and Reformed Publishing Company, 1962), 128.

the vicars of our Most Holy Pope?"[192] Tetzel even resorted to the act of shaming his audience by claiming that dead relatives would remain in torment without their obedience: "Don't you hear the voices of your wailing dead parents and others...?"[193] After heaping upon his audience unbearable guilt and false claims of self-atonement, the credulous masses surrendered their money while Tetzel quipped, "as soon as a coin in the coffer rings the soul from purgatory springs."[194]

This scheme did nothing to absolve the sins of a single soul, but it enriched and empowered[195] those who proffered their blasphemous wares. Wherever money can be made through the offer of the false Gospel of self-atonement, you will find eager profiteers spreading their message of shame.

2. The *Power* of the Doctrine of Self-Atonement: Not only was the false Gospel of self-atonement profitable for Rome, but it also secured tremendous power over the people. In a system of superstitious belief which held that the Pope had the power to forgive sins, the people lived in fear for their lives beneath the capricious dictates of a mere mortal.

As Rome sought to secure greater control over the people, it established the Roman Inquisition which was designed to try and prosecute individuals who questioned papal authority. The members of the inquisition were given

---

[192] Hillerbrand, *The Reformation*, 41.

[193] "Don't you hear the voices of your wailing dead parents and others who say, 'Have mercy upon me, have mercy upon me, because we are in severe punishment and pain. From this you could redeem us with a small alms and yet you do not want to do so.'" Ibid., 42-43.

[194] Ibid.

[195] Thus, if one could remove from history the doctrines of Purgatory and papal indulgences, the coffers of Rome would have been emptied long ago. In his book, *Roman Catholicism,* Loraine Boettner aptly describes the heart of Rome's financial engine: "The doctrine of purgatory has sometimes been referred to as 'the gold mine of the priesthood' since it is the source of such lucrative income. The Roman Church might well say, 'By this craft we have our wealth.'" Boettner, *Roman Catholicism,* 222.

direct authority from the Pope to execute judgment on the accused with no due process. Such inquisitions often included "executioners to conduct tortures, stranglings, and burnings; physicians to oversee the torture; surgeons to repair body damage caused by torture; clerks to record the proceedings and confessions in Latin."[196]

The cruelties that were carried out *in the name of justice* are difficult to grasp. The people had no recourse or means of making an appeal. They had come to believe that the Pope had absolute authority over their eternal souls, and the Inquisition acted as his representative. This false notion of authority was clearly depicted on the aforementioned papal banner containing two keys in an opposing position[197] which signified the Pope's authority over the souls of

---

[196] John Foxe offers a glimpse into the Inquisition's brutalities: "Pope Gregory IX entrusted this heinous task to the Dominican and Franciscan order of friars, and gave them the exclusive rights to preside over the various courts of Inquisition, unlimited powers as judges in his place, and power to excommunicate, torture, or execute any whom were accused of the slightest heresy or opposition to the papal government. Each Inquisition was comprised of about twenty officials: a grand inquisitor; three principal inquisitors or judges; a finance supervisor; a civil officer; an official to receive and account for money fines; a similar one for confiscated property; several assessors to evaluate property; a jailer; counselors to interview and advise the accused; executioners to conduct tortures, stranglings, and burnings; physicians to oversee the torture; surgeons to repair body damage caused by torture; clerks to record the proceedings and confessions in Latin; doorkeepers; and familiars who wormed their way into the confidences of those suspected of heresy and then testified against them. Each trial also had witnesses or informers against the accused, and favored visitors, who were sworn to keep secret any procedures and proceedings that they witnessed." John Foxe, *Foxes Book of Martyrs* (ReadHowYouWant) 70-72, Kindle.

[197] "The symbolism of the keys is brought out in an ingenious and interpretative fashion by heraldic art. One of the keys is of gold (or), the other of silver (argent). The golden key, which points upwards on the dexter side, signifies the power that extends even to Heaven. The silver key, which must point up to the sinister side, symbolizes the power over all the faithful on earth. The two are often linked by a cordon Gules as a sign of the union of the two powers. The handles are turned downwards, for they are in the hand of the Pope, Christ's lieutenant on earth.

men such that "...he can release whatever souls he pleases from further suffering [in Purgatory] and those whom he refuses to release are continued in their suffering, the decisions he makes on earth being ratified in heaven."[198] Such symbolism stood as an ominous reminder to the people that the fate of their own souls, as well as the souls of loved ones in Purgatory, depended entirely on the one who was said to be *the father of princes and kings* and *the ruler of the world.* Such superstition produced a thick cloud of fear which immobilized the masses and left them in a hopeless state.

These artifacts from history should remind us of the manner in which history repeats itself. As such, wherever the masses are manipulated, controlled, and abused by corrupt leaders, one will find brutality and bloodshed. The one *predictably* leads to the other. Whether one considers those who perished at the hands of the Roman Inquisition or the millions who were slaughtered in the Soviet Union's Gulags, Pol Pot's labor camps, or in Mao's Cultural Revolution, the repeated lesson from history remains the same: any philosophical movement or false religion which garners great wealth, power, and absolute control over the people will end up producing division, destruction, and death. *It is the way of the fallen kingdoms of this world.*

When we examine SJI's amassed wealth, power, and inflexible dogmas we should not be surprised that this movement *is spreading throughout modern society with the fervor of a religious cult.* In order to examine this dynamic further, we will consider how SJI, like any other man-made religion, has its own *creed and system of self-atonement:*

1. SJI's Creed: Perhaps what is most central to SJI's creed is the re-definition of the word *race.* As already mentioned, one of SJI's earliest prophetic voices,

---

The wards point upwards, for the power of binding and loosing engages Heaven itself." Bruno Bernhard Heim, *Heraldry in the Catholic Church: Its Origin, Customs and Laws* (Van Duren: 1978), 54.

[198] Boettner, *Roman Catholicism*, 128.

Theodore Allen, posited the very definition of race that has become canonized within SJI. In his seminal work, *The Invention of the White Race*, he argues that the *white race was invented as a ruling-class social control formation*[199] whereby the *ruling elite, in its own class interest, deliberately instituted a system of racial privileges to define and maintain the "white race"*[200] which became *ruinous to the interests of African Americans [and] European-American workers.*[201]

This definition by Allen well represents what the advocates of SJI mean when speaking of race and racism. In a sense, this definition bears a contorted melding of two fundamental components: *societal privilege (or lack thereof)* and *skin color*. Based upon this redefinition of the word race, one can simply look at the epidermis of another human being and immediately pronounce a simple, binary judgment: white skin = *racist oppressor*; dark skin = *oppressed*. Without any further nuance than this "white"-"black" oppressor-oppressed binary, the entire history of America's progress as a melting pot vanishes in thin air. By claiming that America's "original sin" *is the sin of racism*[202] and that racism is "the very air we breathe embedded into fabric of our country,"[203] SJI seems to claim that all of modern America is the antebellum South, *on steroids*.

During the civil rights movement it was understood that living in a *colorblind* society was the pathway forward. As such, being colorblind meant that an individual was to be judged by the content of their character rather than by the color of their skin. Now, with the re-defined world of SJI, with all its lexical innovations, colorblindness "is a mask to hide racism."[204] And those

---

[199] Jeffrey Perry, Introduction to *The Invention of the White Race*, Part 1, by Theodore Allen (Veso Books), 1, Kindle.

[200] Ibid.

[201] Ibid.

[202] Ibram X. Kendi, "Pass an Anti-Racist Constitutional Amendment" (Politicomagazine, 2019), https://www.politico.com/interactives/2019/how-to-fix-politics-in-america/inequality/pass-an-anti-racist-constitutional-amendment/.

[203] Chanequa Walker-Barnes, "The Curse of Reconciliation" (Biola University September 20 2016): https://www.youtube.com/watch?v=FDBTwMQ70Y4.

[204] The language of color blindness—like the language of "not racist"—is a mask to hide racism. Kendi, *How to Be an Antiracist*, 10.

who fail to agree with such dogma will receive further charges of racism for the simple reason that *one's denial of racism is racism*. As Kendi has opined: "The very heartbeat of racism is denial…when people say they're not racist, they're sharing the words that white supremacists use."[205]

2. SJI's System of Self-Atonement: SJI's system of absolution has at its core the requirements of *confession* and *commitment (confession of wrongdoing and a commitment to reverse one's sins of racism)*. Kendi outlines his standards of such confession and commitment in his book, *How to Be an Antiracist*. In the following examples, he specifies the very words that should be uttered, in the first person singular:

a. "I stop using the 'I'm not a racist' or 'I can't be racist' defense of denial."[206] This requisite confession is consistent with Kendi's claim that *the very heartbeat of racism is denial*. Disregarding any consideration of individual's personal thoughts, beliefs, or character, admission of guilt is foundational for those who are deemed as guilty. Until such a confession of guilt takes place, no progress can be made for the individual.

b. "I admit the definition of racist (someone who is supporting racist policies or expressing racist ideas)."[207] This confession reveals the requirement of agreeing with the aforementioned credal definition of racism. As already reviewed, SJI argues that *race* is an invented concept, created by "the white ruling class" in order to oppress and impoverish others. Yet they insist on using this flawed definition rather than seeking to restore the word's actual meaning and value. By this they reveal a rather troubling belief system which suggests that it is best to fight error with error, *rather than fight error with truth*. Despite the illogic of this, those seeking absolution must submit to this

---

[205] Newscenter Ibram X. Kendi: 'The very heartbeat of racism is denial' https://www.rochester.edu/newscenter/ibram-x-kendi-the-very-heartbeat-of-racism-is-denial-470332/.
[206] Kendi, *How to Be an Antiracist*, 226.
[207] Ibid.

standard if they wish to pursue personal restoration with the advocates of SJI.

c. "I confess the racist policies I support and racist ideas I express...I accept their source (my upbringing inside a nation making us racist)."[208] Nested within this confession is the broader charge against the entire nation: [America is] "making us racist." This reinforces the aforementioned determinism found within SJI authors. Rather than individuals growing, learning, and developing *as individuals*, SJI posits a determinism which makes the population of an entire nation nothing more than slaves of *the system*. The disciples of this SJI religion must accept the reality of their personal ignorance and resultant need for the expositors of SJI dogma; or as DiAngelo says: "How can I say that if you are white, your opinions on racism are most likely ignorant, when I don't even know you? I can say so because nothing in mainstream US culture gives us the information we need to have the nuanced understanding of arguably the most complex and enduring social dynamic of the last several hundred years."[209]

Should anyone ever hope for final deliverance from all such confessed guilt, they must know that there is no end in sight for those who seek absolution, because "racism must be continually identified, analyzed and challenged; no one is ever done."[210] Such a system of self-atonement is nothing more than a *carrot and stick* scheme that has no end. Yet it is this system of feigned deliverance that keeps SJI running just like any well-oiled religious machine. Such mechanisms of public contrition and repentance have a long and sordid history. They often lead to a form of religious competition to see who can excel in public displays of piety.

This brings to mind yet another artifact from history called flagellation. This primitive, medieval practice consisted of religious zealots who lashed themselves with whips in order to display their piety in

---

[208] Ibid.

[209] DiAngelo, *White Fragility*, 8.

[210] Robin DiAngelo, Seminar on Racism Worksheet, 2012.

public view[211] (something that is commonly referred to as "virtue signaling" in the modern day). As they did this, they would confess their sins while swearing allegiance to a contrived creed or system of religion. Some zealots actually managed to beat themselves to death.[212] During the Middle Ages this practice of public repentance was loudly displayed throughout Europe.[213] During the Black Plague (1346-1353), the practice

---

[211] Matthew 6:5: 5 "And when you pray, you are not to be as the hypocrites; for they love to stand and pray in the synagogues and on the street corners, in order to be seen by men. Truly I say to you, they have their reward in full.

[212] Philip Schaff gives us a sampling of what this looked like in its earliest days: "Peter Damianus (1007-1072 AD) systematized and popularized a method of meritorious self-flagellation in connection with the recital of the Psalms; each Psalm was accompanied with a hundred strokes of a leathern thong on the bare back, the whole Psalter with fifteen thousand strokes. This penance became a rage, and many a monk flogged himself to death to the music of the Psalms for his own benefit, or for the release of souls in purgatory. The greatest expert was Dominicus, who wore an iron cuirass around his bare body (hence called Loricatus), and so accelerated the strokes that he absolved without a break twelve Psalters; at last he died of exhaustion (1063)." Philip Schaff and David Schley Schaff, *History of the Christian Church*, v. 4 (New York: Charles Scribner's Sons, 1910), 788–789.

[213] Philip Schaff gives us a sampling of what this looked like in its earliest days: "Peter Damianus (1007-1072 AD) systematized and popularized a method of meritorious self-flagellation in connection with the recital of the Psalms; each Psalm was accompanied with a hundred strokes of a leathern thong on the bare back, the whole Psalter with fifteen thousand strokes. This penance became a rage, and many a monk flogged himself to death to the music of the Psalms for his own benefit, or for the release of souls in purgatory. The greatest expert was Dominicus, who wore an iron cuirass around his bare body (hence called Loricatus), and so accelerated the strokes that he absolved without a break twelve Psalters; at last he died of exhaustion (1063)." Philip Schaff and David Schley Schaff, *History of the Christian Church*, v. 4 (New York: Charles Scribner's Sons, 1910), 788–789.

of flagellation dramatically increased because of the superstitious belief that such public self-abuse would merit favor with God. Because of such superstition, great pressure was placed on all members of society to participate in this ineffectual and ghastly practice, because "if any would not scourge himself, he was held to be a limb of Satan."[214] Such compulsory rhetoric was *socially persuasive* due to fear. Because the masses feared religious dogmas and social rejection, they complied with tremendous fervor.

As bizarre as this ancient practice was, there is a form of it to be found in the modern day among SJI advocates. For example, during the completion of this manuscript, Tom Hanks wrote an essay for the New York Times in which he argued that the Tulsa Massacre should receive more attention than it has. Hanks was very self-critical in what he wrote, indicating that such history is underreported partly due to his own failure to tell "the history of Black people" and the "horrors of Tulsa." Remarkably, this was not enough for Eric Deggans who wrote an opinion piece for NPR titled: *Tom Hanks Is A Non-Racist. It's Time For Him To Be Anti-Racist.* After surveying a great deal of Hanks' own expressions of contrition and regret, Deggans insisted, "it is not enough...I am saying it is time for folks like Hanks to be anti-racist."[215] In a sense, Deggans' complaint about the inadequacy of Hanks' public expression of contrition well encapsulates SJI's confessional lingo and public flagellation standards. As already noted, a person who says "I am not a racist" is actually a racist who is simply hiding their racism, as Kendi further explains:

"What's the problem with being 'not racist'? It is a claim that signifies neutrality... language of 'not racist'—is a mask to hide racism. This may seem

---

214 Ibid., 877–878.

215 Eric Deggans, "Tom Hanks Is A Non-Racist. It's Time For Him To Be Anti-Racist" (www.npr.org, 13 June 2021).

harsh, but it's important at the outset that we apply one of the core principles of antiracism."[216]

Kendi's interpretation of the negative particle, *not*, reflects yet another linguistic contortion so often found among SJI allies. A negative particle simply *negates* an action, condition, or identity; however, if a person says, "I am not a murderer," is this now to be seen as an insufficient descriptor of an individual who does not commit murder? Must we adopt new confessional standards such that we are now anti-murdering, anti-thieving, anti-lying advocates? Kendi's point is that a person who is anti-*anything* is an individual of action. The use of the word *anti* then becomes a public confession of one's commitment to the SJI cause as a true disciple of its creed, which includes *anti-capitalist* and *pro-LGBTQ* advocacy. All are inseparably tied to one another.

So, for example, in order to be properly counted as an *anti-racist* disciple, one must actively be *anti-capitalist.* Failure to speak out, in a continual and active sense, against capitalism is tantamount to being a "racist." As well, failure to be active in promoting the LGBTQ movement is also racist. Those who wish to be the faithful disciples of this religion must accept its creed *and regularly act accordingly.*

This is why I have referred to SJI as a modern day cult. Its demands for slavish devotion create an oppressive and controlling environment. Like Johan Tetzel, the messengers of Social Justice continue to insist on strict obedience from their followers while shaming anyone who dares to question them. Carrying a message of the shame of "whiteness" and of self-atonement through public displays of contrition, this new religion is gaining tremendous *power and wealth,* the likes of which should give even the casual student of history serious pause.

As we look further at the religious nature of SJI we find that its credal standards can vary, often producing significant philosophical

---

[216] Kendi, *How to Be an Antiracist,* 10.

conflict; however, the core doctrine of this movement remains the same: the constant shaming of "whiteness." Such constant vilification and derogation of human beings on the superficial basis of skin color has never proven to be productive for any society, *and it has always proven to be abominable in the sight of God.*

Yet it is this derogation of "white people" that is essential to the mechanism of SJI. As long as the guilt of "whiteness" can be imputed to those with a light epidermis, SJI's never ending and deeply profitable system of self-atonement can continue, in perpetuity. Barbara Applebaum, associate professor in Cultural Foundations of Education at Syracuse University, offers a familiar derogation of "all white people":

> "The relevant point for now is that *all white people* are racist or complicit by virtue of benefiting from privileges that are not something they can voluntarily renounce."[217]

Clearly, SJI's message is remarkably fatalistic. Similar to the logic of the eugenicist, a person can be deemed as a despised member of the human race simply by virtue of how they were born. For Robin DiAngelo, this meant that her only hope was to "be less white" because, as she claimed, "white people do not exist outside the system of white supremacy." Rhetoric and logic such as this is the fertile soil from which SJI's *racial bigotry* sprouts and flourishes. For example, when Amy Coney Barrett was nominated for the Supreme Court in 2020, the fact that she had two adopted Haitian children stirred Kendi to react with the following:

> Some White colonizers "adopted" Black children. They "civilized" these "savage" children in the "superior" ways of White people, while using them as

---

[217] Barbara Applebaum, *Being White, Being Good* (Lexington Books, Lanham MA, 2010), 16, italics mine.

props in their lifelong pictures of denial, while cutting the biological parents of these children out of the picture of humanity.[218]

As we have already reviewed, SJI tramples underfoot any careful consideration of the individual (thoughts, beliefs, actions) in order to spread its collectivist message of anti-racism and "systemic racism." Time and again we see that the message of "white guilt," "white supremacy," and all things anti-"white" supply the jet-fuel that enables SJI to soar. Like the system of indulgences, SJI's constant guilt-mongering creates the perceived need for its costly and faulty offers of absolution. Those who are eager to escape from SJI's racialist-purgatory (individuals and institutions alike) are often quite eager to place their coins in the coffer with the hope of hearing the ring of freedom.

Because of this, SJI's wealth and influence continues to explode at an alarming rate. In the case of Robin DiAngelo, her message of "white guilt" has catapulted her to fame and fortune. Her speaking fees have reportedly earned her as much as $1.5 million annually, not including her book royalties.[219] Ibram Kendi, who prefers to be called an *anticapitalist* seems to be enjoying the benefits of capitalism nonetheless. In August 2020, the Fairfax School District in Virginia invested $44,000 in order to promote Kendi and his SJI materials. His *one hour* presentation earned him $20,000 with the remaining $24,000 being used to purchase his books.[220]

---

[218] Ibram X. Kendi (Twitter @DrIbram) (26 September 2020). https://twitter.com/DrIbram/status/1309916696296198146.

[219] Charles Fain Lehman, "The Wages of Woke" (The Washington Free Beacon, 25 July 2020). https://freebeacon.com/culture/the-wages-of-woke-2/.

[220] Asra Q. Nomani, "Fairfax, Va. School District Spent $24,000 On Ibram Kendi Books for U.S. History Classes" The Federalist (30 September 2020). https://thefederalist.com/2020/09/30/fairfax-va-school-district-spent-24000-on-ibram-kendi-books-for-u-s-history-classes/.

On a broader scale, the popular organization, Black Lives Matter, received over $90 million dollars in donations in 2020.[221] Remarkably, its founder (Patrisse Khan-Cullors) said in a video posted in 2015 that she and fellow organizer, Alicia Garza, are "trained Marxists."[222] Despite this reality, Khan-Cullors "went on a real estate buying binge, snagging four high-end homes for $3.2 million in the US alone."[223] It is truly hard to say if Marxism and racial bigotry have ever been *this profitable.*

Yet these examples of SJI's power and prominence may soon be dwarfed by what likely lies ahead. As of the writing of this book, the U.S. government, via the Biden administration, has declared its inflexible support for SJI training, likely making the ideology skyrocket in the future. On the day of his Inauguration, January 25th 2021, President Biden signed an executive order in which he spoke of America's need for an "ambitious whole-of-government equity agenda" in view of the nation's "systemic racism." This seemed to open the door for further advancement of SJI advocacy in various government agencies and businesses. Reports continue to surface regarding businesses like Coca-Cola, Walt Disney Corporation, Lockheed Martin (among others) that are promoting much of the SJI narrative by urging their "white employees" to be *less white* while calling for "white males" to *check their privilege.*

---

[221] Aaron Morrison, "Exclusive: Black Lives Matter opens up about its finances" (Los Angeles Times Online, 23 Feb. 2021). https://www.latimes.com/world-nation/story/2021-02-23/ap-exclusive-black-lives-matter-opens-up-about-its-finances.

[222] Yaron Steinbuch, "Black Lives Matter co-founder describes herself as 'trained Marxist'" New York Post (25 June 2020) https://nypost.com/2020/06/25/blm-co-founder-describes-herself-as-trained-marxist/.

[223] Isabel Vincent "Inside BLM co-founder Patrisse Khan-Cullors' million-dollar real estate buying binge" New York Post (10 April 2021). https://nypost.com/2021/04/10/inside-blm-co-founder-patrisse-khan-cullors-real-estate-buying-binge/.

For the federal government itself, the Department of Education is now weighing in heavily on the SJI agenda in K-12 classrooms. On April 19 2021, the DOE issued a federal rule indicating that millions of dollars in taxpayer money will be used for American history and civics education grants which will prioritize materials consistent with the New York Time's 1619 Project and Ibram Kendi's book, How to Be an Antiracist.[224] With the government's legal and financial backing of SJI, we have now entered into uncharted waters: compulsory acceptance of the *ideology* of Social Justice/CRT.

For the religious zealots of SJI, this is a welcome and much needed change. In one recent example of such zeal, Katherine Watkins, an 8th grade teacher at Cedar Park Middle School (Portland OR), insisted in a Zoom call with her peers that teachers must adopt SJI or else be fired:

I'm gonna say something that's not nice and not sweet, but it's true: if you're not evolving into an anti-racist educator, you're making yourself obsolete in this profession. Our district is only getting browner and browner with our children so....obviously, you can't change your melanin, alright, but you can change your mind so that you can actually function in a district that is full of BIPOC (black, indigenous, and people of color) children. So if you're being resistant, I understand that, but you're gonna have to eventually come to the light. Because if you're going to keep all those old views of...colonialism...it's going to lead to being fired. Because you're going to be doing damage to our children...um trauma. So, as we fire the teachers who sexually abuse our children, we will be firing the teachers who do racist things to our children and traumatize them. And, while our district may not be completely on there

---

[224] Kerry McDonald, "Biden Administration Prioritizes 'Wokeism" Critical Race Theory in Schools" (Foundation for Economic Education, April 22, 2021). https://fee.org/articles/biden-administration-prioritizes-wokeism-critical-race-theory-in-schools/.

...NEA is working on it. And so it's just a matter of time...so it's like you either evolve or dissolve.[225]

Watkins' comments hide precious little. They remind us that the most insidious movements, philosophies, *and religions of men* throughout human history have all shared a common trait: the requirement of *compulsory* obeisance. In short, Watkins is employing the language of revolution consistent to that of traditional Marxism:

The Communists disdain to conceal their views and aims. They openly declare that their ends can be attained only by the *forcible overthrow of all existing social conditions.* Let the ruling classes tremble at a Communistic revolution. The proletarians have nothing to lose but their chains. They have a world to win.[226]

Typical of SJI's thinking, critics of their credal standards are vilified in the worst possible fashion: denial of one's racism *is racism;* the promotion of personal responsibility *is colonialism;* and failure to promote SJI/CRT is *child abuse.* Taken to its logical end, Watkins' allusion to child abuse wouldn't just result in the firing of a teacher, but *imprisonment.* Perhaps Watkins didn't think through the logic of her pontifications; or perhaps she did, but her message portends a solemn and sobering reality: the leaders of this movement are not interested in debating their *ideology,* instead they insist on obedience to their commands which currently have the backing of the D.O.E, the N.E.A. Based on this trajectory it may eventually carry the *legal force of the Constitution of the United States.* Seeking the compulsory submission of America's citizenry, Ibram Kendi argues for the full force of a Constitutional Amendment:

---

[225] Mythinformed MKE (Twitter @MythinformedMKE)
https://twitter.com/MythinformedMKE/status/1397977839828361220.
[226] Karl Marx, *Communist Manifesto*, 63.

To fix the original sin of racism, Americans should pass an anti-racist amendment to the U.S. Constitution that enshrines two guiding anti-racist principals [sic]: Racial inequity is evidence of racist policy and the different racial groups are equals. The amendment would make unconstitutional racial inequity over a certain threshold, as well as racist ideas by public officials (with "racist ideas" and "public official" clearly defined). It would establish and permanently fund the Department of Anti-racism (DOA) comprised of formally trained experts on racism and no political appointees. The DOA would be responsible for preclearing all local, state and federal public policies to ensure they won't yield racial inequity, monitor those policies, investigate private racist policies when racial inequity surfaces, and monitor public officials for expressions of racist ideas. The DOA would be empowered with disciplinary tools to wield over and against policymakers and public officials who do not voluntarily change their racist policy and ideas.[227]

Kendi's constitutional prescription for America's "original sin of racism" is bewildering. If passed, would all citizens be required to believe that America's original sin is racism? Moreover, how much authority would this D.O.A. have and who would be its appointed officers? Would Katherine Watkins of Cedar Park Middle School be an ideal official in this department, who believes that the opponents of SJI are guilty of child abuse? Or perhaps Ibram Kendi would be ideal to serve in this capacity; after all, he is a leading voice within the SJI community. How would he apply his postulate of *present discrimination as a remedy for past discrimination* within such a powerful office? And what application of justice might America hope to receive from a man who believes that he has the right to render judgments against the whole nation by saying

---

227 Ibram X. Kendi, "Pass an Anti-Racist Constitutional Amendment" (Politico 2019).
https://www.politico.com/interactives/2019/how-to-fix-politics-in-america/inequality/pass-an-anti-racist-constitutional-amendment/.

"justice has convicted America"[228] when Derek Chauvin was found guilty of murder in the death of George Floyd?

Should the advocates of SJI acquire the power they seek, what exactly would happen to America's liberties which remain the envy of the world? One thing the student of history knows for certain is that the merging of man-made religion with money and power has always proven to be a lethal mixture. To the extent that SJI conducts itself as a new religion and is amassing great wealth and power, we should be on guard for what may come next for our nation, and especially for the church.

Finally, to the extent that SJI bears the form of religion, with its central creed and system self-atonement, it offers no real message of hope. Its only message is that of a *feigned* hope; that which is *fictitious and devised*. As such, it has nothing more than sweeping accusations, unsubstantiated claims,[229] undecipherable language and logic, and a system of self-atonement that never leads to actual reconciliation, but only leads to shame and division. As Robin DiAngelo admits in the beginning of her book, *White Fragility*: "This book does not attempt to provide the solution to racism."[230] Similarly, another popular book, *Divided by Faith*, surmises much about the "race disparities" in the American church but then its authors admit to having no help to offer the reader: "our analysis has not led us to specific solutions for ending racialization..."[231] For Kendi, he offers a tepid expression of hope, however it is one that raises many questions and much doubt:

---

[228] Jordan Davidson, "CBS Produces Segment With Anti-Capitalist Ibram X. Kendi Questioning 'Justice' of Chauvin Conviction" (The Federalist, 21 April 2021):___https://thefederalist.com/2021/04/21/cbs-produces-segment-with-anti-capitalist-ibram-x-kendi-questioning-justice-of-chauvin-conviction/.

[229] "Nor does it (her book, White Fragility) attempt to prove that racism exists; I start from that premise." DiAngelo, *White Fragility*, 5.

[230] Ibid.

[231] Michael O Emerson and Christian Smith, *Divided by Faith* (Oxford University Press: 2000), 171, Kindle.

> There is nothing I see in our world today, in our history, giving me hope that one day antiracists will win the fight, that one day the flag of antiracism will fly over a world of equity. What gives me hope is a simple truism. Once we lose hope, we are guaranteed to lose. But if we ignore the odds and fight to create an antiracist world, then we give humanity a chance to one day survive, a chance to live in communion, a chance to be forever free.[232]

Kendi's conclusion is disturbing because it reveals the bankruptcy of his Liberation Theology and SJI. He carries with him the same dangerous naïveté possessed by Engels, Marx, and the countless additional souls who sought an earthly paradise by means forceful revolution. The bloody legacy of all such revolutions reminds us that the path to destruction is often paved with sincere intentions. Disturbingly, Kendi's singular hope rests in the creation of an *antiracist world* after the image and likeness of his SJI agenda, consisting of *anticapitalist* and *pro-LGBTQ* credal standards.

        With such an agenda as this, we are left to wonder what will happen to those who, in good conscience before God, cannot promote the LGBTQ lifestyle. Or what will happen to those who are opposed to the socialist system of government that Kendi is clearly promoting? Will this Neo-Marxist, and others with him, have to resort to the confessional standards of classical Marxism and enact a *forcible overthrow of all existing social conditions?* Will Christians have to bow the knee to Kendi's mandates or be condemned as "racists" according to his contorted definitions? His conclusion raises more questions than it answers and leaves the reader with more confusion than real hope. Sadly, his notion of antiracism underscores what it means to "live in communion" with others and "be forever free." Because of this, he has clearly chosen to herald that which is temporal, deeply flawed, and corrupted by sin over

---

[232] Kendi, *How to Be an Antiracist,* 238.

the eternal life, forgiveness, and kingdom of Christ that is freely offered in the Gospel.

In all of this it should be quite clear to the reader that this new and powerful movement is utterly bankrupt of any real justice or hope.

JESUS' JUSTICE

Psalm 2:12:
12 Do homage to the Son, lest He become angry, and you perish in the
way, For His wrath may soon be kindled.
How blessed are all who take refuge in Him!

CHAPTER 6

SOCIAL JUSTICE IDEOLOGY
AND THE TALE OF TWO KINGDOMS

As we considered in the previous chapter, Johan Tetzel was not the first person to employ the tactics of manipulation in order to secure wealth and power over the masses; nor will he be the last. This disturbing scheme has played out through the span of history and always will, provided that there are credulous humans and greedy hucksters in the equation. Sadly, this dangerous mixture will persist until *The King of Righteousness is seen* sitting at the right hand of Power and coming with the clouds of heaven (Mark 14:62) to establish *His eternal kingdom (Psalm 110)*. Until that day comes, we will have to face the ebb and flow of philosophers and religionists who seek to subjugate society to *their* will.

Liberation Theology, which is SJI in religious garb, *is* yet another such movement and it seeks to replace the celestial crown of Christ and His kingdom with the *straw, sticks, and dust of this temporal world*, as Ibram Kendi well summarizes:

"Jesus was a revolutionary and…the job of the Christian is to *liberate society from the powers on earth that are oppressing humanity.* Everybody understands that, so, that's Liberation Theology in a nutshell."[233]

As noted in the previous chapter, Kendi's hope rests entirely on the establishment of a Postmodern, Neo-Marxist antiracist *kingdom on earth* rather than in the triumph of Jesus' justice and His eternal kingdom. And the pathway that leads to such earthly bliss, as he imagines it, is one which promotes the oppressor and oppressed binary whereby the world is seen as being engulfed in the plague of "whiteness." Yet we must wonder where all this constant vilification against one sector of humanity will lead us. Where else could it lead us except into the inevitable territory of greater division, distrust, and hate?

SJI's message of racial bigotry obliterates our sense of surprise whenever we see social hostility in its wake. For example, a New York City psychiatrist, Dr. Aruna Khilanani,[234] who spoke at a Yale School of Medicine conference (April 2021), openly emoted her repressed desire for murder, saying "I had fantasies of unloading a revolver into the head of any white person that got in my way, burying their body and wiping my bloody hands as I walked away relatively guiltless with a bounce in my step, like I did the world a favor." Ironically, the title of her lecture was *The Psychopathic Problem of the White Mind.* In a follow up to this disturbing presentation, BNC commentator Marc Lamont Hill interviewed Khilanani and asked this question: "would it be fair to say, based on your expertise, that white people are psychopathic?" She responded by saying, "I think so, yeah." Such rhetoric has been

---

[233] Ibram Kendi, Judson Memorial Church in Manhattan, in August 2019, italics mine.

[234] Samuel Chamberlain, "NYC shrink who talked about shooting white people now says they are 'psychopathic'" (New York Post, June 18 2021). https://nypost.com/2021/06/18/nyc-shrink-who-talked-about-shooting-white-people-now-says-they-are-psychopathic/.

commonplace among the more secular expressions of SJI, and yet these same expressions of hatred are actually becoming normalized and promoted among professing Christians.

In Sarah Bessey's New York Times bestseller, *A Rhythm of Prayer*, we have a stunning example of the hostility and hate that is regularly promoted in SJI. One particular prayer, *Prayer of a Weary Black Woman*, by Chanequa Walker-Barnes, hides precious little regarding the author's disdain for "white people":

Dear God, Please help me to hate White people. Or at least to want to hate them. At least, I want to stop caring about them, individually and collectively. I want to stop caring about their misguided, racist souls, to stop believing that they can be better, that they can stop being racist...[235]

Walker-Barnes, who claims to be a Christian, issues no repentance for her attitude; makes no request for a changed heart or for the grace to love her enemies *as Christ commands*,[236] but instead asks for a "Get Out of Judgment Free card" after treating her readers to the following invectives:

Lord, grant me, then, the permission and desire to hate the White people who claim the progressive label but who are really wolves in sheep's clothing. Those who've learned enough history, read enough books, spent enough time in other countries to make themselves seem knowledgeable even though that

---

[235] Sarah Bessey, *A Rhythm of Prayer: A Collection of Meditations for Renewal*, (Convergent Books, February 2021), 69.

[236] Matthew 5:43–46: 43 "You have heard that it was said, 'YOU SHALL LOVE YOUR NEIGHBOR, and hate your enemy.' 44 "But I say to you, love your enemies, and pray for those who persecute you 45 in order that you may be sons of your Father who is in heaven; for He causes His sun to rise on the evil and the good, and sends rain on the righteous and the unrighteous. 46 "For if you love those who love you, what reward have you? Do not even the tax-gatherers do the same?

knowledge remains far removed from their hearts. Those whose unexamined White supremacy bubbles up at times I'm not expecting it, when I have my guard down and my heart open. Lord, if you can't make me hate them, at least spare me from their perennial gaslighting, whiteman-splaining, and White woman tears. Lord, if it be your will, harden my heart. Stop me from striving to see the best in people. Stop me from being hopeful that White people can do and be better."[237]

The thought of asking God to harden one's heart is more than disturbing, it transcends imagination. Sadly, by virtue of the content of the author's prayer, her petition may have already been granted. Though this passage is stunning, it shouldn't be terribly surprising. SJI advocates preach a message of *vilification and shame* with inflexible certitude, while offering no real hope for reconciliation. This is necessary for the maintenance of "white guilt," which sustains the requisite oppressor and oppressed binary. However, religious leaders who embrace racial bigotry like this, in the name of "justice," are simply demonstrating their disdain for God and His commands.

While it may be fashionable to parade such vitriol for others in the modern day, it has no place among God's people who are called to follow Christ rather than the whims of men. In the case of Chanequa Walker-Barnes, her overt racial bigotry and disdain for "whites" has its roots, not in Scripture, but in Liberation Theology advocates like James Cone:

It is interesting that most people do understand why Jews can hate Germans. Why can they not understand why black people, who have been deliberately and systematically dehumanized or murdered by the structure of this society, hate white people?[238]

---

[237] Bessey, *A Rhythm of Prayer*, 70-71.
[238] Cone, *Black Theology and Black Power*, 15.

Statements like this, which support racial bigotry and hatred, are typical with Cone and his followers. The fact that he frequently quotes from Scripture and invokes the name of Jesus reveals the bankruptcy of his "theology."

However, all such tactics have a familiar ring to them. With Tetzel's messages he *vilified and shamed* his audiences, even evoking the memory of dead relatives in order to sell his faux-forgiveness. This was the very mechanism he employed in order to establish a carefully crafted system of societal persuasion and control, and it bears an ugly likeness to the faux religion of Liberation Theology. Whether we are talking about James Cone or Johan Tetzel, it is clear that neither man proclaimed the Gospel of Christ which promises, not only eternal forgiveness, but the kind of *transformation of life* that can lead one to love others, *even their enemies*:

> Matthew 5:43–45: 43 "You have heard that it was said, 'YOU SHALL LOVE YOUR NEIGHBOR, and hate your enemy.' 44 "But I say to you, love your enemies, and pray for those who persecute you 45 in order that you may be sons of your Father who is in heaven; for He causes His sun to rise on the evil and the good, and sends rain on the righteous and the unrighteous.

The message of the Gospel is one of mercy, grace, forgiveness, love, justice, redemption, and a work of sanctification that is so powerful and miraculous that a person can have a love for their enemy after the pattern of God Himself. No mere *ideology* can do this. The message of Liberation Theology is the very antithesis to biblical revelation because it supplies substitutes for *the Gospel, the Christian's citizenship, and the kingdom of Christ.* We will review these briefly, followed by a consideration of how Liberation Theology contradicts all three Christian beliefs:

1. The Gospel: The word *Gospel* (εὐαγγέλιον, *euaggelion*) simply means *good news.* We saw a preview of the Gospel's message when we looked at Psalm 2:12

where we learned that *all who take refuge in the Son of God are blessed.* Such good news is especially wonderful in light of the context in which that promise is made: "Do homage to the Son, lest He become angry, and you *perish in the way, for His wrath may soon be kindled.*"

The simple message of these passages is quite clear: when Christ comes again He will judge the world in righteousness (Acts 17:31), and only those who take refuge in Him by faith will be saved from His wrath. This same truth was expounded to Nicodemus when Jesus described the supremacy of His salvation over the temporal deliverance supplied by Moses: "And as Moses lifted up the serpent in the wilderness, even so must the Son of Man be lifted up; that whoever believes may in Him have eternal life" (John 3:14-15). Christ then taught Nicodemus that he too could experience eternal salvation rather than perish in wrath: "For God so loved the world, that He gave His only begotten Son, that whoever believes in Him should not perish, but have eternal life." (John 3:16). The deliverance supplied through Moses was limited, temporal, and constrained to this world; but what Christ accomplished when He died on the cross and rose again from the grave achieves *eternal salvation* for all who believe in Him. Only a fool would trade the latter for the former.

What Christ presented to Nicodemus is the same binary message that is throughout Scripture, and it is the only one that matters: "He who believes in Him is not judged; he who does not believe has been judged already, because he has not believed in the name of the only begotten Son of God." (John 3:18). When we contrast the message of the Gospel with the current day discussions of justice, we come to a crucial but troubling reality: had God poured out nothing but His holy justice upon the human race all would be condemned by the eternal judgment of the Almighty; or as it says a few verses later in John 3, "He who believes in the Son has eternal life; but he who does not believe in the Son shall not see life, but the wrath of God abides on him." (John 3:36).

Thus *the good news* is that those who *take refuge in the Son* are spared of wrath,[239] being redeemed by grace through faith; not by any personal merit or

---

[239] Ephesians 2:1–3: 1 AND you were dead in your trespasses and sins, 2 in which you formerly walked according to the course of this world, according to the prince of the power of the air, of the spirit that is now working in the sons of disobedience. 3 Among them we too all formerly lived in the lusts of our flesh,

works.[240] Because of this they understand that they have no reason to boast, except in the Lord alone.[241] Those who are His[242] have a new position in that they are delivered from the domain of darkness and are transferred to the kingdom of the beloved Son (Colossians 1:13). They also have a new nature,[243] by the indwelling Spirit,[244] and bear fruit for God's glory by His strength. This spiritual progress will continue within the child of God amidst an ongoing battle[245] against sin.[246]

Only in eternal glory will this battle of sin end in the final resurrection[247] of God's people.[248] Until that day comes, it is the calling of all believers to be engaged with this world as doers of God's word, not merely hearers who delude themselves (James 1:22). As those who have been saved by grace, believers in Christ are to be gracious and merciful to others (Ephesians 4), loving the Lord their God, loving their neighbor,[249] *and even loving their enemies*[250] to the chief end that God would be glorified in everything.

2. The Christian's Dual Genealogy and Citizenship: God's work of salvation delivers men and women to a new and blessed status whereby they are adopted into the family of God[251] as members of His household.[252] This familial status

---

indulging the desires of the flesh and of the mind, and were by nature children of wrath, even as the rest.

[240] Ephesians 2:8-9; Gal. 2:16.

[241] 2 Corinthians 10:17.

[242] John 6:39: "And this is the will of Him who sent Me, that of all that He has given Me I lose nothing, but raise it up on the last day."

[243] 2 Cor. 5:17, Gal. 2:20.

[244] Romans 8:12-17.

[245] Gal. 5:18-20.

[246] 1 John 1:8.

[247] Phil. 3:20-21.

[248] Phil. 1:6.

[249] Mark 12:28-31.

[250] Matthew 5:43–45.

[251] Ephesians 1:5, Romans 8:14.

brings with it a new, heavenly citizenship; the former establishing the basis for the latter. The Apostle Peter brings these conjoined realities together when he wrote: "But you are A CHOSEN RACE, A royal PRIESTHOOD, A HOLY NATION, A PEOPLE FOR God's OWN POSSESSION, that you may proclaim the excellencies of Him who has called you out of darkness into His marvelous light." (1 Peter 2:9).

When Peter addressed his Christian readers, he employed our now familiar term γένος, *genos* when calling them a chosen *race*. This is yet another reason why the word *race* is important and should be preserved from mutilation by contemporary fads and philosophies. The fact that believers are members of this spiritual race,[253] as the children of God, also means that they serve the highest authority of all as the citizens of heaven. This again brings us to the crucial binary division of humanity as established by God Himself: the children of God and the children of the devil. Thematically speaking this division is found throughout Scripture.[254]

Jesus taught this principle in the parable of the wheat and the tares (Matthew 13:36-43) when He interpreted the lesson for His disciples: "the field is the world; and as for the good seed, these are the sons of the kingdom; and the tares are the sons of the evil one." (Matthew 13:38). Nowhere in Scripture are we given a third category of humanity. This privileged position then means that believers are to *be imitators of God as beloved children*[255] who walk as children of light rather than by the darkness of this world.[256]

---

[252] Ephesians 2:19.

[253] This race, or genealogy, is a spiritual one consisting of all those who are *in Christ* through faith. The Apostle Paul underscores this idea in Galatians 3:15-29 wherein he identifies Christ as the promised seed of Abraham (Genesis 22:18), and all those who are in Christ (through faith) are Abraham's seed, heirs according to promise. Thus, this spiritual lineage through Abraham goes back to Christ Himself such that, in Him, "there is neither Jew nor Greek, there is neither slave nor free man, there is neither male nor female; for you are all one in Christ Jesus." (Galatians 3:28).

[254] 1 John 3:6-11.

[255] Ephesians 5:1: 1 THEREFORE be imitators of God, as beloved children.

[256] Ephesians 5:8: 8 for you were formerly darkness, but now you are light in the Lord; walk as children of light.

And so it is that the children of God have dual genealogies and citizenships. Physically speaking, they are members of the single human race while having a temporal citizenship here on earth.[257] Spiritually speaking, they are members of the spiritual, chosen race of God's household and are the citizens of heaven. We must remember that when Paul calls believers the citizens (πολίτευμα, *politeuma*) of heaven in Philippians 3:20, this word does not speak of a *position* that is devoid of a requisite *practice*. Instead, the Greek root πόλις (*polis*), from which we get the English word *politics*, speaks of the *bond* and *obligations* one has with other citizens and therefore it can refer to an individual's *conduct* as a citizen. Because of this, Paul exhorted believers to manifest the glories of their heavenly citizenship by a *conduct* which magnifies the Gospel: "Only *conduct* (πολιτεύεσθε, *politeuesthe*) yourselves in a manner worthy of the gospel of Christ" (Philippians 1:27).

Such conduct is not the result of *fleshly compulsion* but is derived from a willingness of heart as a result of the Holy Spirit's work in the believer. In all of this, the great calling for all of Christ's servants is to be faithful stewards of their earthly responsibilities *while fixing their eyes on Christ and His kingdom*.[258]

3. The Kingdom of Christ: From the very beginning we have looked briefly at a few key passages that reveal several things about the kingdom of Christ. Our summary of Psalms 2 and 110 reminded us that Christ will triumph over all the kingdoms of the earth as the King of kings and Lord of lords.[259] Though the

---

[257] Romans 13:1-7.

[258] Hebrews 12:1–3: 1 THEREFORE, since we have so great a cloud of witnesses surrounding us, let us also lay aside every encumbrance, and the sin which so easily entangles us, and let us run with endurance the race that is set before us, 2 fixing our eyes on Jesus, the author and perfecter of faith, who for the joy set before Him endured the cross, despising the shame, and has sat down at the right hand of the throne of God. 3 For consider Him who has endured such hostility by sinners against Himself, so that you may not grow weary and lose heart.

[259] Philippians 2:9–11: 9 Therefore also God highly exalted Him, and bestowed on Him the name which is above every name, 10 that at the name of Jesus EVERY

nations rage against the Lord and His anointed Messiah,[260] they will be defeated, subdued, and shattered with a rod of iron (Psalm 2:9; 110:1-2, 5).

The *good news* is that the Messiah, the priestly King of Righteousness (Melchizedek Psalm 110:4, Hebrews 7), will redeem many who will be members of His kingdom and serve Him *willingly and joyfully* (Psalm 110:3). Their willingness of heart glorifies the Savior in view of His salvific and sanctifying work. When the Savior returns He will establish a new heaven and new earth where He will wipe away every tear, for in His eternal kingdom *there shall no longer be any death; there shall no longer be any mourning, or crying, or pain*[261] and "there shall no longer be any night; and they shall not have need of the light of a lamp nor the light of the sun, because the Lord God shall illumine them; and they shall reign forever and ever" (Revelation 22:5). Until that day comes, God's true children are known in this world *not* for their longing for the kingdom *by itself,* but for their intense and eager longing for *the Savior above all.*

Perhaps one of the most lethal aspects of SJI, as manifested within the contemporary church, has to do with its derogation of the above truths. One prominent book that has had a significant role in influencing pastors and congregants alike is *Divided by Faith – Evangelical Religion and the Problem of Race in America,* by Michael O. Emerson and Christian Smith. Several times throughout the book, they criticize what they call the "miracle motif," a degrading euphemism for God's work of salvation and sanctification:

KNEE SHOULD BOW, of those who are in heaven, and on earth, and under the earth, 11 and that every tongue should confess that Jesus Christ is Lord, to the glory of God the Father.

[260] Psalm 2:1–3: 1 WHY are the nations in an uproar, And the peoples devising a vain thing? 2 The kings of the earth take their stand, And the rulers take counsel together Against the LORD and against His Anointed: 3 "Let us tear their fetters apart, And cast away their cords from us!"

[261] Revelation 21:4: 4 and He shall wipe away every tear from their eyes; and there shall no longer be any death; there shall no longer be any mourning, or crying, or pain; the first things have passed away."

"...the miracle motif holds...that society is improved by improving individuals. Because society is viewed as merely the aggregation of individuals, social change is achieved by personal change and renewal—most important, by people becoming Christians."[262]

Emerson and Smith repeatedly refer to the biblical concepts of salvation and sanctification as the *miracle motif,* insisting that "White evangelical solutions to racialization are thus limited and, by themselves, ultimately doomed to failure."[263] The disturbing feature of what is presented in *Divided by Faith* is that it obfuscates the work of God's grace in the life of a child of God.

Contrary to their faulty supposition, salvation is not a mere *motif,* but stands as evidence to the world that He can take rebellious men and women and give them new hearts and desires which lead them to joyful servitude. This is the promised work of the Messiah in Psalm 110:3 as Charles Haddon Spurgeon so excellently summarized:

Psalm 110:3 "Thy people will volunteer freely in the day of Thy power." - "They [God's people] are a willing people...all that they do, they do willingly, for they are constrained by no compulsion, but by grace alone. I am sure we all can do a thing far better when we are willing than when we are forced. God loves his people's services, because they do them voluntarily. Voluntaryism is the essence of the gospel. Willing people are those whom God delights to have as his servants. He would not have slaves to grace his throne, but free men, who, with gladness and joy, should be willing in the day of his power."

Such *voluntaryism* is rooted in love: a love for Christ;[264] a love for the brethren;[265] and a love for one's neighbor.[266] Thus, the children of God are

---

[262] Emerson and Smith, *Divided by Faith,* 117.

[263] Ibid., 132.

[264] 1 Corinthians 16:22.

evident by virtue of their love for the Lord, which also means that they do not love this sinful world[267] because friendship with the world is hostility toward God.[268] They remain in this life as imperfect vessels who battle daily with sin, but are being sanctified by Christ's daily provision of grace. The love that believers possess does not originate from within them, but originates in God alone.[269]

However, Liberation Theology obliterates all these aforementioned points of biblical truth. Though disturbing, this reality is somewhat unsurprising seeing that Liberation Theology denies biblical authority. As Cone has opined, "God was not the author of the Bible...efforts to prove verbal inspiration of the Scriptures results from the failure to see the real meaning of the biblical message: human liberation! Unfortunately, emphasis on verbal infallibility leads to unimportant concerns."[270]

With its denial of scriptural authority and anthropocentric emphasis on *human liberation from earthly oppression,* Liberation Theology is nothing more than a spiritual tomb filled with dead men's bones. Instead of presenting the message of the *Savior,* the Lord Jesus Christ, Liberation Theology bears a striking resemblance to an epistemology of secularism, as already described: *The doctrine that morality should be based solely on regard to the well-being of mankind in the present life, to the exclusion of all considerations drawn from belief in God or in a future state.* Whereas the Gospel of Jesus Christ presents a real hope through the deliverance *from* sin, death, and eternal condemnation unto the heavenly Kingdom of Christ, Liberation Theology

---

[265] John 13:35: "By this all men will know that you are My disciples, if you have love for one another."

[266] Mark 12:28-31.

[267] 1 John 2:15-17.

[268] James 4:4.

[269] Galatians 5:22-23; 1 John 4:19: We love, because He first loved us.

[270] Cone, *A Black Theology of Liberation,* 847, Kindle.

settles for a freedom from earthly oppression, as Cone has delineated: "the Marxists claim that black religion is an opiate, we reply merely that sometimes it is and sometimes it is not...many blacks have found in religion not an opiate but a tonic that gives courage and strength in the struggle of freedom."[271] Though Liberation Theology is fraught with religious language and customs, it is both secular and agnostic in its ultimate focus. Devoid of any Gospel content, Liberation Theology offers nothing more than a mere *tonic* of a secularized religion.

However, the liberation that Jesus did preach was that of a liberation from the slavery of one's sin (John 8:33-36), not governmental oppression in this life. Moreover, Christ promised His followers that they would be hated by all on account of His name and experience considerable oppression (Matthew 10:22). Because Jesus' disciples are members of His *chosen race* and are *citizens of heaven*, they are prohibited from being surprised when the world hates them (1 John 3:13), but they must remember that their pursuit of righteous living in this fallen world will result in persecution. Since they will be persecuted in the likeness of Christ Himself, they should rejoice in the face of such trials:

Matthew 5:10–12: 10 "Blessed are those who have been persecuted for the sake of righteousness, for theirs is the kingdom of heaven. 11 "Blessed are you when men cast insults at you, and persecute you, and say all kinds of evil against you falsely, on account of Me. 12 "Rejoice, and be glad, for your reward in heaven is great, for so they persecuted the prophets who were before you."

By virtue of Christ's repeated use of the word *blessed* (μακάριοι, *makarioi*) we should be reminded that all who take refuge in the Son are *blessed* (Psalm 2:12, LXX: μακάριοι, *makarioi*). They are blessed, *not by an absence of oppression in this world*, but in view of the Son's *work* of salvation, sanctification, and perseverance in their lives; *a work that*

---

[271] Cone, *The Black church and Marxism*, 174-75, Kindle.

remains inviolable within a world that devises vanity and rages against the Almighty.

Clearly, Christ's call to rejoice in the face of trials, in view of one's *heavenly reward*, is the very opposite of Liberation Theology where every form of oppression, whether real or imagined, must be removed by revolution. For Cone and others, this turns the individual from seeking the joy of Christ's eternal kingdom to preaching "Black Power and Black Freedom."[272] Perhaps one of the most disturbing realities of Liberation Theology is that its veil of religion has made it the latest Trojan horse to enter freely into the professing church. And we must wonder where this will lead us in the future, especially if SJI is *given* free rein.

All this brings us to yet another incipient error found within SJI, which similarly undermines the message of the Gospel: *cultural relativity*. In order to evaluate this concept we must first consider the word culture itself. The word has a long and complex etymology, but, as it is used today, it typically refers to the social institutions, customs, arts, literature, and societal accomplishments that are *cultivated* (produced) by any given people-group or nation. As such, this is a metaphorical use of the term's historic connotation: *cultivate*, as in the *cultivation of soil* or *tillage*. Of course, cultures can vary significantly with respect to institutions, customs, arts, literature, and societal accomplishments. Cultural relativity seeks to embrace and accept all societal cultures by eliminating any standards of critical analysis of such cultures. In our modern world of "Social Justice," a modified form of cultural relativity is employed in which SJI-friendly cultures are accepted as normative, while all other all others are rejected. For Kendi, such an interpretive standard for culture isn't an optional concept, but is central to what it means to be an antiracist:

---

[272] "Preaching in its truest sense tells the world about Christ's victory and thus invites people to act as if God has won the battle over racism. To preach in America today is to shout 'Black Power! Black Freedom.'" Cone, *Black Theology and Black Power*, 76, Kindle.

"'All cultures must be judged in relation to their own history, and all individuals and groups in relation to their cultural history, and definitely not by the arbitrary standard of any single culture,' wrote Ashley Montagu in 1942, a clear expression of cultural relativity, the essence of cultural antiracism."[273]

"To be antiracist is to reject cultural standards and level cultural difference...to be antiracist is to see all cultures in all their differences as on the same level, as equals. When we see cultural difference, we are seeing cultural difference—nothing more, nothing less."[274]

In addition to Kendi's *explicit* mention of *cultural relativism* (an interpretation of one's culture apart from any external standards) and *cultural leveling* (communication between cultures leading to commonality), he also *implicitly* advocates the concept of *cultural collectivism* which places its focus on the *collective* as having a higher value than one's personal cultural standards. For the sake of simplicity, from this point forward I will just use the label *cultural collectivism* since this lies at the root of all that Kendi is promoting. As such, it is a system that seeks to *compel cultural change and conformity* according to the standards and definitions of SJI. By adding such a standard to his definition of antiracism, Kendi further tightens the strictures already in place for his readers. His conclusion is simple enough: failure to have a broad-based acceptance of other cultures is *racist.*

Like many other pontifications made by Kendi, it is difficult to imagine that he really seeks to *reject cultural standards and level cultural difference,* as he said. If Kendi were to apply such a standard, then how would he respond to the various cultures of the past and present? The Athenian culture, as we have reviewed, was fraught with religiously fueled

---

[273] Kendi, *How to Be an Antiracist,* 91.
[274] Ibid., 84, 91.

racism enough to make a Klansman blush. Would he charitably embrace this? Or are we to imagine that Kendi would be broad minded enough to embrace the culture of the antebellum South or of the culture of slavery in modern day Sudan?

These questions expose the illusory nature of *cultural collectivism*. When Kendi says, "When we see cultural difference, we are seeing cultural difference—nothing more, nothing less," his statement is rather disingenuous, because he also insists that there should be a "levelling of cultural differences." *Cultural levelling* and *cultural collectivism* refer to the diminishment of cultural differences, requiring an adjustment of certain standards within society. Thus, SJI seeks the *promotion* or *mitigation* of cultural norms in order to bring about conformity with its core tenets. In terms of such *cultural promotion*, questionable societal practices are often advanced with demands for *tolerance*, which is really code for *compulsory acceptance*. For example, the prevalence of "Drag Queen Story Hour" in public libraries continues to spread throughout our nation with supportive cries for tolerance. Those who dare to oppose such things are typically labelled as ignorant and intolerant. By this procedure, the LGBTQ culture is *promoted* in society consistent with SJI standards.

In terms of *cultural mitigation*, many SJI advocates speak of the pervasive dangers of *cultural colonialism*, or the spread of "White Western civilization." Many insist on mitigating or even eliminating literature and scientific resources produced by "whites." More and more we hear about public schools throughout the nation abandoning Shakespeare's works because they are said to promote "white supremacy and intolerance."[275] By this procedure, cultural standards in violation with SJI are *mitigated* for the good of the collective. Much of this *cultural*

---

[275] Harriet Alexander "How 'woke' English teachers have cancelled Shakespeare," (Daily Mail, February 15 2021) https://www.dailymail.co.uk/news/article-9263735/Woke-teachers-cut-Shakespeare-work-white-supremacy-colonization.html.

collectivism is taking place in our nation's educational system and it is all rooted in compulsory activism and control.

Reports continue to surface of parents expressing grave concern over obscene and pornographic books that are promoted in the name of "equity." Joe Mobley of Loudoun County, VA expressed his concerns about the literature being supplied to young children, saying "they have books that are supposed to be teaching equity but what they are really teaching, you know, it is a language that we can't say [on air] here but very sexually explicit stuff."[276] Such examples now appear on a daily basis revealing that the entire premise of *cultural collectivism* is that any and all forms of culture which conflict with the tenets of SJI must be mitigated or entirely eliminated for the sake of "justice." History reveals that this is a very dangerous trend.

In the third chapter we introduced the tragic realities of Christian persecution in the 1st century Roman Empire. Much of this came in a form of *cultural collectivism* as we have been reviewing. Nearly all of Rome's literature, art, entertainment, philosophies, and rituals were deeply rooted in paganism, often making it impossible for Christians to partake in many public activities. We could consult several examples of this, but it would be far better to consider the root source of this divide which clearly distinguishes between the cultures of paganism and Christianity: *the love of God.*

For the disciples of Christ, their culture is inherently different because they seek a cause higher than themselves *via* their *loving servitude for Christ.* Such a priority of love was made evident when Christ identified the commandment of love as being *the foremost of all*: "You shall love the Lord our God with all your heart, and with all your soul, and

---

[276] Joshua Q. Nelson, "Virginia parents blast school board over graphic books," (Fox News: May 13 2021) https://www.foxnews.com/us/virginia-parents-loudoun-school-board-graphic-books-critical-race-theory.

with all your mind, and with all your strength."[277] We should note that the word Christ used for *love* (ἀγαπήσεις > ἀγάπη, *agapē)* was rarely employed in the secular world at the time. Within the Graeco-Roman world, *erōs*-love was heralded as *the foremost*. Such love was deeply *self-oriented* and supplied the breeding ground for a tremendously *hedonistic culture*.

The contrast between these concepts of love could not be greater. The Christian reality of *agapē*-love had a radically different orientation, making the word *erōs*,[278] and its related term *hēdonē* (hedonism), impossible to use in any godly sense. Unlike the self-orientation of *erōs* and *hēdonē*, the word *agapē* is centered in the idea of *union with another (i.e., a relationship)*. For the Christian, the defining element of *agapē*-love is union with Christ.[279] Because of this, Christian love is

---

[277] Mark 12:29–31: 29 Jesus answered, "The foremost is, 'HEAR, O ISRAEL! THE LORD OUR GOD IS ONE LORD;30 AND YOU SHALL LOVE THE LORD YOUR GOD WITH ALL YOUR HEART, AND WITH ALL YOUR SOUL, AND WITH ALL YOUR MIND, AND WITH ALL YOUR STRENGTH.'31 "The second is this, 'YOU SHALL LOVE YOUR NEIGHBOR AS YOURSELF.' There is no other commandment greater than these."

[278] "I observe in conclusion that *erōs, eran, erastes,* never occur in the N.T., but the two latter occasionally in the Septuagint; thus *eran,* Esth. 2:17; Prov. 4:6; *erastes* generally in a dishonorable sense as 'paramour' (Ezek. 16:33; Hos. 2:5); yet once or twice (as Wisd. 8:2) more honorably, not as='amasius, ' but 'amator.' Their absence is significant. It is in part no doubt to be explained from the fact that, by the corrupt use of the world, they had become so steeped in sensual passion, carried such an atmosphere of unholiness about them (see Origen, *Prol. in Cant. Opp.* tom iii. pp. 28–30), that the truth of God abstained from the defiling contact with them; yea, devised a new word rather than betake itself to one of these." Trench, R. C. (2003). *Synonyms of the New Testament.* (9th ed., improved.) (43). Bellingham, WA: Logos Research Systems, Inc.

[279] 1 John 4:7-10: 7. Beloved, let us love one another, for love is from God; and everyone who loves is born of God and knows God. 8. The one who does not love does not know God, for God is love. 9. By this the love of God was manifested in

always grounded in a Christ-centered valuation of everything, including our relationships with a spouse, children, other brethren, and the lost of this world. In this sense, the pre-biblical notion of *agapē* (honoring others) is somewhat preserved in this New Testament usage.[280] Such a concept of honor within *agapē*-love reveals a beautiful expression of harmony between the OT and the NT: children are taught to honor (*appreciate* or highly esteem) their father and mother in the fifth commandment (Exodus 20:12, Ephesians 6:2) as their earliest pedagogy of filial love and devotion. Such are the early *tutorials* that point us to the higher calling of being the children of God. In view of this, it is not difficult to see the strength and centrality of the term *agapē*.

By significant contrast, at the core of *erōs* one will not find such a concept of *otherness* because individual passion remains supreme. It is this self-centered pursuit of pleasure that saturated the 1ˢᵗ century Graeco-Roman *pagan culture* and influenced every aspect of life.[281]

---

us, that God has sent His only begotten Son into the world so that we might live through Him. 10. In this is love, not that we loved God, but that He loved us and sent His Son to be the propitiation for our sins.

[280] "The translators probably preferred the words of the *agapaō* group which convey less affective emphasis since they designate 'a sober kind of love—love in the sense of placing a high value upon some person or thing, or of receiving them with favour' (Warnach, SacVB 518; in this connection see also Joly)." Balz, H. R., & Schneider, G. (1990-c1993). *Exegetical dictionary of the New Testament.* Translation of: Exegetisches Worterbuch zum Neuen Testament. (1:9). Grand Rapids, Mich.: Eerdmans.

[281] "What the Greek seeks in *eros* is intoxication, and this is to him religion. To be sure, reflection is the finest of the flirts which the heavenly powers have set in the heart of man (Soph. Ant., 683 ff.); it is the fulfillment of humanity in measure. More glorious, however, is the *eros* which puts an end to all reflection, which sets all the senses in a frenzy, which bursts the measure and form of all humanistic humanity and lifts man above himself...It is a god, and he is powerful even above the gods: *turannos theon te kanthropon* (Eur. Fr., 132, Nauck). All the forces of

Unsurprisingly, the lack of Christian participation in hedonistic, pagan rituals is what led others to believe that the followers of Christ were the hostile source of all calamities. Society's disdain for such non-participation continued to increase with time, as characterized by Minucius Felix:

"You apprehensive and anxiety-ridden Christians abstain from innocent pleasures. You don't watch the public spectacles, you don't take part in the processions, you absent yourselves from the public banquets, you shrink away from sacred games, sacrificial meat, and altar libations. That's how frightened you are of the gods whose existence you deny!"[282]

In an environment such as this, their own version of *cultural collectivism* produced tremendous pressure upon the Christian community to compromise their consciences before God. Failure to assimilate with a hedonistic society resulted in severe persecution, with many being brutalized and murdered in the name of justice; for Rome and her gods. Non-compliant believers were labelled as the *enemies of humanity* because of their lack of participation in the annual religious festivals which were believed to be necessary for the sustenance of the gods. Over time, the vilification of the Christian community led to the first official persecution of the church as decreed by Nero. A brief account of this development is described by the Roman historian Tacitus:

"But neither human resources, nor imperial munificence, nor appeasement of the gods, eliminated sinister suspicions that the fire had been instigated. To suppress this rumour, Nero fabricated scapegoats – and punished with every

---

heaven and earth are forces of second rank compared with the one and only supreme power of *eros*. No choice is left, nor will, nor freedom, to the man who is seized by its tyrannical omnipotence, and he finds supreme bliss in being mastered by it." Gerhard Kittel ed., *The Theological Dictionary of the New Testament*, (Michigan: Eerdmans Publishing, 1991), 1:35.

[282] Minucius Felix, *Octavius* 8.4, 5; 9.2, 4-7; 10.2, 5; 12:5.

refinement the notoriously depraved Christians (as they were popularly called). Their originator, Christ, had been executed in Tiberius' reign by the governor of Judaea, Pontius Pilatus. But in spite of this temporary setback the deadly superstition had broken out afresh, not only in Judaea (where the mischief had started) but even in Rome. All degraded and shameful practices collect and flourish in the capital. First, Nero had self-acknowledged Christians arrested. Then, on their information, large numbers of others were condemned - not so much for incendiarism as for their hatred of humanity. Their deaths were made farcical. Dressed in wild animals' skins, they were torn to pieces by dogs, or crucified, or made into torches to be ignited after dark as substitutes for daylight."[283]

Tacitus' description of these early Christians reveals how they were falsely labelled *as the haters of humanity,* which resulted in horrific brutality. As we have already reviewed, the Christian community resisted, not out of a hatred for humanity, but out of their love for Christ. They could not, for conscience' sake, participate in the hedonistic and idolatrous culture of the Graeco-Roman world, replete with its sacrifices to the gods and licentious conduct often associated with such worship.[284]

Of course, there will be those who will imagine that these events of yesteryear could not happen in the current day. Yet we must not forget our earlier consideration regarding history's tutelage. In the modern day we find tremendous pressure being placed upon individuals to accept, repeat, and promote the antiracist creed, all of which is centered on an

---

[283] Tacitus, *The Annals of Imperial Rome,* (New York: Barnes & Noble Books, 1993), 365, italics mine.

[284] Minucius Felis: "You apprehensive and anxiety-ridden Christians abstain from innocent pleasures. You don't watch the public spectacles, you don't take part in the processions, you absent yourselves from the public banquets, you shrink away from sacred games, sacrificial meat, and altar libations. That's how frightened you are of the gods whose existence you deny!" Minucius Felix, Octavius 8.4, 5; 9.2, 4-7; 10.2, 5; 12:5.

SJI-centric *cultural collectivism.* In such thinking as this, one is left to wonder who will be required to make cultural accommodations according to SJI's standards *and who will be in charge of pulling the levers of change.* Remember, in Kendi's world of prescribed antiracism he envisions the establishment of a Department of Anti-racism (DOA) *that would be empowered with disciplinary tools to wield over and against policymakers and public officials who do not voluntarily change their "racist" policy and ideas.* The thought of granting a government agency the *power and disciplinary tools* to enforce Kendi's vision of antiracism may seem benign to some, but is not. SJI's persistent language of revolution and cultural collectivism should remind us that ideas printed on paper may appear to be harmless, however they can yield unspeakable disasters for humanity:

> "[an incorrect viewpoint] manifests itself in various ways...[when individuals] hear incorrect views without rebutting them and even...hear counter-revolutionary remarks without reporting them, but instead to take them calmly as if nothing had happened. This is a sixth type [of error]."[285]

The above passage is from a work called, *The Little Red Book,* and was foundational to China's Cultural Revolution (1966-1976) in which as many as 65 million dissidents were brutalized and murdered. Written by Mao Tse-Tung, this booklet warns its readers about the danger of complicity with "incorrect views", which, in this particular quote refers to *liberalism* (L. līberālis: freedom, free thinking).[286] To do this, Chairman Mao listed multiple *types of danger* that arise from free thinking because

---

[285] Mao Tse Tung, *The Little Red Book,* 1653-1654, Kindle.

[286] The word *liberal* has experienced tremendous change over the years. Its core meaning is simple enough. Coming from the French term *libéral* it refers to a *free man.* However, in more recent years it is sometimes used as a political label referring to leftist policies favoring Socialism and even Communism. In such cases as this it represents a total reversal of connotation. In the above citation, Mao is clearly referring to the problem of *free thinkers* as if this were an actual problem.

such freedom elevated individuality while diminishing the nation's collectivist ideals. Like any other Marxist movement, Mao's oppressive Cultural Revolution was rooted in *compulsory obedience,* and those who failed to support his revolution were subjected to public shaming, torture, and death. He was able to do all this because he had secured the *power and disciplinary tools* necessary to enforce his ideology.

In free, multi-cultural societies, the right to agree or disagree with the social institutions, customs, arts, literature, and societal accomplishments of any sector of one's nation is the bedrock of societal liberty. Exercising this liberty isn't inherent evidence of racial bigotry. It is, instead, the right of every citizen who believes in such freedom. More than this, it is the prerogative of all Christians to exercise discernment and sound judgment when assessing the cultures of this world, *issuing criticism or praise according to one's conscience.* However, the absence of such freedom predictably leads to nothing but *compulsory enslavement and brutality.*

All this leads us to a crucial conclusion within this chapter. In stark contrast to the corrupt and worldly realities of human bondage, abuse, and compulsory servitude, the Bible describes the Christian as a *bondslave (δοῦλος, doulos) of Christ,* which depicts a servitude that is rooted in true freedom and joyful voluntarism, *all in the bonds of love.*[287] Servitude such as this is something that the world does not and cannot know. While this language may seem alien to many, such a description is

---

[287] OED correlates the word bondslave with a *bondman* (a man in who is bound). Such imagery is found in 2 Corinthians 4:5 when the Apostle Paul called himself a bondslave (δοῦλος, *doulos*) "for Jesus' sake" and then described the nature of his servitude a few verses later: "For the love of Christ controls (συνέχει, *sunexei*) us..." (2 Corinthians 5:14). The word "controls" (συνέχει, *sunexei*) can also be translated as *constrain.* When we think of Christians as being the bondslaves of God we must remember that their constraints/bonds consist of eternal love.

repeatedly found throughout Scripture (Acts 2:18, 4:29; Romans 1:1, 6:16-17; 1 Corinthians 7:22; 2 Corinthians 4:5; Galatians 1:10; Philippians 1:1; Colossians 1:7, 4:7, 4:12; 2 Timothy 2:24; Titus 1:1; 2 Peter 1:1; Jude 1; Revelation 1:1, 2:20, 10:7, 11:18, 15:3, 19:2, 19:5, 22:3, 22:6). Unlike the worldly mechanisms of slavery, as rooted in kidnapping, compulsory servitude, and abuse; the bondslaves *of God* render a joyful and voluntary servitude as those who are God's *eternal possession,* having *eternal freedom in Christ:*

> 1 Peter 2:15–16: 15 For such is the will of God that by doing right you may silence the ignorance of foolish men.16 Act as free men, and do not use your freedom as a covering for evil, but use it as bondslaves of God.

Peter's description of believers as the *bondslaves of God* flows from what he stated earlier: "you are a chosen race, a royal priesthood, a holy nation, a people *for God's own possession*" (1 Peter 2:9, italics mine). However, God does not *possess or own* His people *as mere chattel* (more on this in the next chapter), but He possesses them as those who are now members of His holy and eternal family. They are His possession because they have been bought with a price (1 Corinthians 6:20, 7:23) and have been freed from their *slavery to sin* (John 8:34; Romans 6:16) in order to serve in the image and likeness of Christ's own humble servitude; a servitude in which He "took the form of a bondslave (δούλου, *doulou*)...humbled Himself and became obedient to the point of death, even the death of the cross." (Philippians 2:7-8). Such sacrificial servitude is the standard set forth for every child of God who lives and serves as the bondslave of God.

Sadly, what the Bible teaches about slavery (δούλου, *doulou*) has been sufficiently confused and abused throughout history, thereby making this term and topic highly controversial. But this scriptural term must not be shunned seeing that it reveals the glory of Jesus' *servitude* as the priestly King of Righteousness who came, not to be served, but to serve and to give His life a ransom for many (Matthew 20:28). Such an example of humble servitude is the holy and true standard for all Christians (Matthew 20:20-27).

In all of this we find an infinite difference between the believer's high and holy calling as a bondslave of God versus the mechanisms of compulsory servitude and abuse as contrived by mere mortals. The former is rooted in true freedom, joy, justice, and love while the latter is fraught with corruption, misery, and injustice. *There is nothing new under the sun*, and history reveals that *cultural collectivism* is yet another form of compulsory slavery that is cloaked beneath a false banner of justice.

Overall, it is quite evident that there is no *cultural collectivism* that can be achieved between the bondslaves of God and the slaves of worldly corruption; between the heavenly crown of Christ, and the straw, sticks, and the dust of this world.

JESUS'
JUSTICE

Exodus 21:16:
16 And he who kidnaps a man, whether he sells him or he is
found in his possession, shall surely be put to death.

CHAPTER 7

WHAT THE BIBLE SAYS
ABOUT SLAVERY AND MAN-STEALING

Anyone who has taken the time to read SJI materials knows that such works share a common focus on the historic subject of slavery. And when it comes to those overtly religious forms of SJI teaching, significant focus is typically placed on the *professing church's* past and present failure in opposing, not only slavery, but its diseased ideological root: racial bigotry.

For example, Jemar Tisby doesn't hesitate to issue his own sweeping accusations when condemning "Protestants, especially evangelicals, [who] have written some of the most well-known narratives of racism in the United States."[288] Thabiti Anyabwile broadly accuses "the church" of being *complicit* with "America's original sin" of racism.[289] Emerson and Smith repeatedly infer that "evangelical religion" continues to manifest complicity with racial bigotry similar to that of the antebellum South. For them, racial bigotry continues to persist in America, only "the form has changed from slavery, to 'Jim Crow'

---

[288] Tisby, *The Color of Compromise*, 16.
[289] Ibid., i.

157

segregation, to the post-Civil Rights-era division."[290] The central problem with such argumentative procedures is that they treat the *professing* church as a monolithic unit. Because of this, it seems likely that those who consume such literature might imagine that the *true church of Jesus Christ* would ever have anything to do with those who promote such racial bigotry.

Nevertheless, as we discussed in the sixth chapter, *A Tale of Two Kingdoms*, there has always been the true and the false church, just as there has always been the *wheat* of Christ's people surrounded by the *tares* of the enemy. Those who fail to recognize this distinction are typically quick to derogate Christ's church while misrepresenting the facts of history. While it might be tempting to count such argumentative methods as being unworthy of a response, failure to address such views would be an abject failure of this or any other book which seeks to confront SJI. Unless *we* are willing to face the good, the bad, and the ugly realities of history, we will only stumble in the darkness of our ignorance. Honesty demands a true and just reckoning of all the facts of history whether we like those facts or not.

Thus, in order to enter into this historical analysis we will examine various aspects of slavery from the 1st century to the American Civil War with a special focus on: *1. the concepts and definitions of slavery, 2. what Scripture teaches about slavery, and 3. what impact the Gospel has had on slavery throughout history.*

1. Concepts and definitions of slavery: Like many other discussions in the modern day, the topic of slavery repeatedly falls victim to a severe lack of historical understanding. This is especially prominent here in America where many assume that the African slave trade typifies the full history of the practice, or that slavery somehow originated in Colonial America. Such misperceptions are now being weaponized by the advocates of SJI,

---

[290] Emerson and Smith, *Divided by Faith*, 8.

thereby creating as much or more division in our nation than existed on the eve of the civil rights era.

However, not only was slavery universally practiced throughout human history, but it continues to persist in places like Africa, China, and Middle Eastern nations. Though great progress has been made over time, contemporary ignorance of this subject has slowed such progress. However, an objective understanding of history helps us to comprehend just how much progress has been made, as Milton Meltzer clearly summarizes in his classic work, *Slavery – A World History*:

> "The institution of slavery was universal throughout much of history. It was a tradition everyone grew up with. It seemed essential to the social and economic life of the community, and man's conscience was seldom troubled by it. Both master and slave looked upon it as inevitable."[291]

Meltzer continues to explain that from ancient history "there is no evidence...that the paradox [of the practice] entered people's minds in the earliest days of slavery. The idea of 'freedom' in a democratic sense did not develop for a long time."[292] Most slaves throughout ancient history were either war captives (by compulsion) or debt slaves (by contract). In the case of a debt slave, "a needy man could borrow money against the pledge of his labor. If he failed to pay his debt, his enslavement redeemed the loss."[293]

Without a broader and deeper perspective of history, it is all too easy to examine the question of slavery through ideological lenses which limit our comprehension of the subject. Meltzer underscores this matter very well:

---

[291] Meltzer, *Slavery I*, 6.

[292] Ibid., 5.

[293] Ibid., 2-3.

"The impact of racism upon certain societies that have known slavery – especially the United States - is of great significance today. But in the ancient world, among the Greeks and Romans as well as other peoples, [skin] color was not a dividing line: whites enslaved whites, by the millions. The European immigrant who slurs black Americans whose ancestors came to the New World in chains probably had ancestors yoked in slavery, too. Most of us – no matter what our color or where in the world we came from – have ancestors who at one time or another were slaves, or to put it morally, shared in the guilt of enslaving others. Many...were both: slaves at one time and masters at another."[294]

So much more could be said about the broad history of slavery, but we must concentrate our attention on the 1st century context in which the New Testament writers addressed this practice. During the reigns of Claudius (41–54 AD) to Trajan (98-117 AD) it is estimated that slaves within the Roman Empire constituted between one third and one half of the total population.[295]

Such a consideration as this is quite remarkable; however, the manner in which this slave population was categorized and managed is of chief importance. Unlike the African slave trade of the 19th century, Rome's standards and definitions of slavery were far more diverse and complex. In his book, *Textbook on Roman Law*, Andrew Borkowski outlines the multiple categories of slavery that were common throughout the Roman Empire, each requiring their own legal definitions and applications. These laws underwent an ebb and flow of change over time, however during the 1st century the following legal standards would have been most applicable:

a. **War Captives**: "This mode of enslavement resulted mainly from the capture in war of foreign prisoners. It also occurred where a foreigner was arrested on Roman territory in times of peace, not having a lawful justification for his

---

[294] Ibid., iv.
[295] Ibid., 128.

presence there. Capture in war became the main source of slaves in the late Republic, campaigns such as those of Julius Caesar in Gaul resulting in the enslavement of large numbers of foreigners. In theory these captives belonged to the Roman people as a whole, but it became the practice for successful generals to hold the captives as booty with a view to their eventual sale. Most enemy prisoners probably became slaves in private hands."[296]

b. Criminal Conduct: *"Crime.* Under the Twelve Tables a thief who was caught stealing became the slave of his intended victim. If the thief was already a slave he would normally be executed, at least in early law. Penal slaves were regarded as ownerless and incapable of being manumitted. A pardon was their only realistic hope of survival. *Evasion of Duty.* Those who evaded being listed in the census, and thus escaped liability to be taxed or to serve in the legions, could be enslaved by the State... *Selling Oneself.* What happened if a freeman tried to sell himself into slavery? Such a sale was invalid, prima facie: a free person could not in theory be the object of a contract of sale. However, attempts to sell oneself were punished – enslavement was imposed to try to deter such behavior...but why would a free person even contemplate selling himself into slavery? In some circumstances slavery might be considered preferable to freedom – for example, where the slave managed the affairs of a powerful and kindly master...*Straying dediticii* ('the capitulated'). Originally, *dediticii* were persons from communities that had taken up arms against Rome and then surrendered."[297]

c. Generational Slavery: *"Birth.* The basic rule (of the *ius gentium*) was that a child took the status that its mother had at the time of the child's birth."[298]

Even a cursory glance at Rome's historic legal standards reveals that the single word *slave* can connote a wide variety of circumstances. Much of

---

[296] Andrew Borkowski, *Textbook on Roman Law*, (New York: Oxford University Press, 2002), 90.

[297] Ibid., 89-90.

[298] Ibid., 91.

this broad connotation has to do with the fact that from the early Roman Republic (509 BC – 27 BC) to the period of the Roman Principate (27 BC – 284 AD) the treatment of slaves varied considerably:

> The law of the Twelve Tables [449 BC] on assault treated slaves just as less privileged adults; the penalty was small, that was all. With the great influx of slaves after the Punic Wars [264-146 BC], when Roman society and economy were transformed, there began Rome's great heyday of 'slave economy', and the chattel status of slaves grew more severe; and then under the Principate [27 BC – 284 AD]...the status was subjected to a long, slow, tentative process of amelioration by legislation on humanitarian grounds.[299]

Such variation led to a broad range of treatment that a slave would receive: from conditions that would be preferable to freedom[300] to that of sheer barbarity and cruelty. The treatment of slaves also depended significantly on whoever served as emperor. Though slaves were legally classified as chattel, Emperor Claudius (41–54 AD) attempted to mitigate this standard[301] in that he "prohibited the killing of a useless slave and ruled that an abandoned sick slave who recovered should become automatically free."[302] In addition to all these factors, the treatment slaves received was ultimately determined by either the beneficence or cruelty of their master. In some cases, those slaves who lived in wealthy households did not consider it to be "worthwhile" to have their freedom restored.[303]

---

[299] J. A. Crook, *Law and Life of Rome 90 B.C.- A.D. 212*, (Cornell University Press, Ithaca, New York: 1967), 56.

[300] Crook, *Law and Life of Rome*, 59-60.

[301] "...anyone who chose to kill a slave rather than abandon him should be arrested on a charge of murder." Jo-Ann Shelton, *As the Romans Did, A Source Book in Roman Social History* (New York: Oxford University Press, 1988), 188.

[302] Will Durant, *Caesar and Christ: The Story of Civilization, Volume III*, (Simon & Schuster), 9094, Kindle.

[303] In his Fifteenth Discourse on Slavery and Freedom, the Greek philosopher and historian of the Roman Empire, Dio Chrysostom, offered this observation of

We should also note the gargantuan difference between the incarceration systems of the past and the present. Roman prisons were not designed for mass and long-term incarceration as they are today, but were temporary facilities[304] used primarily for those awaiting trial or execution.[305] Thus, war captives and criminals, who by modern standards would normally be incarcerated,[306] lived amidst society *as penal slaves.*

---

slavery in the 1st century AD: "...are not many of these, although free men, yet held unjustly in servitude? Some of them have already gone before the court and proved that they are free, while others are enduring to the end, either because they have no clear proof of their freedom, or else because those who are called their masters are not harsh with them. Consider, for instance, the case of Eumaeus, the son of Ctesias, son of Ormenus: he was the son of a man who was altogether free and of great wealth, but did he not serve as a slave in Ithaca in the households of Odysseus and Laertes? And yet, although he could, time and again, have sailed off home if he had so wished, he never thought it worthwhile." Chrysostom, Dio. Delphi Complete Works of Dio Chrysostom - *The Discourses (Illustrated),* (Delphi Ancient Classics Book 81), Kindle.

[304] "...although we know considerably more about the prison at Rome than, for example, that at Athens, punitive imprisonment for any length of time seems to have been infrequent." Norval Morris and David J. Roghman, *The Oxford History of the Prison: The Practice of Punishment in Western Society,* (Oxford University Press, 1998), 19, Kindle.

[305] Crook, *Law and Life of Rome,* 274.

[306] Of course, a lengthy discussion could be pursued regarding various penal systems, past and present. For example, the language of the 13th Amendment is problematic for a number of reasons. Technically, it allows for the continuance of *slavery via* its *modifying exception* (in italics): "Neither slavery nor involuntary servitude, *except as a punishment for crime whereof the party shall have been duly convicted,* shall exist within the United States, or any place subject to their jurisdiction." It would have been better to disconnect the word *slave* from the modifying exception. Perhaps a better rendering would be: "Slavery shall not exist within the U.S., or any place subject to their jurisdiction, however, penal servitude shall be required of those who have been convicted of crime for the

These historic standards of Roman law and practice must be kept in mind when discerning what the biblical writers were addressing in their day.

However, one significant contrast must be considered when comparing their ancient world with that of the transatlantic slave trade which persisted from the 16th to 19th centuries. The key nations involved in this *trade* (the Portuguese, British, Spanish, French, Dutch, and Danish) were not at war with any of the nations within the African continent, nor were Africans seized by these nations on any pretext of penal retribution. Instead, those foreign nations that engaged in the African slave trade were clearly involved in the act of man-stealing (securing and kidnapping humans as mere chattel for profit). And as the slave trade continued, kidnapping *within the continent* became the primary means of supplying the trade, even though some were enslaved by their fellow Africans as war captives or criminals (whether in reality or as a pretext for their commercial sale).[307]

Overall, the conjoined presence of *supply* and *demand* fueled this ongoing barbarity. Early in his reign, Afonso I, King of Kongo, wrote several impassioned letters to the King of Portugal in which he made an appeal for the cessation of the slave trade:

> We cannot reckon how great the damage is, since the merchants are taking every day our natives, sons of the land and the sons of our noblemen and vassals and our relatives, because the thieves and men of bad conscience grab them wishing to have the things and wares of this Kingdom which they are ambitious of; they grab them and get them to be sold; and so great, Sir, is the corruption and licentiousness that our country is being completely depopulated...many of our people, keenly desirous as they are of the wares and

---

duration established by a court of law containing a jury of one's peers." Because of America's past involvement with chattel slavery, the word *slave* had become so fraught with problematic connotations that its legal use (without qualification) would make it utterly useless in any meaningful sense regarding *penal servitude*.

[307] In very rare cases [in times of severe famine] some desperate "Africans would sell themselves or their children to keep from starving." Meltzer, *Slavery II*, 31.

things of your Kingdoms, which are brought here by your people, and in order to satisfy their voracious appetite, seize many of our people, freed and exempt men; and very often it happens that they kidnap even noblemen and the sons of noblemen, and our relatives, and take them to be sold to the white men who are in our kingdoms; and for this purpose they have concealed them, and others are brought during the night so that they might not be recognized. And as soon as they are taken by the white men they are immediately ironed and branded with fire.[308]

Of the many things that can be said about the transatlantic slave trade, it clearly was a disturbing expression of *corruption and licentiousness* that had a wide variety of willing participants and profiteers. And no matter what justifications were made for the enslavement of these individuals within Africa, those foreigners who seized them had no right to purchase them as chattel and relocate them against their will. Jonathan Edwards (the younger) blasted this criminal behavior in a message he delivered to the Connecticut Society in 1791:

Should we be willing, that the Africans or any other nation should purchase us, our wives and children, transport us into Africa and there sell us into perpetual and absolute slavery? Should we be willing, that they by large bribes and offers of a gainful traffic should entice our neighbours to kidnap and sell us to them, and that they should hold in perpetual and cruel bondage, not only ourselves, but our posterity through all generations? Yet why is it not as right for them to treat us in this manner, as it is for us to treat them in the same manner? Their colour indeed is different from ours. But does this give us a right to enslave them? The nations from Germany to Guinea have complexions of every shade from the fairest white, to a jetty black: and if a black complexion subject a nation or an individual to slavery; where shall slavery begin? or where shall it end?[309]

---

[308] Ibid., 27-29.

[309] Jonathan Edwards, *The injustice and impolicy of the slave trade, and of the slavery of the Africans: illustrated in a sermon preached before the Connecticut*

Edwards' condemnation of the slave trade is unimpeachable. The fact that he calls the practice *kidnapping* reminds us that those who were being categorized as chattel were being seized, relocated, and used against their will as *mere property*. All in all, this was an inhumane abuse of fellow members of the human race without an ounce of justification, biblical or otherwise.

2. What Scripture teaches about slavery: When we evaluate the various passages in the New Testament dealing with slavery, it is important to keep in mind the diversity and complexity of the institution itself. Failure to do so will predictably yield much confusion. Because of this complexity, the New Testament addresses the subject with significant nuance. There are only a handful of passages that deal with slavery, and the majority of them are quite brief: Ephesians 6:5-9; Titus 2:9-10; 1 Timothy 6:1-2; Colossians 3:22, 4:1; 1 Corinthians 7:21-23. Philemon, the only book of the bible dealing with slavery *en toto*, will be the capstone of our study, however we will begin with a review of the shorter passages starting with 1 Corinthians 7:21-23.

Just prior to his instructions on slavery in 1 Corinthians 7:21-23, Paul had exhorted his readers to *remain in the condition in which God called them* regarding singleness, marriage, and circumcision (1 Corinthians 7:8-20). Regarding singleness, he encouraged the unmarried to remain in their condition but with an *exception* stipulated in 1 Corinthians 7:9. Regarding marriage, he forbade all marital dissolutions (1 Corinthians 7:8-17) barring one *exception*.[310] When addressing slaves he

---

society for the promotion of freedom and for the Relief of Persons Unlawfully Holden in Bondage, at their annual meeting in New-Haven, (Boston, Wells and Lilly, Sept. 15, 1791), 4.

[310] Paul forbids the dissolution of marriage between two believers (1 Corinthians 7:39), but issues an exception concerning the unequally yoked union in which the unbeliever abandons the union. From the late Republic onward a free marriage

exhorted them to remain in their condition (1 Corinthians 7:24), but with this *exception*: "if you are able also to become free, rather do that" (1 Corinthians 7:21). Prior to this exception, Paul made it clear that those who had no choice but to remain as slaves should serve as the Lord's freedmen, however, the benefits of freedom for the sake of the Gospel were still preferable if such freedom could be secured.

Paul himself modeled this prioritization of freedom for the sake of the Gospel. When he was shackled for ministering the word of God he sought release from his bonds by revealing his Roman citizenship to those who had constrained him (Acts 22:25-29). Once released, he used his earthly liberty to preach the Gospel to those who unjustly sought his bondage. Overall, Paul modelled the very principle that he conveyed to the Corinthians: all believers should strive to secure *undistracted devotion to the Lord (1 Corinthians 7:35) as those who are His eternal possession*:

1 Corinthians 7:23 You were bought (ἠγοράσθητε > ἀγοράζω, *agorazō*) with a price; do not become slaves of men.

Using the distinct terminology of *manumission* (*ēgorasthēte*) Paul reminded his readers that, as the Lord's people, they had been *purchased* (redeemed) out of their enslavement to sin[311] in order to serve their ultimate Master, the Lord Jesus Christ. This same language of

---

could be dissolved as quickly as it was created: "[Free marriage] was created by the cohabitation of the parties, provided that they regarded themselves as man and wife. As soon as such cohabitation began, i.e., with the necessary intent, the marriage came into existence...A true divorce (in free marriage) does not take place unless an intention to remain apart permanently is present." Borkowski, *Roman Law*, 125-27.

[311] John 8:34–36: 34 Jesus answered them, "Truly, truly, I say to you, everyone who commits sin is the slave of sin.35 "And the slave does not remain in the house forever; the son does remain forever.36 "If therefore the Son shall make you free, you shall be free indeed.

manumission was also used in the previous chapter in order to enjoin the Corinthians to flee from sexual immorality: "you have been bought (ἠγοράσθητε > ἀγοράζω, *agorazō*) with a price: therefore glorify God in your body."[312] The Greek word ἀγοράζω (*agorazō*) is derived from the word *market* (ἀγορά, *agora*) and was historically used to speak of commercial activity. Eventually the word was used to speak of the price paid to secure a slave's freedom.[313]

Of course, Paul did not employ this term in order to call his readers *chattel*; instead, this term laid focus on the incalculable price that was paid for their salvation. Instead of expending silver or gold for their emancipation, Christ redeemed His people by the sacrifice of Himself: "Christ redeemed (ἐξηγόρασεν> ἀγοράζω, *agorazō*) us from the curse of the law, having become a curse for us" (Galatians 3:13). This same word is also used in the heavenly song of the Lamb of God in Revelation 5:9:

> Revelation 5:9: And they *sang a new song, saying, "Worthy art Thou to take the book, and to break its seals; for Thou wast slain, and didst *purchase* (ἠγόρασας > ἀγοράζω, *agorazō*) for God with Thy blood men from every tribe and tongue and people and nation.

The importance of all these rich passages should become quite evident when we recognize that the *purchase price* for an individual's emancipation from their slavery to sin *is the sacrifice and shed blood of Jesus Christ, the Lamb of God*. Without such emancipation from King Jesus, *no person on earth is truly free*. This core message of the Gospel

---

[312] 1 Corinthians 6:19–20: 19 Or do you not know that your body is a temple of the Holy Spirit who is in you, whom you have from God, and that you are not your own? 20 For you have been bought with a price: therefore glorify God in your body.

[313] For ye were bought with a price (ἠγορασθητε γαρ τιμης [ēgorasthēte gar timēs]). First aorist passive indicative of ἀγοραζω [agorazō], old verb to buy in the marketplace (ἀγορα [agora]). A.T. Robertson, *Word Pictures in the New Testament*, (TN: Broadman Press, 1933), 1 Co 6:20.

decimated many of the philosophies and ideologies of Roman society. According to the Gospel, the value of every human life in every generation is immutably established by the Creator. However, by the standards of Rome, such a valuation was entirely lost, especially when it came to slavery:

"what is a slave? Is it a thing or is he a person? In Roman society and law this ambivalence is everywhere. The slave is a *res,* a *mancipium,* thing, chattel; *res mortals,* 'mortal objects'."[314]

Even though Roman law revealed some measure of ambivalence in its definitions of slavery, the fact that souls were being purchased and sold as *material possessions* meant that Rome's default standard for the slave was *res: a thing, chattel.* Thus, any opposition to this standard undermined the very foundation of Rome's institution of slavery. This is why Paul's repeated use of manumission terminology (ἀγοράζω, *agorazō*) is so remarkable. It clearly stood as an explosive Gospel rebuke against the pagan ideologies of the day. Clearly, Christ did not shed His blood for mere chattel. Instead, the eternal Son of God[315] "became flesh"[316] as God incarnate,[317] thereby *entering the genealogy of the single human race as the Son of David;* He lived a life of perfect holiness[318] and humbled Himself "by becoming obedient to the point of death, even death on a cross."[319] And by this matchless sacrifice of His, Christ's ransom is sufficient to redeem a vast number of individuals from *every tribe and tongue and people and nation.* Moreover, by this act of humility and suffering, the

---

[314] Crook, *Law and Life of Rome,* 55-56.

[315] John 1:1-4.

[316] John 1:14.

[317] John 1:18.

[318] John 8:29.

[319] Philippians 2:5-11.

Savior is not ashamed to call those whom He redeemed, *brethren,*[320] even those whom the world slandered as *"res"* (chattel).

This dichotomy between the world's standards and the Gospel underscores the vast differences between false and genuine justice. By the standard of the Gospel, the believer was to make the most of their God-given lives by serving Christ above all, whether slave or free. As for those who had the legal recourse to pursue emancipation, Paul instructed them to "do that": "Were you called while a slave? Do not worry about it; but if you are able also to become free, rather *do that* (χρησαι, *xrēsai)"*[321] (1 Corinthians 7:21). Of course, this injunction does not constitute a universal call for all slaves to abandon their stations. Such a call would have resulted in incalculable mayhem, especially in view of Rome's complex system of slavery and penal retribution. For example, those who were enslaved as war captives, thieves, fraudsters, traitors, and other criminals would be released into a world that had no system of penal incarceration. Not only would this wreak havoc on society[322] but, more

---

[320] Hebrews 2:9-11.

[321] Χρησαι [Chrēsai] is second person singular aorist middle imperative of χραομαι [chraomai], to use, old and common verb. μαλλον χρησαι ([mallon chrēsai]). Make use of what? There is no "it" in the Greek. Shall we supply ἐλευθεριᾳ [eleutheriāi] (instrumental case after χρησαι [chrēsai] or δουλειᾳ [douleiāi])? Most naturally ἐλευθεριᾳ [eleutheriāi], freedom, from ἐλευθερος [eleutheros], just before. In that case εἰ και [ei kai] is not taken as although, but και [kai] goes with δυνασαι [dunasai], "But if thou canst also become free, the rather use your opportunity for freedom." A.T. Robertson, *Word Pictures*, 1 Co 7:21.

[322] "Slavery was in-woven into the texture of society; and to prohibit slavery was to tear society into shreds. Nothing less than a servile war with its certain horrors and its doubtful issues must have been the consequence. Such a mode of operation was altogether alien to the spirit of the Gospel." Joseph Barber Lightfoot, *Saint Paul's Epistles to the Colossians and to Philemon*, 8th ed., Classic Commentaries on the Greek New Testament (London; New York: Macmillan and Co., 1886), 321.

importantly, the Gospel would be conflated with a confused and corrupt message of lawlessness. Realities such as these reveal why Paul's instructions in 1 Corinthians 7:20-24 offer such important nuance.

Yet it is crucial that we recognize the fact that the Bible does in fact refute Rome's institution of slavery *by decimating its fundamental pretext: that the enslaved are mere chattel.* Not only does the Gospel destroy this dehumanizing standard, but it heralds the emancipating and transforming work of the King of Righteousness. Such a transformation as this leads the bondslaves of Christ away from worldly compromise and compulsory servitude to that of true freedom in the Lord.

For this reason Paul issued a *stern prohibition* based on the believer's manumission in Christ: *You were bought with a price; do not become slaves of men* (1 Corinthians 7:23). At its core this command reveals that, no matter what their earthly obligations were, *whether slave or free*, these Corinthian believers were not to become the slaves of men *by their own choices and actions*;[323] nor were they to herald anything or anyone above Christ as their true Lord and Master.[324] Having been

---

[323] Some who were categorized as slaves enjoyed unique levels of liberty and advantage to such an extent that some would likely be tempted to remain in their station. "…those who sold themselves into slavery, often to pay off a debt, but with funds remaining which could form the nucleus for savings or 'earnings' through which the person concerned might hope to redeem his or her freedom. Some choice might be exercised within this category of self-sale concerning the identity of the master. In certain circumstances to sell oneself to a prestigious and successful master whose fairness one trusted could even be perceived as an investment for future prosperity and present protection, always, however, with risk." Anthony C. Thiselton, *The First Epistle to the Corinthians: A Commentary on the Greek Text, New International Greek Testament Commentary* (MI: W.B. Eerdmans, 2000), 563.

[324] Commentators vary somewhat on the connotation of Paul's command: "do not become the slaves of men." Is Paul speaking of spiritual or physical enslavement? In either connotation, his prohibition is a clear rebuke of the

delivered by Christ, they could never subject themselves as *the property of men* because they were the eternal possession of the Lord Jesus (1 Corinthians 6:19-20; 7:23). Thus, the believer's value and purpose is established by the Lord and *no one else*, not even Roman law. If the implications of these truths meant denying the ruthless and licentious demands of an earthly master,[325] then so be it. Civil disobedience for the sake of the Gospel is an integral part of the believer's witness to this lost world. Paul himself was seized and shackled three times by Roman authorities (Acts 21:11-23:22) because of the riots which resulted from his preaching the Gospel, but at no time did he compromise the truth for his personal safety. As Peter and the apostles declared before the Council of the Sanhedrin: "we must obey God rather than men."[326]

Overall, the one *openly rebellious* message that was blasted against Rome's institution of slavery, along with every other mechanism of wickedness that Rome represented, was that Jesus is the King of kings, the Lord of lords, and the Sovereign Ruler over every emperor, patrician, plebian, and slave; and all those who are ransomed by His blood, which

---

world's standards of subjugation and derogation, neither of which honored the value of human life nor Christ's redeeming sacrifice: "Ye were bought with a price (τιμης ἠγορασθητε [timēs ēgorasthēte]). See on 6:20 for this very phrase, here repeated. Both classes (slaves and freemen) were purchased by the blood of Christ. Become not bondservants of men (μη γινεσθε δουλοι ἀνθρωπων [mē ginesthe douloi anthrōpōn]). Present middle imperative of γινομαι [ginomai] with negative μη [mē]. Literally, stop becoming slaves of men. Paul here clearly defines his opposition to human slavery as an institution which comes out so powerfully in the Epistle to Philemon." Robertson, *Word Pictures*, 1 Co 7:23.

[325] Not only is the relationship between 1 Corinthians 6:15-20 and 1 Corinthians 7:20-24 obvious in view of the repeated expression, "you were bought with a price" (6:20, 7:23), but they are, to some extent, conceptually connected by virtue of the related practices of prostitution and slavery. Many of the enslaved at that time were forced into prostitution, but such *wicked or depraved inclinations* were to be rejected by Christ's bondslaves (1 Corinthians 6:15-20; 7:23).

[326] Acts 5:29.

flowed from mortal veins, are *His possession* forever, even those whom the world despised as *mere merchandise.*

Unlike the compulsory servitude demanded by Rome's masters, the child of God serves Christ in view of the Savior's love for His own. It is this message of true emancipation that became the death knell to Rome's institution of slavery and proved to be far more powerful than any political policy that ever could have been promoted or enacted:

> It follows from the consideration of Christian brotherhood that, although it finds many slaves, yet it shall gradually raise them to a state of freedom. It trees[327] their souls at once. They become "the Lord's freemen" (1 Cor. 7:22), and the body cannot always remain bound when the soul is free. Thus, though it does not cut down the tree (of slavery), it severs the roots, and a state of slavery cannot therefore permanently flourish among Christians.[328]

And so it is that when we examine texts that call on slaves to be subject to their masters (Titus 2:9-10, 1 Timothy 6:1-2), we see that they were to do so ultimately unto Christ (Ephesians 6:5-8) with reverence towards Him above all (Colossians 3:22). In like manner, masters were to conduct themselves with restraint and beneficence knowing that they served the same Master in heaven (Ephesians 6:9, Colossians 4:1). Though Paul knew many things about the believers whom he addressed in these letters, at no time are we informed about the exact circumstances of those who had been enslaved.

However, when Paul wrote to the church at Corinth, he acknowledged that many in the church were converted out of a life of

---

[327] This word isn't commonly used in modern English, but it speaks of something or someone seeking freedom: "trans. To drive into or up a tree; to cause to take refuge in a tree" OED.

[328] H. D. M. Spence-Jones, ed., *Philemon, The Pulpit Commentary* (London; New York: Funk & Wagnalls Company, 1909), 9.

depravity and criminal behavior, but now they were washed, sanctified, and justified by the grace and power of God (1 Corinthians 6:9-11). It is most probable that some of those who were previously "thieves" and "swindlers" (1 Corinthians 6:10) were penal slaves among those addressed in 1 Corinthians 7:21-23. As such, similar circumstances likely prevailed throughout the early church. In the end, *all* were to remember that they had been bought with the incalculable price of the shed blood of the Lord Jesus Christ.

We now come to the brief epistle of Philemon which Paul wrote while he was in prison. Philemon was likely a well-known member of the Colossian church who was converted some time during Paul's ministry in Ephesus. Onesimus, Philemon's escaped slave, sought refuge with Paul while he was in prison. Through Paul's ministry of the Gospel, Onesimus came to saving faith in Christ which resulted in a strong bond of Christian fellowship between the two. So intense was their bond that Paul called Onesimus "my child, whom I have begotten in my imprisonment." (Philemon 10). We are never told how long they were together, but it was long enough for Paul to develop such a confidence in Onesimus that he was able to write to Philemon: "...I have sent him back to you in person, that is, *sending my very heart*" (Philemon 12, italics mine). Paul actually desired to retain Onesimus that he might minister to him in his "imprisonment for the gospel" (Philemon 13), and yet he chose to return Onesimus along with his epistolary appeal.

What is especially unique about this letter is that it was written in such a highly personal nature. Paul clearly knew both men, Philemon and Onesimus, and the warmth of his regards for them makes this epistle quite special. Unlike all the other passages dealing with slaves and masters, this text stands above the rest in light of Paul's personal involvement. Because of this, his gentle but strong directives to Philemon are unlike any other when it comes to slave and master instructions within the New Testament.

Some have argued that Paul dutifully returned Onesimus in view of the mandates of Roman law. Since the state viewed slaves as property possessing no legal rights, a runaway was *considered a criminal because he had stolen himself.* They were often tracked by professional slave-hunters, and heralds were typically dispatched to notify the public about the escapee's name and identity.[329] While this was the world's method of responding to such circumstances, Paul was operating on an entirely different level. Rather than deferring to Rome's godless and dehumanizing standards, Paul instead deferred to the greatest authority of all: the authority of King Jesus. Of course, every epistle that Paul wrote did this, but some unfortunately overlook this in Philemon.

From the very outset of the letter, Paul directs our attention to Christ's supremacy by indicating that "every good thing" that was in Philemon was *for Christ's sake (Philemon 6).* Paul recognized Christ's sovereignty in view of his imprisonment and so he referred to himself as "a prisoner of Christ Jesus" (Philemon 9). And alluding to his authority as an Apostle of Christ, he told Philemon that he had "enough confidence in Christ to order [him] to do that which is proper" (Philemon 8), but instead he chose to make a tender appeal.[330]

---

[329] Shelton, *As the Romans Did*, 180.

[330] "But though the apostle declared, indeed, to Philemon the master, (v. 14.) 'without thy mind, would I do nothing;' yet this by no means proves the right of the master, but only that the apostle, in love and courtesy to Philemon, desired, that 'the benefit' which he required of him, 'Should not be as it were of necessity, but willingly,' vs. 14., for the apostle's right to have retained even without the master's consent, is sufficiently implied in a preceding verse, (viz. 8.) 'though I might by much bold in Christ, to enjoin, (or command)' that which Is convenient, let, (said the apostle,) 'for LOVE'S SAKE, I rather beseech.'" Granville Sharp, *The Just Limitation of Slavery: In the Laws of God, Compared with the Unbounded Claims of the African Traders and British American Slaveholders With a Copious Appendix,* (B. White, and E. and C. Dilly), 1240-1252, Kindle.

All this brings us to the heart of the epistle. Rather than dropping an avalanche of orders on Philemon "to do that which is proper," Paul instead made his appeal on behalf of Onesimus "for love's sake" (Philemon 9). Paul was not seeking *compulsory* obedience from Philemon; this was the way of the world and had no place in Christ's kingdom where His people serve Him *willingly*. This formulates the central reason why Paul sent Onesimus back to Philemon. Paul didn't return Onesimus out of some obeisance to Roman standards of chattel slavery or property theft. Paul had one thing in view when dispatching Onesimus and it was to encourage his brother in Christ, Philemon, to respond in *willing obedience as a bondslave of King Jesus*: "but without your consent I did not want to do anything, that your goodness should not be as it were by compulsion, but of your own free will." (Philemon 14, italics mine).

And what *exactly* did Paul want Philemon to do? To answer this we must seek out the imperatives supplied in this letter, of which there are only a few. The key imperative that regulates much of the epistle is clearly revealed when Paul wrote: "If then thou countest me a partner, *receive* (προσλαβοῦ, *proslabou*) him as myself" (Philemon 17, ASV, italics mine). I have supplied the ASV translation for this verse because it captures the bare, literal expression which conveys the idea of *substitution*. Paul wasn't asking Philemon to *receive* Onesimus *in a similar manner* to how he would receive Paul. Instead, Paul directed Philemon to receive Onesimus *"as me"* (ὡς ἐμέ, *hōs eme*), doing so with the cohortative force of an imperative. It is as though Paul had stripped away any and every possible inclination within Philemon to treat Onesimus in a derogating manner. Of course, Paul was not telling Philemon to engage in a fantasy when he said, "receive him as me," but he did want Philemon to give careful consideration to what he wrote in the preceding verses:

Philemon 15–16: 15 For perhaps he was for this reason parted from you for a while, that you should have him back forever, 16 no longer as a slave, but more than a slave, a beloved brother, especially to me, but how much more to you, both in the flesh and in the Lord.

When we consider Paul's instruction regarding how Onesimus should be treated, beginning with his use of the emphatic negative ("have him back *no longer*[331] (οὐκέτι, *ouketi*) as a slave"), coupled with what follows ("but *more than* (ὑπέρ, *huper*) a slave"), and then align all this with his imperative in the next verse, "*receive!* him as me (ὡς ἐμέ, *hōs eme*)," we are left with a stunning exhortation. For Philemon to treat Onesimus as the Apostle Paul meant that, *not only was the legal standard of chattel slavery completely obliterated, but Onesimus would be elevated as an invaluable co-laborer for the Gospel and friend in Christ.*

Whatever Roman legal constructs that existed in the slave and master relationship between Onesimus and Philemon would be subordinated beneath the matchless authority of King Jesus, who made them both brothers by a blood-bought emancipation whereby Christ Himself was not ashamed to call them brethren (Hebrews 2:11). This very humility, as modeled by Christ, was worthy of imitation, and Paul desired that Philemon would obediently (Philemon 21) engage in such imitation by his own free will (Philemon 14).

We are never informed in this epistle how Onesimus became a slave in the first place. Nor does it contain an *explicit* directive for his emancipation, however, Paul's strong exhortations make it difficult to imagine that Philemon would do anything less: "Having confidence in your obedience, I write to you, since I know that you will do even more

---

[331] "Paul mentions to Philemon the receiving [of] Onesimus forever [*that thou shouldest receive him forever. Ver. 15*] yet it would be most unreasonable to conceive that the apostle meant that he should receive him forever a slave!" Granville Sharp, *The Just Limitation of Slavery: Appendix*, (B White and E. & C. Dilly, 1776), 1310, Kindle.

than what I say." (Philemon 21).[332] Church tradition[333] asserts that Onesimus was eventually appointed to serve as the bishop of Ephesus, further strengthening the likelihood that Philemon responded in obedience to Paul's instructions.[334]

In the end, Paul's gentle but firm assertion of Onesimus' brotherhood, in the flesh and in the Lord, laid a crucial foundation for generations to come. As such, the Gospel's focus on our shared humanity, as well as Christ's emancipating work, eventually produced an environment in which Rome's system of slavery couldn't possibly survive:

---

[332] (16 verse.) "if he hath wronged thee..." (in which expression even the supposed debt of service may be included,) "put that on my account," (said the apostle, vs. 18.) which must be a complete discharge of all the master's temporal demands on Onesmus; and therefore it is a strange perversion of the apostle's meaning to cite this epistle, in favour of slavery, when the whole tenor of it is in behalf of the slave!" Granville Sharp, *The Just Limitation of Slavery: Appendix*, (Hardpress.net, 2017), 1263-1269, Kindle.

[333] Not a few slaves died martyrs, and were enrolled among the saints; as Onesimus, Eutyches, Victorinus, Maro, Nereus, Achilleus, Blandina, Potamiaena, Felicitas. Tradition makes Onesimus, the slave of Philemon, a bishop. The church of St. Vital at Ravenna—the first and noblest specimen of Byzantine architecture in Italy—was dedicated by Justinian to the memory of a martyred slave. But the most remarkable instance is that of Callistus, who was originally a slave, and rose to the chair of St. Peter in Rome (218–223). Philip Schaff and David Schley Schaff, *History of the Christian Church*, v. 2 (New York: Charles Scribner's Sons, 1910), 350.

[334] "Seeing, then, that we have become acquainted with your multitude4 in the name of God, by Onesimus, who is your bishop, in love which is unutterable, whom I pray that ye love in Jesus Christ our Lord, and that all of you imitate his example, for blessed is He who has given you such a bishop, even as ye deserve [to have]. Ignatius of Antioch, *The Second Epistle of Ignatius to the Ephesians*, in The Apostolic Fathers with Justin Martyr and Irenaeus, ed. Alexander Roberts, James Donaldson, and A. Cleveland Coxe, vol. 1, The Ante-Nicene Fathers (Buffalo, NY: Christian Literature Company, 1885), 101.

When the Gospel taught that God had made all men and women upon earth of one family; that all alike were His sons and His daughters; that, whatever conventional distinctions human society might set up, the supreme King of Heaven refused to acknowledge any; that the slave notwithstanding his slavery was Christ's freedman, and the free notwithstanding his liberty was Christ's slave; when the Church carried out this principle by admitting the slave to her highest privileges, inviting him to kneel side by side with his master at the same holy table; when in short the Apostolic precept that 'in Christ Jesus is neither bond nor free' was not only recognized but acted upon, then slavery was doomed. Henceforward it was only a question of time.[335]

Lightfoot is right when he says that, with the advancement of the Gospel "slavery was doomed. Henceforward it was only a question of time." However, the Gospel's progress in this matter did not come without setbacks and stumbling blocks. Sadly, during the 18th and 19th centuries, there were many who manipulated Scripture in order to justify the transatlantic slave trade here in America and in England. In both countries, the tactics of these pro-slavery advocates were strikingly similar in that they heralded the Law of Moses *to a fault* insisting that England and America were to be governed by the unique commands and prescriptions entrusted to ancient Israel.

Such an exaltation of the Mosaic Law is no benign matter, but can lead to a great number of errors like those found in the ancient church of Galatia. At Galatia, many failed to understand that the Mosaic Law was not an end, but a means to a greater end of serving as a tutor that leads us to Christ (Galatians 3:24). Their failure to understand this led Paul to issue some of the harshest rebukes recorded in Scripture whereby he called them *fools* who were being *bewitched* in their efforts to be saved through the works of the Law. Paul even argued that those troubling Judaizers, who were pressing the Mosaic standard of circumcision, should mutilate themselves (Galatians 5:12).

---

[335] Lightfoot, *Saint Paul's Epistles to the Colossians and to Philemon*, 323.

The severity of these warnings should remind us of the danger of heralding the Law of Moses above Christ, after all, "the Law was given through Moses; grace and truth were realized through Jesus Christ" (John 1:17). Ironically, those who sought to justify the transatlantic slave trade by means of the Law fell under the Law's condemnation in view of its clear prohibition against kidnapping.[336]

Paul warned his "child in the faith", Timothy, concerning those who were "wanting to be teachers of the Law" but who failed to understand the Law's overall purpose of revealing our sin and resultant need for Christ. In 1 Timothy 1:9-10, he stipulated the Law's usefulness with reference to those who are lawless and rebellious, followed by a list of transgressions to include "kidnappers." The Greek word that he used, translated as kidnapper, is ἀνδραποδισταῖς, (*andrapodistais*). This term is a construct of two words: *anēr* (man) and *pous* (foot).[337] The etymology of this term suggests that it was an adaptation of the word τετράποδα (*tetrapoda*) denoting four footed animals, as Moulton and Milligan clarify in *The Vocabulary of the Greek Testament*:

[this combination of *tetrapoda* and *andrapoda*] reminds us of the etymology of the word, which is merely an analogy-formation from τετράποδα, with which it is so often associated—just as electrocute is made out of execute, to take a modern instance of a common resource of language. The word, which was normally plural...was never an ordinary word for slave: it was too brutally obvious a reminder of the principle which made quadruped and human chattels differ only in the number of their legs.[338]

In relation to the above, the English word *chattel* is etymologically related to the word *cattle*, denoting property, goods, money, and livestock. At the

---

[336] Exodus 21:16.

[337] Robertson, *Word Pictures*, 1 Ti 1:10.

[338] James Hope Moulton and George Milligan, *The Vocabulary of the Greek Testament*, (London: Hodder and Stoughton, 1930), 40.

core of Scripture's prohibitions against kidnapping is a sharp rebuke against the *dehumanizing nature* of the act. Not only is this dehumanizing act a grave offense to the one who is kidnapped, but, more importantly, it is an offense to the Almighty to such an extent as to warrant grave judgment. This is especially evident in Revelation 18:13 where we find that those who commercially buy and sell *slaves* (*sōmatōn*, bodies) and *human lives* (*psuxas*, souls) like chattel, along with *things* like flour, wheat, cattle and sheep, do so as the cobelligerents of demons and unclean spirits (Revelation 18:2). A. T. Robertson notes that the term (*andrapodistais*) in 1 Timothy 1:10 speaks of "...enslavers, whether kidnappers (men-stealers) of men or stealers of the slaves of other men. So slave-dealers. By the use of this word Paul deals a blow at the slave-trade (cf. Philemon)."[339]

With all of this in view, it seems impossible to imagine that so many sought to defend slavery in America *by means of Scripture*. This effort required several nuanced definitions and interpretations. For example, many of the defenders of slavery in America made a moral distinction between the transatlantic slave trade and the domestic slave trade. They decried the former as an injustice while promoting the latter as a *domestic necessity*. This form of reasoning saw the culpability for kidnapping (*via* the transatlantic slave trade) as no longer being in effect once these individuals were relocated and resold in America.[340] The logic of this strains credulity. If you, the reader, experienced the tragic kidnapping of a family member who was then sold to your next door neighbor, I doubt that you would *let bygones be bygones*. The reality is that two parties are now guilty of kidnapping *with the neighbor serving as an accomplice to the original crime*.

---

[339] Robertson, *Word Pictures*, 1 Ti 1:10.

[340] The Act Prohibiting Importation of Slaves was passed by the US Congress, February 13th 1807 and enacted on March 2nd 1807.

In the end, the Bible does clearly address the subjects of slavery *and kidnapping*. Should we conflate and confuse these concepts, we will fail to see the unique atrocities of the transatlantic slave trade.

3. The Gospel's historic impact on slavery: The inhumane commerce known as the transatlantic slave trade, which spanned from the 16th to the 19th centuries, resulted in the transport of between 10 to 12 million African slaves to Portuguese America (Brazil, 38.5%), the British West Indies (18.4%), the Spanish Empire (17.5%), the French West Indies (13.6%), and British North America (9.7%).[341] The undoing of this monstrous practice did not take place overnight, but came as the result of several hard-fought battles for abolition.

It is oftentimes the case that when the abolitionist cause during this era is considered, names like William Wilberforce and John Newton immediately come to mind, as in the case of the 2007 movie, *Amazing Grace,* which highlighted the co-labors of Newton, Wilberforce, as well as Thomas Clarkson. The film well summarized the anti-slavery battles these men faced, however, it managed to leave out one key individual by the name of Granville Sharp (GS). Today, that name is most commonly known by Greek grammarians because of his grammatical rule called the Granville Sharp rule. This important rule has been an essential component in understanding a great number of biblical passages, especially those that affirm Christ's deity. However, beyond his renown as a highly disciplined Greek grammarian and biblical scholar, GS's tremendous labors for the cause of abolition have led many to conclude that he is the *father of the anti-slavery movement in Britain.*

Overall, it would be impossible to understand the efforts of Wilberforce, Clarkson, and Newton without first examining the foundational work of Sharp, whose zeal in this cause was rooted in his desire to glorify God by advancing the teaching of the Scriptures. In view

---

[341] Anthony Appiah and Henry Louis Gates, *Africana: the encyclopedia of the African and African American experience* (Basic Civitas Books, New York, NY).

of this, as we examine the Gospel's impact on slavery in Britain and American, we will review several contributions made by Sharp; contributions that effectively toppled several pillars of slavery and eventually contributed to Britain's Slave Trade Act of 1807 and the Slavery Abolition Act of 1833. Of Sharp's many labors, we must begin with his defense of *Jonathan Strong*:

1765 – Defense of Jonathan Strong: Sharp's entry into the abolitionist cause began when he first learned about the case of Jonathan Strong, an enslaved man from Barbados who was nearly beaten to death by his owner, David Lisle. Granville's brother, William Sharp, an eminent surgeon, gave aid to Strong in the form of medical assistance, money, clothing, and eventually had Strong admitted to a hospital in which he received 4 ½ months of needed care.[342]

William and Granville then secured an opportunity for Strong to work for a trusted apothecary (Mr. Brown), however, after only two years of this arrangement, Lisle came upon his former slave, had him seized, imprisoned, and committed for sale to a Jamaican planter by the name of James Kerr. When GS sought to intervene, Lisle challenged him to a duel[343] but was instead confronted with the promise that their real battle would be carried out in

---

[342] Jonathan Strong's account of these events: "I meet with a man – told him my case – he recommended to Mr. William Sharp in Mincing Lane, Fenchurch Street: I took his advice and went to Mr. Sharp. I could hardly walk, or see my way, where I was going. When I came to him, and he saw me in that condition, the gentleman take charity of me, and give me some stoff to wash my eyes with, and some money to get myself a little necessaries till next day. The day after, I come to the gentleman, and he sent me into the hospital, and I was in there for months and a half. All the while I was in the hospital, the gentleman find me in clothes, shoes, and stockings, and when I come out, he paid for my lodging, and money to find myself some necessaries, till he get me into a place." Prince Hoare, *Memoirs of Granville Sharp, ESQ* (London: Henry Colburn & Co., 1820), p.33.
[343] Thomas, Hugh, *The Slave Trade: The Story of the Atlantic Slave Trade*, (Simon & Schuster), 485, Kindle.

court.[344] This triggered a legal contest into which Granville fully immersed himself, even though he was not a lawyer.

Against all odds, GS sought the help and support of many legal professionals in his studies, but none came to his aid; even his own lawyers were against him in the cause.[345] However, he was given significant latitude to prepare his defense such that for a period of two years he amassed significant legal knowledge on his own. His legal research centered on whether or not English law supported slavery at all, especially in view of the dehumanizing pretext of the practice: chattel slavery.

It was during this same time that GS wrote one of his most persuasive books rebuking the evils of slavery, titled, *Extract from a Representation of the Injustice and Dangerous Tendency of Tolerating Slavery*. With meticulous detail supplied in his *Extract...of Tolerating Slavery*,[346] GS demonstrated that English law, *as written,* supplied no positive law supporting slavery but instead preserved the right of liberty to *all* who fell beneath its purview. Central to his overall argument was the Golden Rule which upheld the dignity of all humanity as well as the principles of love and justice: "All laws ought to be founded upon the principle of 'doing as one would be done by.'" This tract had become so well circulated in England and so well regarded by several legal authorities, that "the lawyers employed against...Strong were intimidated"[347] and, because of their delayed pursuit of the case the plaintiff was "compelled to pay treble costs for not bringing forward" a viable argument.[348]

---

[344] Charles Stuart, *A memoir of Granville Sharp: to which is added Sharp's Law of passive obedience, and an extract from his Law of retribution,* (American Anti-Slavery Society), 66-68, Kindle.

[345] Haore, *Memoirs,* 39.

[346] For the sake of simplicity, all references to GS's *Extract from a Representation of the Injustice and Dangerous Tendency of Tolerating Slavery* include his separately published "Appendix" (An Appendix to the Representation of the Injustice and Dangerous Tendency of Tolerating Slavery, 1769) will be referred to as, *Extract...of Tolerating Slavery.*

[347] "Lisle, finding the nature of the person with whom he had to deal (GS), invendted various pretexts for deferring the suit against him, and at length offered a compromise, which Mr. Sharp rejected." Hoar, *Memoirs,* 39.

[348] Ibid., 40.

Though this particular case did not change English law, it was the first domino to fall in a long series that would eventually lead to the fall of slavery in England and elsewhere in the world.

1769 Publication - *Extract from a Representation of the Injustice and Dangerous Tendency of Tolerating Slavery*: Not only did GS's aforementioned *Extract...of Tolerating Slavery* have a significant impact in England, but it also had a powerful influence within the American Colonies. Prominent abolitionist Anthony Benezet[349] helped to distribute this work throughout the colonies[350] which fueled a greater desire "to abolish slavery as well as the Slave Trade."[351] Consistent with all of his anti-slavery literature, GS reminded his readers that his arguments were founded in the true source of all authority: "The Scriptures (which are the only true foundation of all laws)."[352] He forcefully rebuked the classification of Africans as "*res*" chattel, calling this a "disgrace of human nature."[353]

We should pause and note the remarkable fact that the Declaration of Independence, which came seven years later, originally included an anti-slave trade clause which contained similar language to that of GS's *Extract...of Tolerating Slavery*. Such similarities include mentions of the *piratical* nature of

---

[349] "...it is remarkable, that Mr. Benezet reprinted that tract (*Extract...of Tolerating Slavery*) at Philadelphia, without knowing that the author had paid the same compliment to his former work (*Some Historical Account of Guinea with an Inquiry into the Rise and Progress of the Slave-trade*) in 1767." Hoar, *Memoirs*, 97.

[350] "The tract 'on the Injustice of Slavery,' and the dispersion of it throughout America by Benezet...during the course of three successive years (from 1769), had already produced the most powerful effect." Ibid., 103.

[351] Ibid., 104.

[352] Sharp, *Extract...of Tolerating Slavery*, 33.

[353] Ibid., 29-30. Also see: Granville Sharp, *An Appendix to the Representation of the Injustice and Dangerous Tendency of Tolerating Slavery*, (London, printed 1771), 7.

slavery;[354] the hypocrisy of a Christian supporting the trade;[355] slavery's contradiction against the dignity of "human nature"[356] as well as its violation of the principle of "life and liberty" and "happiness."[357] Clearly, the anti-slave trade clause is quite alien to Jefferson's personal views, especially since he too owned slaves; however, while it could never be proven that GS's ubiquitous booklet had any influence[358] on the Declaration's original rough draught,[359] one

---

[354] Declaration's Rough Draught: "This piratical warfare, the opprobrium of infidel powers..."; GS's *Extract...of Tolerating Slavery*: "There is such a thing as justice to which the most sacred regard is due. It ought to be inviolably observed. Have not these unhappy men a better right to their liberty, and to their happiness, than our American merchants have to the profits which they make by torturing their kind? Let therefore our colonies be ruined, but let us not render so many men miserable. Would not any of us, who should be snatched by pirates from his native land, think himself cruelly abused, and at all times entitled to be free?" Sharp, *Extract...of Tolerating Slavery*, 38-39.

[355] Declaration's Rough Draught rebuked the hypocrisy of a "Christian king" promoting the piracy of slavery: "This piratical warfare the opprobrium of infidel powers, is the warfare of the CHRISTIAN king of Great Britain."

[356] In opposition to the pretext of *res* (chattel) slavery, GS refers to the dignity of "human nature" three times in his *"Extract...of Tolerating Slavery"* and twice in his "Appendix."

[357] "Have not these unhappy men [slaves] a better right to their liberty, and to their happiness, than our American merchants have to the profits which they make by torturing their kind?" Granville Sharp, *Extract...of Tolerating Slavery*, 39.

[358] Jefferson's principal reliance on Franklin and Adams (as stipulated in his 1823 letter to James Madison) for the development of the Declaration's content does raise questions about the document's original and final formulation. This is especially the case since Franklin himself had such a profound deference for GS's abolitionist work.

[359] In his 1823 letter to James Madison, Thomas Jefferson addressed Timothy Pickering's speculations about the original development of the Declaration of Independence, thereby revealing the manner in which the document was originally drafted: "I consented [to write the draft]: I drew it; but before I reported it to the committee, I communicated it separately to Dr. Franklin and

thing had become quite clear in the years leading up to 1776: many of the inhabitants of England and the Colonies[360] began to grapple with fact that if liberty was to be established for one, then liberty must be established for all on the basis of a *shared humanity*. As GS clearly argued, the toleration of domestic slavery was an affront to the Creator and greatly contradicted the Colony's expressed desire for liberty.[361]

---

mr Adams requesting their corrections; because they were the two members of whose judgments and amendments I wished most to have the benefit before presenting it to the Committee; and you have seen the original paper now in my hands, with the corrections of Doctor Franklin and mr Adams interlined in their own hand writings-their alterations were two or three only, and merely verbal. I then wrote a fair copy, reported it to the Committee, and from them, unaltered to Congress...Pickering's observations, and mr Adam's in addition, 'that it contained no new ideas, that it is a commonplace compilation, it's [sic] sentiments hacknied in Congress for two years before, and it's [sic] essence contained in Otis's pamphlet,' may all be true. Of that I am not to be the judge. Rich H. Lee charged it as copied from Locke's Treatise on government. Otis's pamphlet I never saw, & whether I had gathered my ideas from reading or reflection I do not know. I know only that I turned to neither book or pamphlet while writing it. I did not consider it as any part of my charge to invent new ideas altogether & to offer no sentiment which had ever been expressed before." Thomas Jefferson, Letter to James Madison, 30 August 1823.

[360] In a personal letter to GS (May 14 1772), Benezet mentioned Benjamin Franklin's important assistance to the abolitionist community. Further evidence of such assistance was revealed when Franklin distributed Sharp's book, *A Declaration of the People's Natural Right to a Share in the Legislature, in Support of the American colonists*, throughout the colonies. Hoare, *Memoirs*, 99, 172-173.

[361] This, in part, encapsulates Sharp's message in his *Extract...of Tolerating Slavery,* and was more specifically articulated in his *Declaration of the People's Natural Right to a Share in the Legislature* which was printed and distributed in the Colonies in 1774.

1772 - Somerset v. Stewart: GS quickly developed a reputation of being a staunch defender of the enslaved, not only because of his labors on behalf of Jonathan Strong, but especially in view of his well distributed *Extract...of Tolerating Slavery* which rebuked the continuation of slavery in England and the colonies. Because of this, he was frequently sought out for legal protection by those in need. This resulted in five additional court battles after Strong,[362] including the case of James Somerset in Somerset v. Stewart.

Somerset had been acquired as a slave in the Colony of Virginia by Charles Stewart before being transported to England in 1769. Two years later, Somerset managed to escape from Stewart and eventually sought GS for help in January 1772. Sharp offered his assistance to Somerset's legal counsel[363] and Lord William Mansfield, who had become very familiar with GS's advocacy on behalf of the enslaved, was overseeing the case.

This particular situation would test Sharp's carefully crafted argument in his *Extract...of Tolerating Slavery* as to whether or not English law, *as written,* preserved the rights of *all* who fell beneath its purview. In the case of Somerset, the core issue was whether or not he was protected by English law the moment he stepped foot on British soil in 1769.

Though Mansfield had delayed the case for months, a final judgment was given in favor Somerset's freedom. Mansfield had conceded, as Sharp had been strenuously arguing for years, that there was no "positive law" supporting slavery and therefore English law could do nothing else but affirm his freedom. On June 22 1772 James Somerset was declared a free man, which profoundly advanced the cause of abolition.

---

[362] Hoare, *Memoirs*, 248.

[363] Mr. Hargreaves then proceeded with the defence. "If," said he, "the claim of Stewart over Somerset, be here recognized, domestic slavery, with its horrid train of evils, may be lawfully imported into this country, at the discretion of ever)' foreigner or native. It will come, not only from our own Colonies, but from Poland, Russia, Spain and Turkey—from the coast of Barbary; from the eastern and western coasts of Africa; from every part of the world, where it still continues to torment and dishonor the human species." Charles Stuart, *A memoir of Granville Sharp*, 216-220.

1774 Publication - *A Declaration of the People's Natural Right to a Share in the Legislature, in Support of the American colonists*: By this time, GS had a growing concern for the American colonies in their pursuit of freedom *for all*. Having become well-known in the Colonies, he decided to make good use of his growing influence by promoting a tract he wrote in 1774, titled, *A Declaration of the People's Natural Right to a Share in the Legislature, in Support of the American Colonists*. GS gave two hundred and fifty copies of this booklet to Benjamin Franklin who subsequently dispatched them to America. Thousands of copies of the tract were printed in Boston, New York, and Philadelphia and were then distributed throughout the colonies.[364]

This particular work directed the "thoughts of many among the colonists to constitutional points, which, however momentous, had before lain unexamined by them, as not hitherto called into view by the relative dependencies of the two countries; and he thus became, unintentionally, though not unconsciously, an instrument[365] in the great work of American Independence."[366] Remaining faithful to his focus on abolition, GS warned his readers that the lawful protection of liberty and justice *for one* necessitated liberty and justice for all. As such, he sought to promote a legal standard

---

[364] Hoare, *Memoirs*, 172-173.

[365] Daniel B. Wallace expands upon the similarities between America's Declaration of Independence and that of GS's *Declaration of the People's Natural Right to a share in the Legislature*" but admits that it could never be proven that the former was influenced by the latter: "Incidentally, there is some evidence that this slender volume [by GS] may have influenced Thomas Jefferson, both verbally and conceptually. A cursory look at Sharp's work suggests some remarkable similarities with the Declaration of Independence. Nevertheless, establishing literary dependence in a case such as this is notoriously difficult and quite beyond the scope of this paper." Daniel B. Wallace *"Granville Sharp: A Model of Evangelical Scholarship and Social Activism"* Bible.org https://bible.org/article/granville-sharp-model-evangelical-scholarship-and-social-activism#_ftnref31.

[366] Hoare, *Memoirs*, 172.

whereby "…the laws of natural equity, justice, and liberty…be strictly observed, and the abomination of domestic as well as political slavery abolished!"[367]

Concerning America's toleration of domestic slavery, he issued this solemn warning: "The toleration of domestic slavery in the Colonies greatly weakens the claim or natural right of our American brethren to liberty. Let them put away the accursed thing, that horrid oppression from among them, before they presume to implore the interposition of divine justice; for whilst they retain their brethren of the world in the most shameful involuntary servitude, it is profane in them to look up to the merciful Lord of all, and call him Father!"[368]

Sharp's warning was quite stark, but it was needful. The hypocrisy of crying for God's just intervention for the cause of liberty, while harboring the grave injustices of slavery, was an unconscionable act that warranted such a warning.

1776 Publications - *The Law of Liberty; The Law of Retribution; The Just Limitation of Slavery in the Laws of God*: By 1776, GS's warnings against slavery had taken on an intensity and solemnity comparable to that of a prophet. In his work, *The Law of Liberty,*[369] he presented an exposition of the foremost commandment of love as well as the Golden Rule. Not only did he establish a basis for the gracious and fair treatment of all members of the human race, but he issued severe warnings against those who violated such standards.

In his work, *The Law of Retribution,* he rebuked those who sought to justify the kidnapping and enslaving of Africans on the basis of Scripture, while revealing the promised judgment that would fall on those who did so. The subtitle of this work is, quite fittingly, "*Or A Serious Warning to Great Britain and her Colonies, Founded on Unquestionable Examples of God's Temporal*

---

[367] Granville Sharp, *A Declaration of the People's Natural Right to Share in the Legislature which is the Fundamental Principle of the British Constitution of State*, (London, 1774), 28.

[368] Sharp, *A Declaration*, 28.

[369] The full title of this work is: *The Law of Liberty, or, Royal Law, by Which all Mankind will Certainly be Judged!*

Vengeance Against Tyrants, Slave-holders, and Oppressors." By itself, this is GS's lengthiest and most severe rebuke against English and American slavery.

Finally, his work, *The Just Limitation of Slavery in the Laws of God,* rebuked fallacious uses of Scripture in defense of slavery which included a directed refutation of Reverend Thompson, who employed the specious argument of the "curse of Ham" for the enslavement of Africans. All of these works were, above all other considerations, a heralding of the glory of God through a defense of *sacred Scripture*: "But it is not enough, that the Laws of England exclude Slavery merely from this island, whilst the grand Enemy of mankind triumphs in a toleration, throughout our Colonies, of the most monstrous oppression to which human nature can be subjected! And yet this abominable wickedness has not wanted advocates, who, in a variety of late publications, have attempted to palliate the guilt, and have even ventured to appeal to Scripture for the support of their uncharitable pretensions; so that I am laid under a double obligation to answer them, because it is not the cause of Liberty alone for which I now contend, but for that which I have still much more at heart, the honour of the holy Scriptures, the principles of which are entirely opposite to the selfish and uncharitable pretentions of our American Slaveholders and African Traders."[370]

In all of this, GS remained committed to his call for a liberty which was rooted in justice, and he repeatedly sought to influence other reputed abolitionists to this same standard, including Benjamin Rush, John Jay, General Lafayette, and John Adams. His emphasis always remained focused on the complete and total abolition of slavery rather than a partitive approach which sought "a *gradual Abolition* of the Colonial oppression [in the hope that], if *the Trade was abolished,* some prudent regulations would of course be soon adopted to supersede the other."[371] For Sharp, the most principled way to approach the slave trade, as well as domestic slavery, was to establish "an immediate declaration that the whole '*System of Colonial Law*' is totally

---

[370] Granville Sharp, *Extract...of Tolerating Slavery,* 2-3.
[371] Granville Sharp, *The System of Colonial Law Compared with the Eternal Laws of God,* (Richard Edwards, London, 1807), 9-10.

illegal"[372] in view of its continuance of slavery (see Appendix III, The Honour of the Holy Scriptures).

1781 - The Zong Massacre: Though public opinion continued to grow in its opposition against slavery, far greater progress was needed in England and America. Tragically, the Declaration of Independence had been signed and ratified without the anti-slave trade article originally contained in the rough draft. Though this article would not have been enough to end slavery in its entirety, it could have supplied further progress towards that end. As well, its stipulations would have helped to expose the horrors of the slave trade where humans were being "captivated" and "carried" into slavery, with some incurring a "miserable death in their transportation" to the colonies. When one considers this omitted article, the language of its warning seems prophetic in view of the unspeakable tragedy that would take place five years later aboard the slave ship named, *Zong.* Of course, every slave ship experienced the tragic loss of human life seeing that kidnapped souls were packed into these vessels like animals with little food or water. Such abusive treatment resulted in high mortality rates somewhere between 15%-20% on average. However, the tragic story of the Zong went well beyond the common horrors of the day because it involved the *deliberate murder of 132 Africans.*

Though the details of this case aren't entirely clear, a key witness alleged that the ship veered off course due to navigational errors, leading to a significant delay in the journey across the Middle Passage. This resulted in a panic within the crew over crucially needed supplies, the greatest of which was drinking water.[373] Because of this, the ship's captain claimed that it was

---

[372] Ibid.

[373] The complexity of the Zong case far exceeds the scope of this book, but this enigmatic case extended into two trials. The original ship's log had been lost or destroyed making the recounting of events on the ship quite difficult. The original claim of insufficient water was later contradicted by additional testimony (in the second trial) indicating that there was a significant supply of rain the day before slaves were thrown off the ship. By itself, this nullified the claim that the killing of the enslaved was in any way *necessary.* Moreover, Walvin reveals the additionally horrific detail regarding the testimony of the Zong's first mate, James Kelsall, "Rumour had spread among the shackled Africans that they were being

necessary to throw a number of the enslaved overboard to preserve their limited supplies. However, it is most likely that this barbaric act was done in order to mitigate financial losses to the owners of the Zong. This was due to the fact that maritime insurance provided no compensation for those who died of "natural causes" while enroute to their destination, but they did provide compensation for a ship's losses at sea whenever cargo was *necessarily* sacrificed in order to preserve what remained. Because the enslaved were classified as *res* (chattel), their cold-blooded murder was seen as nothing more than "a sensible jettisoning of objects."[374] So traumatizing was this grotesque event that an additional ten slaves jumped overboard to their deaths.[375]

Despicably, the ensuing legal contest over the Zong did not consist of a mass-murder trial, but instead entailed a dispute between the ship's owners and the insurers regarding monetary compensation. The first trial concluded in favor of the ship's owners whereby the insurers were ordered to pay compensation for the Zong's claimed losses.

Not long after the insurers appealed this ruling, GS became involved and began to campaign "against the crew and the owners of the ship both inside and outside the courts, and tried to bring murder charges against the men involved."[376] He made direct appeals to the British Admiralty, underscoring the fact that the "Zong killings were an 'extreme wickedness', and any justification for the killings [was] a 'damnable doctrine.'"[377]

---

killed because the ship's supplies were running short: 'they begged they might be suffered to live and they would not ask for either Meat or Water but could live without either till they arrived at their determined port.'...This despairing plea – little more than a throwaway line in a legal statement – is as haunting a fragment of evidence as any that has come down to us from the ranks of millions of Africans consigned to the bellies of the slave ships." James Walvin, *The Zong: A Massacre, the Law & the End of Slavery*, (Yale University Press, 2011), 158, Kindle.

[374] Ibid., 146.

[375] Ibid., 97.

[376] Ibid., 117.

[377] Ibid., 167.

Though Mansfield ruled in favor of the insurers in the second trial, Sharp's appeals for a conviction of murder were ignored. However, rather than quenching the abolitionist cause, this concluding judgment in the Zong case became an accelerant to the anti-slavery movement's fiery zeal.

By now, GS had developed a very significant, collaborative network of abolitionist cohorts, and he moved quickly in order to mobilize this growing force: "Sharp, the political and legal busybody, was determined to make the most powerful men in the nation aware of the Zong...Bishops with seats in the Lords were showered with Sharp's tracts, hot from the press. To ensure that they got the message, he also approached them individually."[378]

Eventually, the Zong massacre gained national and international attention, causing the winds of change to blow much more strongly in favor of liberty.

One cannot rightly consider the vigorous labors of Granville Sharp without first appreciating the fact that he was nothing more than an imperfect vessel of God's grace whose desire it was to magnify the Lord by *means of honoring the holy Scriptures.*

Having read most of his works on slavery, two of his memoirs, along with other related materials, it is this author's opinion that so very few know about this man because of his profound humility. He did not seek the limelight, nor was he chasing after the praise of men. He was a simple servant who sought to magnify the name of Christ against tremendous opposition. His redemption in Christ was not a *mere motif* or contrivance having no effect. His boldness for the Gospel was like that of the Apostle Paul's, who wrote: "For I am not ashamed of the gospel, for it is the power of God for salvation to everyone who believes, to the Jew first and also to the Greek." (Romans 1:16).

In time, this powerful Gospel would transform hearts and lives in such a manner that would impact the world; even a world that was engulfed in slavery. As previously noted, J. B. Lightfoot was right when he wrote: "when...the Apostolic precept that 'in Christ Jesus is neither bond

---

[378] Ibid.

nor free' was not only recognized but acted upon, then slavery was doomed. Henceforward it was only a question of time."[379] In God's providence, the end of the slave trade in England was made a certainty when the Gospel continued to grip the hearts of individuals like Newton, Wilberforce, and Clarkson, among many others.

Newton, formerly a slave ship captain of many years, wholly relented of the wickedness of his life when he was converted. The Lord's transformative work made him another fierce contender for the abolitionist cause. In his book, *Thoughts upon the African Slave Trade*, published in 1788, Newton offered this sobering reflection: "It will always be a subject of humiliating reflection to me, that I was once an active instrument in a business at which my heart now shudders."[380] Newton's popular hymn, *Amazing Grace*, begins with that familiar line: *"Amazing grace, how sweet the sound that saved a wretch like me! I once was lost, but now am found, was blind, but now I see."* This was not an expression of feigned humility for Newton, but it reveals his serious and solemn perspective regarding his former life:

"I was formerly one of his [Satan's] active undertemptors and had my influence been equal to my wishes I would have carried all the human race with me. A common drunkard or profligate is a petty sinner to what I was."[381]

Newton's profound testimony would eventually have a significant impact on the young parliamentarian, William Wilberforce. When Wilberforce had a crisis of conscience regarding his future in politics he sought

---

[379] Lightfoot, *Saint Paul's Epistles to the Colossians and to Philemon*, 323.

[380] Newton, John, *Thoughts upon the African slave trade*, (London: Printed for J. Buckland, in Pater-Noster Row; and J. Johnson, in St. Paul's Church-yard, 1725-1807), 170, Kindle.

[381] Bill Moyers, (director), "Amazing Grace with Bill Moyers," Public Affairs Television, Inc. (1990).

Newton's council which gave him a new level of clarity concerning the manner in which he might be used in England's world of politics. On October 28 1787, Wilberforce made a record of his renewed resolve: "God has set before me two great objects, the suppression of the slave trade and the reformation of *manners* [*modes of procedure*]."[382]

In addition to Sharp and Newton, Wilberforce was strongly assisted by another co-laborer in the Gospel, Thomas Clarkson, whose strong opposition to slavery was clearly revealed in his classic work, *The History of the Abolition of the African Slave-Trade by the British Parliament*, published in 1808. His stalwart collaboration with Wilberforce helped to advance the abolitionist cause in England:

> No subject is more pleasing than that of the removal of evils. — Evils have existed almost from the beginning of the world; but there is a power in our nature to counteract them — this power increased by Christianity. — Of the evils removed by Christianity one of the greatest is the Slave Trade. — The joy we ought to feel on its abolition from a contemplation of the nature of it; and of the extent of it; and of the difficulty of subduing it.[383]

All of these men, Sharp, Newton, Clarkson, and Wilberforce, had come to the same point of determination and Gospel resolve even though they came from very different facets of society.

When the Slave Trade Act was passed in 1807, this was a great victory, but it did not bring an end to domestic slavery. In order to confront this, Wilberforce wrote *An appeal to the religion, justice and humanity of the inhabitants of the British Empire on behalf of the negro slaves in the West Indies* in 1823 which became another key contribution for the abolitionist cause. Throughout this work, he openly and

---

[382] Kevin Belmonte, *William Wilberforce* (Michigan: Zondervan, 2002), 100, Kindle, italics mine.

[383] Thomas Clarkson, *The History of the Abolition of African Slave-Trade by the British Parliament,* (Musaicum Books), 1, Kindle.

unreservedly rebuked those who ignorantly established dehumanizing justifications for slavery, like that of Edward Long's book, *The History of Jamaica*, which presented degrading comparisons between native Jamaicans and baboons:

.

> ...in the gradations of being, Negroes were little elevated above the Oran outang, "that type of man." Nor was this an unguarded or a hastily thrown out assertion. He institutes a laborious comparison of the Negro race with that species of baboon; and declares, that "ludicrous as the opinion may seem, he does not think that an Oran outang husband would be any dishonor to a Hottentot[384] female."[385]

As well, Wilberforce issued solemn and direct challenges to his colleagues in Parliament, urging them to contemplate the inhumanity of slavery in view of their "common Creator":

> ...is there, in the whole of the three kingdoms, a parent or a husband so sordid and insensible that any sum, which the richest West Indian proprietor could offer him, would be deemed a compensation for his suffering his wife or his daughter to be subjected to the brutal outrage of the cart-whip—to the savage lust of the driver —to the indecent, and degrading, and merciless punishment of a West Indian whipping? If there were one so dead, I say not to every liberal, but to every natural feeling, as that money could purchase of him such concessions, such a wretch, and he alone, would be capable of the farther sacrifices necessary for degrading an English peasant to the condition of a West Indian slave. He might consent to sell the liberty of his own children, and to barter away even the blessings conferred on himself by that religion which declares to him that his master, no less than himself, has a Master in heaven—a

---

[384] The word hottentot was used by 17th century Dutch settlers as a moniker for the native Khoisanids in South-West Africa.
[385] William Wilberforce, *An Appeal to the Religion, Justice, and Humanity of the Inhabitants of the British Empire: In Behalf of the Negro Slaves in the West Indies*, (J. Hatchard and Son), 142, Kindle.

common Creator, who is no respecter of persons, and in whose presence he may weekly stand on the same spiritual level with his superiors in rank, to be reminded of their common origin, common responsibility, and common day of final and irreversible account.[386]

Wilberforce's *Appeal* stirred no small measure of controversy. To a culture that had become complicit with slavery, his rebukes began to expose England's open wound of this long held practice. This brought many pro-slavery advocates out into the open, leading to a series of contests. One such contest involved Reverend George Wilson Bridges, the Rector of Mandeville (Manchester parish, Jamaica), who published a refutation against Wilberforce's *Appeal*, titled: *A Voice from Jamaica in reply to William Wilberforce, ESQ. M. P. (1823)*. In this work, Bridges attempted to defend Edward Long's degrading "Hottentot" comment and mocked Wilberforce's efforts, calling them all an "unworthy means."[387] Yet in God's good and sovereign purposes, those contrarian efforts set forth by Bridges and others like him actually had a very different effect:

In the end, the charges of hypocrisy and falsehood brought against Wilberforce and his colleagues furthered the cause they were intended to obstruct. The charges forced the abolitionists to conduct a painstaking investigation of the colonial slave system, which eventually resulted in much more widespread knowledge of the abuses connected with slavery. As Wilberforce's sons phrased it: "Then was laid open that prison-house abhorred by God and man, and those secrets were revealed which posterity will view with equal wonder and abhorrence."[388]

How ironic it is that Bridges' efforts to dissuade the abolitionist movement actually backfired, triggering its greater progress and eventual triumph.

---

[386] Wilberforce, *An Appeal*, 524-532.
[387] Belmonte, *William Wilberforce*, 281.
[388] Ibid., 282.

Despite such opposing efforts, the Gospel prevailed in the lives of many who fought for the glory of Christ and for genuine justice. This very goal was well represented in Wilberforce's *Appeal* by means of two biblical texts cited on the title page. The first such passage was Jeremiah 22:13: "Woe to him who builds his house without righteousness and his upper rooms without justice, who uses his neighbor's services without pay and does not give him his wages." The second text is an abbreviated reference to Micah 6:8, *"do justice and love mercy."* Taken together, both passages clearly herald Wilberforce's message and mission for *justice* in his virulent opposition to slavery.

In all of this we must receive the tutelage that this segment of history supplies: whenever and wherever the Lord's people uphold the Gospel and the message of Jesus' justice, God's saving and sanctifying light will shine brilliantly amidst this world of darkness. England's example of *Gospel fidelity* became a strong rebuke to a world that continued in the debaucheries of slavery. England's example *of wisdom* made certain that slavery would eventually degrade and perish, and this has been *most true* wherever the Gospel has been greatly upheld. And this same wisdom would continue to spread, take root, and flourish within the nation whose originating confession was that *all men are created equal*, as Jonathan Edwards (the younger) clearly articulated in his sermon on the Golden Rule (Matthew 7:12):

"...It is a principle, the truth of which hath in this country been...universally acknowledged...*that all men are born equally free.* The Africans are by nature equally entitled to freedom as we are; and therefore we have no more right to enslave [them] than they have to do the same to us. They have the same right to their freedom which they have to their property or to their lives."[389]

---

[389] "Therefore to enslave them is as really and in the same sense wrong, as to steal from them, to rob or *to murder them.*" (*italics mine,* c.f. Exodus 21:16) Edwards, *The Injustice and Impolicy of the Slave Trade,* 5.

While the advocates of SJI are right to observe that the *professing church* has frequently failed in the mission of the Gospel, they are catastrophically wrong to ignore the remarkable triumphs of the *true church* throughout history for the cause of genuine justice.

The inhumanity of the transatlantic slave trade needed to be exposed for the monstrous evil that it was and the sword that was required to slay this beast was the great truth that is inseparable from the Gospel message itself; that the Lord made all the nations of men through one blood; that *all* are the *genos* (race/genealogy) of God who desperately need Jesus, the great emancipator and King of Righteousness.

J E S U S'
J U S T I C E

---

1 Peter 4:17:

17 For it is time for judgment to begin with the household of God; and if it begins with us first, what will be the outcome for those who do not obey the gospel of God?

CHAPTER 8

JUDGMENT BEGINS
WITH THE HOUSEHOLD OF GOD

As our world continues to be engulfed in accusations of "systemic racism" and "systemic white supremacy," one must wonder what will result from this chorus of condemnation. Such a chorus undermines genuine wisdom and repeatedly obfuscates the clear and much needed lessons of history.

For decades the advocates of SJI have claimed to be the fair and objective arbiters of history, *par excellence,* and those who dare question their "wisdom" are typically treated to no small measure of belittlement and scorn. Yet even the most modest evaluation of their teaching reveals that their stilted version of the past leads them to a despicable vilification of an entire segment of the human race *via* "systemic white supremacy." Their negative view of *nearly everything* makes them incapable of seeing any good or any progress in this nation or elsewhere in the world.

As was mentioned in the previous chapter, the Christian church is repeatedly vilified by SJI authors as being the past and present cohort of racial bigotry, and this constitutes a very troubling accusation. In his book, *The Color of Compromise,* Tisby unreservedly connects white supremacy to the church: "At the outset of the nineteenth century, the United States could have become a worldwide beacon of diversity and equality. Fresh from the Revolutionary War, it could have adopted the noble ideals written in the Declaration of Independence. It could have crafted a truly inclusive Constitution. Instead, *white supremacy became more defined as the nation and the church solidified their identities.*"[390] Similarly, he even goes so far as to link Christianity with that of the KKK:

...the KKK crafted a vision of a white America and, more specifically, a white Christian America. Only native-born Protestant men, and a few women, were allowed to join. Many Klan members actively participated in their local churches, and some of the same men who conducted night rides on Saturday ascended to the pulpit to preach on Sunday...The KKK's dedication to race and nation rose to the level of religious devotion because of its overt appeal to Christianity and the Bible.[391]

Passages such as these remind us that any historical analysis can be manipulated and abused to serve faulty agendas. They also remind us that *guilt by association* arguments, though faulty, thrive within SJI materials. However, while it is tempting to dismiss faulty or excessive arguments, doing so would be counterproductive. Though few would give credence to Tisby's association of Christianity with the KKK, there is a need to acknowledge the grave shortcomings of those who have *claimed to uphold the Gospel but failed to do so.* Thus, it is crucial that we examine history *objectively*, knowing that there will be a broad sampling of good and evil throughout.

In the previous chapter, we examined what powerful impact the Gospel had on the slave trade *via* individuals like Sharp, Wilberforce, Clarkson, Newton and others. These were flawed and imperfect people, but they fought against the monstrous injustice of slavery in their service

---

[390] Tisby, *The Color of Compromise*, 57, italics mine.
[391] Ibid., 100-103.

to Christ. We have also considered the disturbing realities of false religionists like Johann Tetzel and Reverend George Wilson Bridges, charlatans who proffered their ideological wares to the masses. Though Tetzel and Bridges claimed to be followers of Christ as well, their lives and doctrine clearly belied their profession. False religion such as this plagues the whole of human history and often manifests itself beneath the labels of *conservative* and *liberal.* Even the *conservative Pharisees* and *liberal Sadducees*[392] revealed the commonality of their corruption when they joined forces to crucify Christ. Clearly, their *confession* of being the followers of God was undermined by the *bad fruit* of their conduct. In the end, many individuals, under a variety of labels, claim allegiance to the Lord, however, all will ultimately be known by their life and doctrine.

With this in view, our focus in this chapter will be set upon those whose mishandling of the Scriptures have tarnished the Gospel's message and the church's reputation. This is especially needful for those who fail to see a distinction between the true and false church. Rather than wasting our time on unrelated extremists, like the KKK, we will address those whose reputation has placed them more squarely within the visible, professing Evangelical church. The point of this procedure is not to render judgments concerning the eternal state of such individuals, after all only "the Lord knows who are his" (2 Timothy 2:19). Instead, we will examine those who have marred the reputation of Christ by means of significant *corruptions of the Gospel*, both *in history* and *in the present*.

1. Historic Corruptions of the Gospel: Two years after America's costly Civil War, Robert Lewis Dabney, a Presbyterian pastor and former

---

[392] The Pharisees were by nature the rigidly legal, the Sadducees in the first instance only the aristocrats, who certainly were driven by the historical development into that opposition to Pharisaic legality, which however formed no fundamental element of their nature. Emil Schürer, *A History of the Jewish People in the Time of Jesus Christ* (Capella Press), 9965, Kindle.

Confederate States Army chaplain, wrote a book defending the practice of slavery, titled, *In Defense of Virginia [and through her of the South] in Recent and Pending Contests Against the Sectional Party*. Throughout his work, Dabney employed passages from the Old and New Testaments in his effort to justify compulsory labor from the enslaved:

> ...the cavils, objections and special pleadings of the Abolitionists teem like the frogs of Egypt, engendered in the mire of ignorance and prejudice, so numerous because so worthless...Whatever may have been the leniency of the [O.T.] system [of slavery], the state of the Gentile slaves showed the essential features of slavery among us, the right to the slave's labour for life without his consent, property in that labour, the right to buy, sell and bequeath it; the right to enforce it on the slave by corporal punishments, which might have any degree of severity short of death. (See Exod. xxi. 20, 21.) Virginians had no interest to contend for any stricter form of slavery than this.[393]

This particular passage from Dabney's *Defense* is both stunning and telling. The thought of seizing fellow human beings against their will, compelling their servitude by force (theirs and their progeny), and beating them just short of death, *all in the name of Jesus Christ,* surpasses credulity.[394]

We should take special note of Dabney's mention of Exodus 21:20-21 in this citation, especially with respect to the exegetical habit that it reveals. Throughout his book, Dabney consults passages from both the OT and NT, however, he leans most heavily on the Mosaic Law, *to a fault,* in a manner that was similar to many other pro-slavery advocates at

---

[393] Robert Lewis Dabney, *In Defense of Virginia* (E. J. Hale and Son), 1318-31, Kindle.

[394] In his book, *In Defense of Virginia*, Dabney expends significant energy trying to justify slavery in America. He attempts to distance himself from the charge of kidnapping through a number of arguments, including that of *domestic slavery.* For more information relating to Dabney, as well as other matters relevant to this book, go to www.thearmoury.org in order to search the article database.

the time. As the Galatian errorists of the 1st century advanced the root-rot of *another Gospel* (*via* their abuse of Mosaic law), those who promoted the continuance of 19th century slavery in America proffered *similar* abuses of Scripture to their generation.

As we have already reviewed, Granville Sharp confronted such manipulations of Scripture in his day. In his work, *The Just Limitation of Slavery*, GS refuted those who abused biblical texts in order to justify slavery, justly rebuking the grave error of likening American slavery to the unique permissions and prescriptions granted to Israel in the Old Testament. He rightly insisted that *there is no sense in which* "the Israelites, under the dispensation of the Law, either in killing, dispossessing, or enslaving...should justify our modern acts of violence and oppression, now that we profess obedience to the Gospel of Peace."[395]

Yet Dabney's efforts to defend the enslavement of kidnapped persons and their progeny, *via* the text of Exodus 21:20-21, should remind us of the need for caution when wielding the sword of God's Word. Had Dabney given more careful consideration to the logic of his argument; had he considered the reality that domestic slavery continued the commercialization of kidnapped souls and their progeny;[396] and had he

---

[395] Sharp, *The Just Limitation of Slavery*, 166-176.

[396] As will be discussed further in the eighth chapter, many slave trade advocates attempted to justify domestic slavery and trading as a societal necessity. Congress passed the Act Prohibiting Importation of Slaves on February 13th 1807; it was signed into law March 2nd 1807 and made effective January 1st 1808. Though this was supposed to end the transatlantic slave trade, slaves were still smuggled into America. Even apart from this consideration, the fact that most slave trading was done domestically simply means that kidnapped souls, *and their progeny*, continued to be used as chattel. To pretend that the criminal reality of kidnapping and chattel slavery ended at this point in time is a pure fantasy crafted by those who sought to retain the practice.

more carefully examined the context of the passage he used to justify his position (Exodus 21:20-21), he may have considered changing his views:

> Exodus 21:16: "And he who kidnaps a man, whether he sells him or he is found in his possession, shall surely be put to death."

How striking it is that just four verses prior to Dabney's proof-text for the continued enslavement of kidnapped Africans (Exodus 21:20-21), we actually find the *lawful standard of capital punishment* for all who sustained this practice. As well, his conflations of the capital crime of kidnapping with the Scriptural teachings on slavery reveal a profoundly disturbing message.

Dabney's broad and significant influence as a pastor and chaplain made his problematic teaching even more disturbing. But Dabney was not alone in this. Many who sought to justify the enslavement of Africans did so *via* similar interpretations of biblical passages, yielding disastrous effects. Just the title *and subtitle* of his book reveals the theological contests that persisted in the South: *In Defense of Virginia [and through her of the South] in Recent and Pending Contests Against the Sectional Party.* Dabney's mention of the *Sectional Party* refers to those abolitionist factions that would eventually formulate the Republican Party. These were among the abolitionists whom Dabney rebuked when he wrote, "the cavils, objections and special pleadings of the Abolitionists teem like the frogs of Egypt, engendered in the mire of ignorance and prejudice, so numerous because so worthless."[397] Such commentary clearly reflects the vehemence of pro slavery advocates against abolitionists, all of which reveals the persistent contests which continued in early America over the cause of abolition.

Additionally, the qualifying phrase, *and through her of the South,* makes it clear that Dabney believed his *Defense of Virginia* was a representative vindication of the confederacy, and in many respects it

---

[397] Dabney, *In Defence of Virginia*, 1319, Kindle.

was. Many pro-slavery advocates at this time promoted various versions of the pseudo-doctrine of the "curse of Ham" based upon Genesis 9:20-25. We find an example of this in the book titled, *Slavery: A Treatise Showing That Slavery Is neither a Moral, Political, nor Social Evil,* (1844), written by Patrick H. Mell, president of the Southern Baptist Convention (1863-1871). In it he argued that slavery was "essential to the existence of civil society" with this contrived basis:

> "From Ham were descended the nations that occupied the land of Canaan and those that now constitute the African or Negro race. Their inheritance, according to prophecy, has been and will continue to be slavery. "Slavery is advantageous both to the white and the colored race, and until it becomes a pecuniary evil, so long as we have the Bible, our reason, and our independence, we expect to maintain it."[398]

Though this line of reasoning thrived for a while, it did not endure for the simple reason that it was exegetically implausible and logically bankrupt. Dabney employed an alternate form of this teaching, arguing that the curse of Canaan (son of Ham) established the *origin of domestic slavery as a general principle* which he used to justify the enslavement of Africans:

> It [curse of Canaan] does in the first place, what all secular history and speculations fail to do: it gives us the origin of domestic slavery. And we find that it was appointed by God as the punishment of, and remedy for (nearly all God's providential chastisements are also remedial) the peculiar moral degradation of a part of the race. God here ordains that this depravity shall find its necessary restraints, and the welfare of the more virtuous its safeguard against the depraved, by the bondage of the latter. He introduces that feature of political society, for the justice of which we shall have occasion to contend; that although men have all this trait of natural equality that they are children of a

---

[398] R. Albert Mohler, Jr., "Report on Slavery and Racism in the History of the Southern Baptist Theological Seminary," December 12 2018.

common father, and sharers of a common humanity, and subjects of the same law of love; yet, in practice, they shall be subject to social inequalities determined by their own characters, and their fitness or unfitness to use privileges for their own and their neighbours' good.[399]

His argument was that "part of the race" of humans possessed "a peculiar moral degradation" and therefore required "bondage" for the welfare of the "more virtuous." What is key to this viewpoint is that those who claimed the high ground of virtuous living believed they had license to enslave those who possessed *a peculiar moral degradation.* The pivotal point in all of this is that Dabney was defending *one especially toxic idea.* He believed that, by the presumption of moral supremacy, he possessed this prejudicial license:

> *The right to judge an entire segment of humanity as being uniquely defective; worthy of derogation and subjugation.*

It was this right of *judgment,* he believed, that granted him the license to enslave others. I would ask the reader to remember this point for what follows later in this chapter. For Dabney, apparently his definition of *virtue* did not exclude reprehensible conduct like *kidnapping and chattel slavery.* Moreover, with a remarkable sleight of hand, Dabney makes further attempts to justify domestic slavery by means of "the golden rule" (Matthew 7:12) as well as the truth regarding the singularity of the human race:

> Golden Rule: [all are]...equal in their common humanity, and their common share in the obligations and benefits of the golden rule. All men are reciprocally bound to love their neighbors as themselves...Men have by nature, a general equality in this; not a specific one. Hence, the general equality of nature will by no means produce a literal and universal equality of civil condition; for the simple reason that the different classes of citizens have very

---

[399] Dabney, *In Defence of Virginia,* 1068-1073, Kindle.

different specific rights; and this grows out of their differences of sex, virtue, intelligence, civilization, etc., and the demands of the common welfare. *Thus, if the low grade of intelligence, virtue and civilization of the African in America, disqualified him for being his own guardian, and if his own true welfare (taking the "general run" of cases) and that of the community, would be plainly marred by this freedom; then the law decided correctly, that the African here has no natural right to his self–control, as to his own labour and locomotion.*[400]

Of the many comments that can be made about this condescending and disturbing passage, I will offer only a brief summary. In the above text, Dabney manages to issue a rather obvious contradiction regarding the golden rule. While he summarized the principle of the rule well enough, "All men are reciprocally bound to love their neighbors as themselves," we are still left to wonder how such reciprocity of love would justify one man forcibly enslaving another.[401] For example, if Dabney believed that his interpretation was correct, would he have gladly submitted to enslavement by someone who possessed greater intelligence and virtue than he? We think not. As well, he claimed a right to seize the African's *right of self-control and labor,* even though he concedes elsewhere that

---

[400] Robert L. Dabney, *Systematic Theology*, electronic ed. based on the Banner of Truth 1985 ed. (Simpsonville SC: Christian Classics Foundation, 1996), 721, italics mine.

[401] Within this passage Dabney cites Job 31:13-15 which warrants two qualifications. *First*, this particular quote is found amidst Job's efforts to justify himself before God; a self-justification effort that leads to several rebukes from Elihu and culminates in a stern rebuke from God Himself. Because of this, great care and caution should be exercised when drawing from such sections of Scripture. *Second*, the book of Job antedates much of Holy Writ (including the Mosaic Law) leaving us with little understanding regarding the nature of Job's relationship with his servants. Thus, while the text affirms the principle of the Golden Rule in general, how this can be used to justify the American slave trade leaves much to the imagination.

stealing is a violation of the Golden Rule: "The essence of theft is in the violation of the Golden Rule as to our neighbor's property. The essence of stealing is the obtaining our neighbor's goods without his intentional consent and without fair market value returned."[402] Dabney is right when he argues that the essence of theft is in the violation of the Golden Rule, but he fails miserably when seeking to apply that point *fairly*.

By seeking to justify the theft of an enslaved person's freedom and labor, Dabney was violating the creation ordinance which establishes work as an inseparable part of human stewardship.[403] As such, he was ultimately violating the *freedom, personal conscience, and material stewardship* of the enslaved which is nothing more than *an act of man-stealing*, being promoted through a twisted eisegesis of several passages *including the Golden Rule*.

GS was right to blast those who abused the Scriptures in this manner when he reminded his readers that they could not "justify slavery under the Christian dispensation."[404] He was especially right to warn those who persisted in this treachery, stipulating that the "[merchants of slavery] may, perhaps, plead custom and prescription (to their shame be it said) for their actions, yet, as they cannot, like the Israelites, produce an authentic written commandment from God for such proceedings, the offenders can no otherwise be esteemed than as lawless robbers and oppressors, who have reason to expect a severe retribution from God for their tyranny and oppression."[405]

Ultimately, the persistence of this evil culminated in America's Civil War, from 1861-1865, in which a vast sum of blood and treasure was lost, that is, 850,000 souls and 96 billion dollars.[406] When one considers the collective brutality and bloodshed of the slave trade, along with the

---

[402] Dabney, *Systematic Theology*, 497.

[403] Genesis 1-3.

[404] Sharp, *The Just Limitation of Slavery*, 2116.

[405] Ibid., 166-176.

[406] This total factors in inflationary differences between 1865 and 2021.

war that would secure its end, the overall toll of human suffering is inestimable. Tragically, those who sought to defend and justify this monstrosity *by Scripture* ultimately scarred the reputation of the professing church.

In the Lord's sovereign providence this is all history now, but one must wonder what *might have happened* if leaders like Dabney relented of their corrupt views.[407] Dabney, by virtue of his significant position as a pastor and Confederate chaplain, could have been an influence in the likeness of Sharp, Newton, Clarkson, and Wilberforce. What impact could there have been if prominent men like him rejected the prevailing influences of the culture around them, standing fast on the Gospel's affirmation of the *value and singularity of the human race?* Sadly, we will never know. Instead of being a beacon of light to a needy nation, he succumbed to a religious culture that contentedly cohabitated with the evils of man-stealing under the pretext of scriptural authority.

Dabney's defense and representation of Virginia *and the South* should remind us of the corrupting culture that persisted within many *professing churches* at the time. Yet despite such betrayals of scriptural authority, there were faithful voices in America and Britain who opposed such corruption, as in the case of the British pastor Charles Haddon Spurgeon who had no hesitation expressing his abhorrence for slavery:

> "although I commune at the Lord's table with men of all creeds, yet with a slave-holder I have no fellowship of any sort or kind. Whenever one has called upon me, I have considered it my duty to express my detestation of his wickedness, and I would as soon think of receiving a murderer into my church....as a man stealer."[408]

---

[407] Luke 22:20: And in the same way He took the cup after they had eaten, saying, "This cup which is poured out for you is the new covenant in My blood.

[408] Godfrey Holden Pike, *The Life and Work of Charles Haddon Spurgeon*, (UK: Banner of Truth Trust, 1992), 333

Similar to Sharp, Spurgeon's views on slavery had become widely known in England as well as America; but not all were eager to hear from this abolitionist preacher. When Spurgeon was invited to preach at a church in New York City, news of this provoked much hostility in the American South. One Alabama newspaper reported that the abolitionist preacher, Spurgeon, would receive a beating "'so bad as to make him ashamed.'"[409] Christian T. George in, The Lost Sermons of C. H. Spurgeon, best summarizes the hostility which persisted in the South against Spurgeon:

> February 17, 1860, citizens of Montgomery, Alabama, publicly protested the "notorious English abolitionist" by gathering in the jail yard to burn his "dangerous books": Last Saturday, we devoted to the flames a large number of copies of Spurgeon's Sermons. . . . We trust that the works of the greasy cockney vociferator may receive the same treatment throughout the South. And if the Pharisaical author should ever show himself in these parts, we trust that a stout cord may speedily find its way around his eloquent throat. On March 22, a "Vigilance Committee" in Montgomery followed suit and burned Spurgeon's sermons in the public square. A week later Mr. B. B. Davis, a bookstore owner, prepared "a good fire of pine sticks" before reducing about sixty volumes of Spurgeon's sermons "to smoke and ashes." British newspapers quipped that America had given Spurgeon a warm welcome, "a literally brilliant reception." Anti-Spurgeon bonfires illuminated jail yards, plantations, bookstores, and courthouses throughout the Southern states. In Virginia, Mr. Humphrey H. Kuber, a Baptist preacher and "highly respectable citizen" of Matthews County, burned seven calf-skinned volumes of Spurgeon's sermons "on the head of a flour barrel." The arson was assisted by "many citizens of the highest standing."[410]

---

[409] George, Christian T., The Lost Sermons of C. H. Spurgeon Volume I: (B&H Publishing Group), 1, Kindle.
[410] Ibid.

George continues his summary regarding the remarkably ill treatment Spurgeon received throughout the South: "In Florida, Spurgeon was a 'beef-eating, puffed-up, vain, over-righteous pharisaical, English blab-mouth.' In Virginia, he was a 'fat, overgrown boy'; in Louisiana, a 'hell-deserving Englishman'; and in South Carolina, a 'vulgar young man' with '(soiled) sleek hair, prominent teeth, and a self-satisfied air.' Georgians were encouraged to 'pay no attention to him.' North Carolinians 'would like a good opportunity at this hypocritical preacher' and resented his 'fiendish sentiments, against our Constitution and citizens.' The Weekly Raleigh Register reported that anyone selling Spurgeon's sermons should be arrested and charged with "circulating incendiary publications."'[411] The hostilities continued to rage against Spurgeon in view of his Gospel stand against slavery.

History's tutelage can be quite unsettling, but we must never ignore its lessons no matter how challenging they may be. Many in the American South developed a complex religious *ideology* that was used to justify criminality. Their use of the Scriptures was clearly stilted enough so as to produce remarkable harm against fellow members of the human race. Sadly, much of this ignorance and hostility from the past persists in the modern day by those who claim allegiance to Christ and His church.

2. Present Corruptions of the Gospel: Though it may seem difficult to imagine, several of the aforementioned Gospel-corruptions in America's past are being either whitewashed or openly reproduced in the present day. In this section, we will focus on a few key examples of these dangerous tendencies, beginning with those whose habit it is to *whitewash* the sins of the past. Such whitewashing can come in a variety of forms, but a particularly popular version of this problem comes by means of the faulty presumption that nearly all of America's founding

---

[411] Ibid.

fathers were Christians. I often refer to this as the *Christianizing of American history* and it is this very procedure which retools the historical record in order to make America's founding appear to be far more scripturally based than reality reveals. Such a viewpoint of America's beginnings is remarkably popular among *Christian Reconstructionists* who see the Mosaic Law as the principal pathway towards reform in America.

However, a more honest dissection of America's history reveals that this nation's founders and founding documents reflect a blending of both religious and secular influences. While the colonies possessed many Christians in her ranks, and a great number of Judeo-Christian principles were implemented in her founding, there were also a great number of individuals who possessed no more than a superficial attachment to the tenets of Christian thinking.

A classic example of this is the case of Thomas Jefferson. Multiple books have been written since America's founding arguing vociferously in defense of the idea that Jefferson was a Christian who submitted to scriptural authority. While such a position may satisfy the hopes and expectations of many, it resultantly places a significant stain on the reputation of Christ and the church. By placing a Christian label on those who lacked fidelity to biblical authority, great confusion results *every time*.

Christian Reconstructionist authors like David Barton have labored strenuously to defend founders like Jefferson in this manner, but have fallen short of such an objective. Though Jefferson did refer to himself as a Christian in his private letters, what he meant by that label represented a very minimalistic notion of deistic morality. This is perhaps best illustrated in what is commonly called, *The Jefferson Bible*, a highly redacted version of the Gospels in which references to Christ's miracles, deity, and resurrection were removed. He boastfully described his sense of license and authority to edit God's Word in this manner within the introduction of his work:

There will be found remaining the most sublime and benevolent code of morals which has ever been offered to man. I have performed this operation for my own use, by cutting verse by verse out of the printed book, and arranging the matter which is evidently his and which is as easily distinguished as diamonds in a dung-hill.[412]

Thus, Jefferson titled his work *The Life and Morals of Jesus of Nazareth*. In a sense, this title even summarizes his view of Christianity as that which is a *moralistic* religion and nothing more. In a letter written to John Adams, May 5 1817, Jefferson well summarized his religious beliefs:

...if the moral precepts, innate in man, and made a part of his physical constitution, as necessary for a social being, if the sublime doctrines of philanthropism and deism taught us by Jesus of Nazareth, in which we all agree, constitute true religion, then, without it, this would be, as you again say, "something not fit to be named even, indeed, a hell."[413]

When we consider the collective writings of Jefferson, it seems quite clear that he was content to reduce Christ to a moralistic philanthropist and mere mortal whose corpse remains in the grave to this very day, *thus inferring* that He was a blasphemer who declared equality with God, feigned various miracles, and falsely claimed the power and authority to forgive sin. For Jefferson, this *faux*-Jesus, replete with a beneficent philanthropy and deistic morality, constituted "true religion." Without this, life would be "a hell." In reality, Jefferson's version of Jesus produced a vacuous, deistic ideology which secures *actual hell* for those who would believe it.

---

[412] Thomas Jefferson, *The Jefferson Bible*, (Neeland Media LLC), 282, Kindle.

[413] Thomas Jefferson, *Complete Works of Thomas Jefferson (Illustrated)* (Delphi Series Ten Book 4), 6348-6349, Kindle.

In many ways, Jefferson's belief system makes his indifference towards the slave trade compromise rather predictable. Jefferson was not ruled by the authority of God's word. His conscience was not governed by the biblical truth that all are members of the single human race. He instead believed the prevailing fantasy of *polygenesis,* or multiple races of men, some of whom were *inherently inferior* to others:

> ...for a century and a half we have had under our eyes the races of black and of red men, they have never yet been viewed by us as subjects of natural history. I advance it, therefore, as a suspicion only, that the blacks, whether originally a distinct race, or made distinct by time and circumstances, are inferior to the whites in the endowments both of body and mind. It is not against experience to suppose that different species of the same genus, or varieties of the same species, may possess different qualifications. Will not a lover of natural history then, one who views the gradations in all the races of animals with the eye of philosophy, excuse an effort to keep those in the department of man as distinct as nature has formed them? This unfortunate difference of color, and perhaps of faculty, is a powerful obstacle to the emancipation of these people. Many of their advocates, while they wish to vindicate the liberty of human nature, are anxious also to preserve its dignity and beauty. Some of these, embarrassed by the question, "What further is to be done with them?" join themselves in opposition with those who are actuated by sordid avarice only. Among the Romans emancipation required but one effort. The slave, when made free, might mix with, without staining the blood of his master. But with us a second is necessary, unknown to history. When freed, he is to be removed beyond the reach of mixture.[414]

Jefferson's corrupted thoughts strongly reflected, not Scripture, but the depraved machinations of those who would later seek racial hygiene in the name of social Darwinism and scientific racism. Jefferson never gave evidence that he believed the Gospel. Even his moralistic version of Christianity was something that he preferred to keep from public view: "I

---

[414] Ibid., 188-189.

not only write nothing on religion, but rarely permit myself to speak on it."[415]

Such a superficial affinity to the authority of the Scriptures would become far more evident in June 1776 when the Continental Congress established a Committee of Five to draft a Declaration of Independence for the American colonies. That committee consisted of John Adams of Massachusetts, Benjamin Franklin of Pennsylvania, Roger Sherman of Connecticut, Robert Livingston of New York, and Thomas Jefferson of Virginia who wrote the draft under the advisement of the other committee members. When Jefferson wrote his "Rough draught" of America's Declaration of Independence, he included 24 refutations against "the present King of Great Britain" (King George III). His final refutation specifically rebuked the African slave trade, *as was mentioned in the previous chapter*:

he has waged cruel war against human nature itself, violating its most sacred rights of life & liberty in the persons of a distant people who never offended him, captivating & carrying them into slavery in another hemisphere, or to incur miserable death in their transportation thither. This piratical warfare, the opprobrium of <u>infidel</u> powers, is the warfare of the <u>Christian</u> king of Great Britain. <u>Determined</u> to keep open a market where MEN should be bought & sold, he has prostituted his negative for suppressing every legislative attempt to prohibit or to restrain this execrable commerce: and that this assemblage of horrors might want no fact of distinguished die, he is now exciting those very people to rise in arms among us, and to purchase that liberty of which <u>he</u> has deprived them, & murdering the people upon whom he also obtruded them; thus paying off former crimes committed against the <u>liberties</u> of one people, with crimes which he urges them to commit against the <u>lives</u> of another.

This anti-slave trade clause, which was omitted in the final document, seems rather alien to Jefferson's own beliefs and practices. The reader

---

[415] Jefferson, *The Jefferson Bible,* 289, Kindle.

should note the underlined words *infidel* and *Christian* in the above reference to King George III. This is a clear rebuke of the king's contradictory profession of Christian faith. Though King George III was an avowed Anglican, he was an unapologetic advocate of the slave trade. As well, Jefferson delivered his rebuke against the king based on the slave trade's violation against "human nature," calling it "piratical warfare" and thereby exposing the criminality of the trade in which "MEN should be bought & sold" as mere chattel.

Though his rebukes of King George III were *logically* sound, Jefferson lacked the *moral resolve* to uphold them. In his autobiography, Jefferson explained why this important clause was finally removed:

"The clause...reprobating the enslaving the inhabitants of Africa, was struck out in complaisance to South Carolina and Georgia, who had never attempted to restrain the importation of slaves, and who on the contrary still wished to continue it. Our Northern brethren also I believe felt a little tender under these censures; for tho' their people have very few slaves themselves, yet they had been pretty considerable carriers of them to others."[416]

Jefferson's description of this compromise reminds us that, while there were those who earnestly sought to end the slave trade at the time, there were others who sought its preservation. But it is especially impossible to ignore the contrast between Jefferson's *passionate* opposition to slavery in the draft and his *dispassionate* description of its omission. What constituted a pivotal moment in America's beginning appears to be treated as nothing more than another item of business for Jefferson. Two key factors account for this.

---

[416] Jefferson, *The Works of Thomas Jefferson, Autobiography of Thomas Jefferson* (Optimized for Kindle), 18.

First, Jefferson was in a state of contradiction himself, having as many as 600 slaves throughout his life.[417] Though he often sought the amelioration of the harsh conditions of slavery, he clearly was not an abolitionist.

Second, whatever can be said about the original authorship of the anti-slave trade passage in the draft, Jefferson did not possess the spiritual and intellectual conviction to defend its stipulations. This is due in part to his moral compromise, as already specified. But his willingness to compromise on such a key issue also points us to the bankruptcy of his deistic philosophical beliefs which fell short of the scriptural truth regarding the singularity of the human race: *a crucial truth that was absent in his redacted version of the Bible.*

The resulting compromise, which GS and others warned against, yielded a profound contradiction between the Declaration's words and the nation's actions. This did not go unnoticed by many abolitionists, like Thomas Day who wrote in 1776: "If there be an object truly ridiculous in nature, it is an American patriot, signing resolutions of independency with the one hand, and with the other brandishing a whip over his affrighted slaves."[418]

In the end, the only thing that is produced by forcing the label *Christian* upon Thomas Jefferson is profound confusion about the Gospel; and such a whitewashing procedure as this resultantly blasphemes the reputation of Christ and His true church.

In addition to this error of whitewashing America's past errors is this other problem of *repeating those past errors in the present.* We have already examined the manner in which many in the 19th century tried to justify the enslavement of Africans by means of the Mosaic Law.

---

[417] Thomas Jefferson/Monticello, Slavery FAQs - Property https://www.monticello.org/slavery/slavery-faqs/property/

[418] David Armitage, *The Declaration of Independence: A Global History* (London: Harvard University Press, 2007), 611-612, Kindle.

Remarkably, many Christian Reconstructionists today promote an epistemology that would likely repeat this error once again:

"The Reconstructionists believe that the Law of God, or Biblical Law, as codified in the OT should be instituted as the law of the United States and every nation on earth before the return of Christ. This is a striking position: If Reconstructionists succeed, and are consistent with their theory, blasphemy would be a criminal offense, homosexuality a capital crime, and slavery (in some form) reinstituted."[419]

In their book, *Dominion Theology: Blessing or Curse? An Analysis of Christian Reconstructionism,* Wayne House & Thomas Ice warn their readers regarding such a Reconstructionist advancement of the Mosaic Law over the Gospel, and they are right to do so.

While many might label such a movement as conservative or "right wing," the reader should note that *there is also a "left wing" manifestation of the same error.* Ironically, many SJI authors also dabble in various forms of Dabneyan eisegesis by overemphasizing the Mosaic Law. For example, when arguing for civic and ecclesiastical reparations for blacks in America, Jemar Tisby offered this injunction on the basis of Numbers 5:7:

"Under Old Testament law if a person wrongs another person, the wrongdoer should confess the sin. But saying 'I'm sorry' is not enough. Expressing remorse may begin the process of healing, but somehow that which was damaged must be restored. The law goes on to state that the wrongdoer 'must make full restitution for the wrong they have done, add a fifth of the value to it and give it all to the person they have wronged' (Num. 5:7)."[420]

---

[419] H. Wayne House and Thomas Ice, *Dominion Theology: Blessing or Curse? – An Analysis of Christian Reconstructionism* (Portland OR: Multnomah Press, 1984), 27.

[420] Tisby, *The Color of Compromise,* 198.

Tisbey's error is twofold: not only does he herald the Mosaic Law to a fault,[421] but he engages in a very basic contradiction of logic. Taken at face value, Numbers 5:7 calls for the one who has sinned *to confess his sin* and make restitution *"for his wrong."* As such, it is impossible to interpret this passage as teaching anything other than *personal culpability and responsibility for sin.* However, Tisby falls in line with other SJI authors who heap the guilt of America's past on "white people" in the present. Such thinking formulates the basis of his application of Numbers 5:7 and this yields some disturbing implications.

If Tisby can allow himself license to implicate an entire segment of humanity for the sins of others committed in the past, then what would prevent him from extending his demand for money to other penal and compensatory standards from the Old Testament? In particular, if modern day "whites" have a share in the guilt of historic slavery, then what would prevent Tisby and others from demanding the penal prescription of Exodus 21:16? If he wishes to herald the Mosaic Law in this manner, by what logical standard is he allowed to press for the application of one passage while ignoring others?

Those who tamper with Scripture in this manner often fail to realize that they are playing a dangerous game of Russian roulette; only in this case the gun is pointed at the heads of others.

---

[421] Numbers chapter 5 deals mostly with the issue of dealing with the defilement of sin "within the camp" of the nation of Israel and is steeped with particulars that are not repeated in the New Testament such as "adding one-fifth (Num. 5:7) or giving what is owed to the priest, in addition to the "ram of atonement" if the next of kin cannot be found (Num. 5:8-10). While the principle of repayment of debt is universally scriptural, it is ultimately summed up for the NT Christian in the commandment of love: Romans 13:7–8: 7 Render to all what is due them: tax to whom tax is due; custom to whom custom; fear to whom fear; honor to whom honor. 8 Owe nothing to anyone except to love one another; for he who loves his neighbor has fulfilled the law.

Of course, the "systemic white supremacy" blame game is no game at all. It is one of the key ideological building blocks of SJI that has become foundational for many professing churches. The explosion of this influence in the modern day is quite stunning, but if we were to seek a key inception point for this current trend, we would have to consider the 2012 conference titled, *Race and the Christian*, featuring John Piper, Tim Keller, and Anthony Bradley. Bradley, who is a professor of religion, theology, and ethics at King's College in New York City and author of *Liberating Black Theology (2010)* concluded his presentation by exhorting "white evangelicals" to engage with Neo-Marxists James Cone and Cornel West.[422]

Perhaps the most striking presentation given at this event came from Tim Keller whose message was entitled, *Racism and Corporate Evil: A White Guy's Perspective.* Keller spoke with the typical self-deprecating language that has become all too familiar among "white" SJI advocates. His overall argument was fraught with the familiar pontifications of *white guilt* and *systemic white supremacy via* his description of *racism and corporate evil.*

Keller sought to defend his position with various proof texts, suggesting that his critics were plagued with ignorance due to their cultural upbringing: "…if you're a New Yorker and you have some kind of objection to some part of the Bible you find offensive, I want you to realize it's your cultural location that's causing the offense."[423] His overall

---

[422] "He (Bradley) ended by exhorting white evangelical leaders to engage with black theologians like James Cone and Cornel West and listen to black evangelicals laboring in evangelical institutions." John Starke, "The Gospel Explains and Undermines Racism," (The Gospel Coalition, March 19 2012): https://www.thegospelcoalition.org/article/the-gospel-explains-and-undermines-racism/.

[423] Desiring God, "Race and the Christian – An Evening with John Piper, Tim Keller, and Anthony Bradley," (New York City), March 28 2012: https://www.desiringgod.org/messages/race-and-the-christian.

argument was founded upon three briefly reviewed texts: Joshua 7 (Achan's sin), Daniel 9 (Daniel's prayer), and Romans 5 (Adam's federal headship). Since Keller's presentation of these passages has been replicated by others within the SJI community, we will review them in this section.

First, Keller employed Joshua 7 in his presentation which describes the discovery of Achan's sin of stealing some of the banned treasure from Jericho and burying it in his family's tent. When Achan's crime was uncovered, he was executed along with his children and all he possessed. Keller presented this as his initial evidence for corporate guilt. However, the brevity and simplicity of this section of Scripture leaves us with as many questions as there might be answers. Because of this, we should be reminded of the simple hermeneutical principle which warns against attempting to derive too much detail from historically descriptive narratives, especially those that are vague and lacking detail. In the case of the narrative of Joshua 7, most commentators agree that Achan's children[424] were likely executed because of their partnership[425] with their

---

[424] "Thus, in the case before us, the things themselves had been abstracted from the booty by Achan alone; but he had hidden them in his tent, buried them in the earth, which could hardly have been done so secretly that his sons and daughters knew nothing of it. By so doing he had made his family participators in his theft; they therefore fell under the ban along with him, together with their tent, their cattle, and the rest of their property, which were all involved in the consequences of his crime." Carl Friedrich Keil and Franz Delitzsch, *Commentary on the Old Testament*, vol. 2 (Peabody, MA: Hendrickson, 1996), 61.

[425] "Perhaps his sons and daughters were aiders and abettors in the villany, had helped to carry off the accursed thing. It is very probable that they assisted in the concealment, and that he could not hide them in the midst of his tent but they must know and keep his counsel, and so they became accessories ex post facto— after the fact; and, if they were ever so little partakers in the crime, it was so heinous that they were justly sharers in the punishment. However God was hereby glorified, and the judgment executed was thus made the more

father's sin, but because very little detail is supplied about Achan's family, this is nothing more than an inferential argument. In his presentation, Keller also affirmed this concept but then employed Joshua 7 in order to advance a form of *societal determinism*, one that eerily reflects Marx's aforementioned notion of *materialistic determinism*:[426] "Most people in most places do understand [unlike "white westerners"]: you are not the product of your individual choices, *you are the product of your community* [italics mine]."[427] Within this formulation of his, Keller substitutes the biblical concept of *personal responsibility* with his notion of *societal determinism*, as if this were the point of Joshua 7. If Achan's children acted as cohorts in his crime (as Keller seemed to concede), then this event affirms nothing other than the principle of personal responsibility (Ezekiel 18:20, Deuteronomy 24:16). Beyond this, we must guard against exceeding what is supplied within this historical narrative. As we reviewed in the first chapter, SJI's Neo-Marxist concept of *determinism* utterly destroys the biblical teaching of personal responsibility and thereby undermines the individual's culpability for sin; all of which results in a corruption of the Gospel call itself.

Second, Keller utilized the example of Daniel's prayer of repentance, for himself and the nation of Israel, as another example of corporate evil. This was his most benign example of the three. The

---

tremendous." Matthew Henry, *Matthew Henry's commentary on the whole Bible*: Complete and unabridged in one volume, (Peabody: Hendrickson, 1996), Jos 7:16–26.

[426] "It is not the consciousness of men that determines their existence, but, on the contrary, their social existence determines their consciousness." Karl Marx, *A Contribution to The Critique Of The Political Economy*, Kindle.

[427] "if you can do something bad, the fact that you can do it; what helped you become the kind of person that could do it was to a great degree your family. Your family produced you directly or at least failed to keep you from becoming that [a wrongdoer] and therefore either actively or passively, your family participates in your guilt." Keller, Race and the Christian.

concept of confessional prayer for one's sin and the sins of a nation simply affirms the reality of the universality of sin. Daniel's prayer for his sin, and the sin of his people, does highlight the beauty and importance of humility in view of humanity's universal guilt. Daniel was a prophet of God[428] whose piety was so distinguishable that God identified him, along with Noah and Job, as being uniquely righteous.[429] Yet Daniel's unique godliness did not exempt him from the fact that *all have sinned and fall short of the glory of God* (Romans 3:23). As a pastor I often pray corporately, in the first common plural, regarding *our sins* as a nation. Since no one honors God as He deserves, all of us can pray, confessionally, that we all fall short of God's righteousness. Such a focus of prayer is not designed to target certain groups or individuals, but is an acknowledgment of the ubiquitous nature of sin. Thus, Daniel's general expression of contrition did not lead him to go after particular individuals or Jewish sects to the exclusion of others. A proper understanding and application of Daniel's prayer would prevent anyone from using it as a retributive weapon against "white people." Had Keller employed this example from Daniel fairly, he would have appealed to his audience *to join him in repentance* and confess the manner in which all have fallen short of honoring God as the creator of the single human race. Such an exhortation would be inclusive of "white supremacy" as well as those who repeatedly express their vitriol against "white people" in the name of Social Justice. Though such an exhortation would have been more in keeping with the principle of prayer found in Daniel 9, it could never fit within Keller's white-guilt motif.

Third, Keller concluded his survey of Scripture by using Romans 5 whereby he employed *classic Federal Theology* as further evidence for his claims. Of the three passages he consulted, this was the most stunning example of his overall argumentative scheme: "...just by virtue of being in

---

[428] Matthew 24:15.
[429] Ezekiel 14:14.

the entire human race you are responsible for things that you didn't individually do." At no time did Keller explain to his audience that the doctrine of Federal Theology within Romans 5 points to *two unrepeatable events in history: 1. Adam's original sin and 2. Christ's one act of righteousness.* Keller's illogical application of this text is rather breathtaking. If the unique and unrepeatable[430] doctrine of Federal Theology were to be universalized *and repeated* in the development of his view of corporate guilt, then every individual would be guilty *of their own sins* as well as the sins *of everyone else* on planet earth. In such "logic" as this, a 19th century enslaved African would share in the guilt of every member of the KKK throughout history, among countless others. Keller's utilization of Romans 5 was the shortest portion of his defense of the concept of corporate evil and systemic racism, and it was the most bankrupt of them all. Despite all this, his audience offered not an ounce of pushback to his fantastic claims. Overall, Keller's contributions in this conference offered a dangerous sense of affirmation to the false doctrines perpetuated by SJI.

What Keller proffered within his broader message of white guilt is strikingly similar to the fraudulent teachings of *generational guilt,* a form of thinking that is often found among Prosperity Gospel teachers. Those who advance such teaching argue that children inherit the guilt of their parents. As a proof text, Exodus 20:5 is typically consulted wherein God promises to deal justly with the wicked and their descendants: "I, the Lord your God, am a jealous God, visiting the iniquity of the fathers on the children, on the third and the fourth generations of those who hate Me." Those who promote the idea of generational guilt typically utilize this text in order to advance a form of *determinism* which assumes that the sin and guilt of a parent is *automatically passed on to future generations.*

---

[430] Adam's Federal Headship is a unique doctrine in view of the *singular event of original sin*: "Therefore, just as through one man sin entered into the world, and death through sin, and so death spread to all men, because all sinned." Romans 5:12.

However, the profound misinterpretation and misapplication of this text is easily detected when we notice the concluding clause in the passage: *"...of those who hate Me."* Rather than teaching a form of passive determinism and generational guilt, this passage instead emphasizes the scriptural principle of personal responsibility. In fact this same principle is underscored further in the very next verse: "...but showing lovingkindness to thousands, to those who love Me and keep My commandments." (Exodus 20:6).

Once again, such texts reveal the most primitive categorization of the human race in all of Scripture: *those who love the Lord versus those who hate him; those who take refuge in the Son versus those who rage against the Lord and His Anointed.*[431]

Remarkably, Keller made no effort to reconcile what he said with those texts that *clearly* decimate the fallacious teachings of generational guilt:

Ezekiel 18:20 "The son will not bear the punishment for the father's iniquity, nor will the father bear the punishment for the son's iniquity; the righteousness of the righteous will be upon himself, and the wickedness of the wicked will be upon himself."

Deuteronomy 24:16: "Fathers shall not be put to death for their sons, nor shall sons be put to death for their fathers; everyone shall be put to death for his own sin."

---

[431] Much more could be said about the difference between God's general, cohortative call of repentance (Ezekiel 18:32; Acts 18:30) versus His secret decrees related to salvation and condemnation (Deuteronomy 29:29); however, such a massive topic would exceed the scope of concern expressed in this section. At the most fundamental level, the priority of the Gospel call is to herald Christ to *all without distinction.*

In the final day of judgment, Christ will issue His just recompense "to every man *according to what he has done.*" (Revelation 22:12). Clearly, there is not an ounce of generational guilt or societal determinism to be found within this sobering promise. The harmonious promise of Scripture, in both Old and New Testaments, is that God will "recompense a man according to his work." (Psalm 62:12; 28:4, Matthew 16:27, Romans 2:6, 1 Corinthians 3:8, Revelation 2:23).

In the end, Keller's effort to dump the guilt of America's past upon the shoulders of "white westerners" in the present is nothing but a shameless exercise. That he willingly twisted the Scriptures in order to promote this SJI motif is purely despicable. By proffering this corruption of the Gospel, Keller stained the reputation of Christ and the church. Rather than using his highly public platform to promote biblical wisdom, Keller's brief presentation in 2012 further propelled the SJI community in this dangerous matter of imputing the sins of the past upon many in the present.

A more recent example of this dangerous tactic occurred on April 20th 2021 when Derek Chauvin was found guilty for the murder of George Floyd. Ibram Kendi quickly weighed in on this judicial pronouncement by video. Though he agreed with the conviction of officer Cauvin, he was quick to issue words of condemnation for the *entire nation*:

> "So now what? Chauvin is headed to jail, but is America headed to justice? Is justice convicting a police officer, or is justice convicting America?"

It should be apparent to the reader that Kendi's concluding query is not an actual question, but is only a rhetorical devise used to stage his unambiguous charge of guilt at the conclusion of his statement: "Justice has convicted America." Of course, SJI's language, terminology, and ideology are all consistent with Kendi's comments. And yet we are left to wonder how it is that an entire country be found guilty for the actions of a single police officer.

Whatever one thinks of Derek Chauvin, George Floyd, or anything else relating to this case, the thought of imputing the guilt of one individual onto an entire nation is, in fact, a gargantuan *and dangerous* leap of logic. And yet, *this is* an example of the "logic" of SJI. When Kendi indicts all of America for the killing of George Floyd, he well represents the movement's common tactics. Such a willingness to blame others in this fashion reflects a very dangerous and twisted god-complex, devoid of any measure of true justice. With all of this we must consider the core lessons of these past and present corruptions of the Gospel.

First, it should be clear that the reputation of Christ and His people can easily be degraded in the public square by the professing allies and enemies of the church. Those authors who seek to Christianize America's founding, despite the realities of actual history, resultantly create many dark associations that can be as problematic as Tisby's conflation of Christianity with the KKK. In either case, those who treat history as a tool for their own agenda should resign from the solemn duty of reporting the facts of yesteryear. *Actual history*, as we have already noted, is an important and needful tutor for present and future generations and therefore those who trifle with such tutelage are corrupting history's crucial pedagogy.

The unpolished facts of history can be quite hard hitting and difficult to grasp, but they are what we need the most. Such *real history* teaches us that whenever and wherever the light of the Gospel burns brightest, its brilliance will be most evident amidst this world's darkness. But whenever and wherever that light is dimmed, darkness will predictably loom over the land. The 19th century Anglican bishop, J.C. Ryle, said it ever so well:

> Whenever a church avoids Christ crucified or puts anything whatever in that foremost place that Christ crucified should always have, from that moment a church ceases to be useful. Without Christ crucified in her pulpits, a church is little better than a hindrance, a dead carcass, a well without water, a barren fig

tree, a sleeping watchman, a silent trumpet, a dumb witness, an ambassador without terms of peace, a messenger without tidings, a lighthouse without fire, a stumbling block to weak believers, a comfort to infidels, a hotbed for formalism, a joy to the devil, and an offense to God.[432]

Our review of past and present corruptions of the Gospel has disclosed a wide variety of ways in which the *visible church* can be a *joy to the devil and an offense to God.* From R.L. Dabney to Southern Baptist President, Patrick H. Mell, it is quite evident that the pro-slavery South generated incalculable confusion before a watching world. Their efforts to justify racial bigotry, by Scripture, obfuscated and undermined the Gospel. But when we examine the teachings of modern day SJI advocates, we find a remarkably similar problem. They too are proffering a message of *racial bigotry* through a twisting of the Scriptures.

In fact, when we evaluate the core message of Dabney, Mell, Tisby, Kendi, and Keller, all of them have asserted *a license to judge an entire segment of humanity as being uniquely defective; worthy of derogation and subjugation.* For the advocates of SJI, "white people" are worthy of such derogation, condemnation, and, at a minimum, *subjugation* to SJI ideology. What their maximal demands for subjugation will be are not yet fully known, but one thing is for certain: many who claim the label, *Evangelical Christian*, have eagerly received this Neo-Marxist movement into the ranks of the professing church and have erected their own Decalogue, promising *to visit the iniquity of the fathers on the children...of all those who hate the god Social Justice Ideology.* Rather than serving as an aid and support to the Gospel, this ideology is a blasphemous affront to Christ Himself.

In view of all this, there is a bitter irony in place when we consider the SBC's transition from President Mell to the present day. In Mell's time, the SBC promoted racial bigotry against Africans. Today, by the

---

[432] J. C. Ryle, *The Cross: Crucified with Christ, and Christ Alive in Me* (Aneko Press), 24, Kindle.

influences of SJI, many in the SBC promote racial bigotry against "whites." In either generation, nothing has really changed. All is done in the name of justice and everything is rooted in an abuse of Scripture. Should the SBC continue down this SJI-friendly pathway they will have merely replaced one filthy garment for another.

Second, our considerations of these past and present corruptions of the Gospel raise further questions about the spiritual origins of such problems. Having advanced many criticisms against individuals who have professed faith in Christ, the reader may be inclined to think that I am adjudicating their salvation (or lack thereof), but this is not my agenda. My only focus in our study has been to evaluate the fruit of those who have assumed the task of teaching the Scriptures to others.

It is one thing to evaluate the life and doctrine of others, ascertaining the fruit of their lives thereby, but it is quite another thing to assume God's sole prerogative of exercising judgment over others. Ultimately, Jesus enjoins Christians to do the former (Matthew 7:15-18) but prohibits them from doing the latter (Matthew 7:19-23, 13:28-30; Romans 12:19). This priority supplies a very challenging tension for the church. The reality is that there are cases in which the Gospel has been obscured and even blasphemed by those who *appeared to be* members of the true church, but were not. As the Apostle Paul taught in 1 Timothy 6:24, "the sins of some men are evident"; but for others their sins "follow after" them, being made evident in time. Scripture supplies examples of this as in the case of Korah, Judas, Hymenaeus, Alexander, Diotrephes, and Demas. In other cases, believers can be led astray and enter into temporary disobedience against the Word before relenting and returning to the priority of the Gospel (Galatians 2:11-21).

Thus, the complexity of knowing the difference between a believer who has momentarily entered into sin versus an apostate who has nothing more than the appearance of religion can be like discerning the difference between wheat and tares. This is why Christ's parable of the wheat and tares in Matthew 13:1-23 is so important. After the enemy planted the tares amidst the wheat, the servants asked the landowner if he wanted them to gather up the tares. The landowner answered by saying:

> Matthew 13:29–30: 29 "... 'No; lest while you are gathering up the tares, you may root up the wheat with them. 30 'Allow both to grow together until the harvest; and in the time of the harvest I will say to the reapers, "First gather up the tares and bind them in bundles to burn them up; but gather the wheat into my barn."'"

This parable reminds us that when the King of Righteousness returns to judge the living and the dead, He will gather the wheat of His true church, while binding and burning the tares of His enemies. It is this *eschatological judgment* that is Christ's prerogative alone because "the Lord knows those who are His" (2 Timothy 2:19) with a perfect, Omniscient knowledge. Mere mortals do not and cannot possess this *ultimate and immutable* knowledge.

Yet, as previously noted, believers are called to evaluate the life and doctrine of those who claim the banner of Christian faith *in order to determine whether or not we should affirm their professions of faith*. When Spurgeon promised that he would not fellowship with the enslavers of men, he was applying this very principle.

For you, dear reader, your task is to consider whether or not you affirm those who *falsely claim a license to judge an entire segment of humanity as being uniquely defective; worthy of derogation and subjugation*. If you choose to affirm such individuals and teaching, then you are nothing more than a co-belligerent of *racial bigotry* and a practitioner of *injustice*. However, if you choose to reject this for the apostasy that it is, you will have taken a stand for God's true justice. Most importantly, if you embrace the beautiful, life-giving message of the Gospel, then you have made a truly wise and eternally life-saving choice.

JESUS' JUSTICE

Isaiah 46:9–10:

9 "Remember the former things long past, For I am God, and there is no other; I am God, and there is no one like Me,
10 Declaring the end from the beginning And from ancient times things which have not been done, Saying, 'My purpose will be established, And I will accomplish all My good pleasure'

CHAPTER 9

GOD'S SOVEREIGNTY
OVER THIS WORLD OF SYSTEMIC EVIL

With all the criticisms that have been issued thus far regarding SJI's teaching on "systemic white supremacy," it must be admitted that there is such a thing as *systemic evil* in this world which consists of all forms of sin, not just white supremacy. In fact, this important concept of systemic evil is repeatedly mentioned throughout the Bible.

Writing to the 1st century churches in Asia Minor, the Apostle John warned Christians about the mass proliferation of false teachers and charged them to guard themselves from idols (1 John 5:21). Amidst these solemn words, he also issued a stark but important reminder regarding the world they faced when he wrote, "the whole world lies in the power of the evil one." (1 John 5:19).

Such a declaration as this is quite stunning. It reminds us just how easy it is to be lulled into a dangerous sense of false security, especially when we lose sight of the prevailing reality of evil in this world. In times of relative peace, it is too easy to imagine that this fallen world is actually a place of *peace*. Thankfully, there is a coming day in which peace will prevail and the Prince of Peace, Jesus Christ, will reign in His eternal kingdom, but until that day comes we are left with the brutal realities of human sin (1 John 1:6, 8, 10), the Devil's schemes (1 John 3:8), and his demonic dominion over the entire world (1 John 5:19).

A profound reminder of this truth raised its ugly head during the month of August, 2021, when the world watched in horror as human beings fell to their deaths from U.S. cargo planes departing from the Hamid Karzai International Airport, Kabul Afghanistan. Such images made it impossible for government officials in Washington D.C. to hide their poorly planned evacuation of American civilians and Afghan allies. Online media was saturated for weeks with video and pictures revealing the desperation of those who knew that remaining in the Taliban controlled nation of Afghanistan would result in their certain torture and likely death.

Few progressives in the West are willing to admit it, but between the well-known realities of Taliban oppression and Afghanistan's history of human trafficking,[433] many of those men, women, and children who remain in country will be subject to several forms of brutality, to include chattel slavery and human trafficking. Such unspeakable oppression should awaken us to a better understanding as to why it is that people

---

[433] "In its annual trafficking report, the State Department put Afghanistan, along with China and Russia, in a small group of countries assessed as failing to make significant efforts to combat the trade in people. Afghanistan was among the countries singled out for a 'government' policy or pattern' of human trafficking, including in Afghanistan's case the employment of child soldiers by security forces and a widespread practice called bacha bazi, which amounts sexual slavery of boys on government compounds, a senior State Department official told reporters, speaking on the condition of anonymity under ground rules set by the department." Missy Ryan, "On eve of military exit, U.S. names Afghanistan among world's worst on human trafficking," (The Washington Post, July 1, 2021): https://www.washingtonpost.com/national-security/afghanistan-human-trafficking/2021/07/01/1e418804-da7e-11eb-ae62-2d07d7df83bd_story.html.

would cling to the wheel wells of outbound cargo planes. Realities such as these seem entirely alien to the freeborn citizens of the U.S. who continue to enjoy incomparable liberty; and yet such atrocities must remind us that desperate souls will often do anything to avoid brutality and torture, like those who jumped to their certain death off the slave-trade vessel, the Zong.[434]

As disturbing as the circumstances in Afghanistan are, they do supply the world with a powerful dose of reality regarding the ongoing horrors of *chattel slavery* in a world that *still lies in the power of the evil one*. Such abuses of human life continue, not only in Afghanistan but also in several African nations, the Middle East, and especially in China which possesses as many as 1.5 million slaves in Xinjiang's reeducation camps. Wherever such abuse of human life persists, we can be sure that this is the result of sin and rebellion against Almighty God. Of course, there are a great number of sins other than chattel slavery, but no matter what form of evil one considers, they all consist of *human acts of rebellion (1 John 1:6, 8, 10)* that act in concert with *the Devil's schemes (1 John 3:8)* and constitute a *systemic evil* amidst *the demonic realm of this world (1 John 5:19)*. It is this reality of *systemic evil* that reveals the important connection between human sin and the Devil.

Such a truth as this is often abused or ignored altogether. This is unfortunate since the Bible frequently mentions this truth in order to help us understand just how universally offensive all sin is in the sight of Almighty God. For the Apostle John, he earnestly desired that his readers would comprehend the severity and gravity of any transgression against

---

[434] Much of the cruelty that took place on the Zong came through the prolonged and torturous nature of the mass murder. Not all 132 slaves were drowned at once, but were thrown overboard in "batches" within view and earshot of the other slaves, as Walvin describes: "A third batch of thirty-eight Africans were killed some time later: ten Africans, realising what was about to happen, jumped overboard to their deaths." Walvin, *The Zong*, 98.

God. To do this he reminded his readers that sin is an act of co-belligerence with the Devil himself: "the one who practices sin is of the devil; for the devil has sinned from the beginning." (1 John 3:8a). John then concluded this passage by affirming the *Lord's sovereignty* over all *systemic evil* along with the Devil himself: "The Son of God appeared for this purpose, that He might destroy the works of the devil." (1 John 3:8b).

These important truths must be addressed, especially in view of how SJI advocates confuse, obfuscate, and even ignore them. All SJI authors speak of the reality of evil, but their identification of the nature and source of evil is grossly skewed. Because of their inability to identify societal corruption correctly, SJI authors resultantly proffer ineffectual and even dangerous solutions. As a result, their quest for destroying the presence of evil in this world consists of a Christless and hopeless creed; one that is entirely incompatible with Christianity. For this reason, we will first consider how SJI teaching undermines *the reality of systemic evil,* and, second, we will observe how this ideology obfuscates *the reality of God's sovereign providence.*

1. The Reality of Systemic Evil: The now familiar narrative of SJI literature is that the central source of evil within this world is that of *white supremacy.* If the SJI community were to write their own rendition of the Bible, their version of 1 John 5:19 might read, "the whole world lies in the power *of systemic white supremacy.*" Though *white supremacy* is evil, I can assure the reader that the Devil's list of vices is much greater than this one alone. Not only does SJI's limited form of thinking fallaciously vilify one segment of society on the basis of skin color, as already reviewed, but it grossly obscures the biblical reality of *universal sin* and *systemic evil.* By their constant demonization of "white people," SJI advocates create, by default, a faux category of innocence for all those who are outside the realm of "whiteness." Thus, when Nickole Hannah-Jones echoed the sentiment that "…whites have always been an unjust, jealous, unmerciful, avaricious, and blood-thirsty set of beings, always seeking after power and authority"[435] we are left to wonder if all those with a darker epidermis are innocent of the same charge. Thinking such as this is a gross contradiction to God's word which asserts that *both Jews and Greeks are all under sin (Romans 3:9)*, such that *"there is none righteous, not even one; there is none who understands, there is none who seeks for God; all have turned aside, together they have become useless; there is none who does good, there is not even one; their throat is an open grave, with their tongues they keep deceiving, the poison of asps is under their lips; whose mouth is full of cursing and bitterness; their feet are swift to shed blood, destruction and misery are in their paths, and the path of peace have they not known; there is no fear of God before their eyes."* *(Romans 3:10-18).*

Hannah-Jones' fixation on "whites" is representative of many other SJI advocates, who, by virtue of this same fixation, contradict Christ who taught that "everyone who commits sin is the slave to sin." (John 8:34). Those who falsely believe that they are naturally exempted from such slavery, imagining that they are *without sin,* are those who "lie" (1 John 1:6), "deceive" themselves (1 John 1:8), and "make Him (God) a liar" (1 John 1:10).

The Bible repeatedly reminds us that there are only two masters to serve in this fallen world: The Lord Jesus Christ or the Devil, and every decision ever made by any member of the human race is a decision to serve one or the other, regardless of one's epidermis. Despite these crucial truths, the SJI community continues to engage in dangerous fantasies about how to improve the world through the elimination of "whiteness," and for some this should include the complete eradication of "whites" from the human race. Duquesne University professor, Derek Hook, recently echoed this sentiment by suggesting that "white people should

---

[435] David Walker in his 1829 Appeal as quoted in Nickole Hannah-Jones, Letter to the Editor (The Observer Newspaper, Notre Dame), 1995.

commit suicide as an ethical act."[436] Dangerous rhetoric such as this is becoming more and more commonplace, reflecting much of the same neuroses that are now common among such ideologues. Imagining that the world can be improved by removing all pale-skinned members of the human race makes as much sense as insisting that a gallon of polluted water can be wholly purified by extracting just one quart from its contents. Though this procedure *would* remove some of the pollution, it would still leave three quarts of equally polluted water behind. By this analogy, the removal of any portion of the human race could never eradicate the *systemic evil* of human sin, along with the spiritual realm of evil that is overruled by the Devil and his demonic cohort.

The Apostle Paul expanded upon this crucial idea in greater depth when he wrote to the church at Ephesus, reminding them of the spiritual context of their salvation. Like any other Christian, they were not saved because they were morally or spiritually in better standing than anyone else. They were instead saved by God's merciful love and redeeming grace *alone*. In order to magnify this great truth, he reminded his readers of the nature of their violent enmity against God at the time they were redeemed:

Ephesians 2:1–5: 1 AND you were dead in your trespasses and sins, 2 in which you formerly walked according to the course of this world, according to the prince of the power of the air, of the spirit that is now working in the sons of disobedience. 3 Among them we too all formerly lived in the lusts of our flesh, indulging the desires of the flesh and of the mind, and were by nature children of wrath, even as the rest. 4 But God, being rich in mercy, because of His great love with which He loved us, 5 even when we were dead in our transgressions, made us alive together with Christ (by grace you have been saved)...

---

[436] Duquesne University Professor, Derek Hook, quoting Terblanche Delport, a South African philosophy professor at the University of Pretoria. https://www.thecollegefix.com/video-white-people-should-commit-suicide-as-an-ethical-act-duquesne-professor-says/.

Rather than beginning with the discussion of God's redeeming love, Paul began with the reality of his readers' *sin and rebellion*: "...and *you* were dead in your trespasses and sins"; a point that he repeats again in v. 5. Every member of the church at Ephesus, before they were redeemed and joined together as the people of God, lived their individual lives as perpetual violators of God's standards. Moreover, their spiritual death-march consisted of a *broader cooperation with the spiritual forces of evil in this world* such that they all walked "...according to [κατὰ, *kata*, "in relationship to"] the course of this world, according to the prince of the power of the air, of the spirit that is now working in the sons of disobedience." This broader viewpoint of sin, as Paul described, reveals a dangerous *co-belligerence* with the Devil (the prince of the power of the air) and all of fallen humanity (the sons of disobedience).

Simply put, what the Apostle is describing in these verses is the reality of *systemic evil.* This principle is important because it teaches that an individual's act of rebellion against God is an expression of *solidarity*[437] with the evil of this world; a *systemic evil* that is perpetually instigated by the Devil and all members of the human race who rage against the Lord and His anointed (Psalm 2). Additionally, this solidarity with evil is global in view of the broad array of the Devil's cohort of demons, which comprises of the "...the rulers...the powers...the world forces of this darkness...the spiritual forces of wickedness in the heavenly places." (Ephesians 6:12). This additional layer of truth reminded Paul's readers that they were surrounded by the Devil and his demonic cohort, not only in the city of Ephesus or even the Roman Empire, but it engulfed *the*

---

[437] This idea of *sinful solidarity* simply speaks to the shared rebellion of all members of the human race as those who rage against the Lord and His anointed Messiah (Psalm 2:1-3). However, such solidarity does not undermine personal culpability for sin seeing that God will "recompense a man according to his work." (Psalm 62:12; 28:4, Matthew 16:27, Romans 2:6, 1 Corinthians 3:8, Revelation 2:23).

entire fallen world. Such a stark lesson as this reveals the binary nature of the world in which we live as well as the binary choices that we must make on a daily basis, consisting of either *justice or injustice; righteousness or evil; the glory of God or the glory of the Devil and his fallen angels.*

This spiritual contest was well illustrated when Peter rejected Christ's disclosed will to suffer as the Messiah (Matthew 16:21-22). In that moment, Jesus turned and rebuked him for his *co-belligerence with evil,* saying "Get behind Me, Satan! You are a stumbling block to Me; for you are not setting your mind on God's interests, but man's." (Matthew 16:23). Though this rebuke likely shocked Peter in the moment, it supplied a crucial lesson for him and for everyone in every generation: *any act of rebellion against the Almighty is an act of solidarity with the Devil and the systemic evil of this world.*

Without such truths, we may be tempted to think that an act of sin is nothing more than a personal event having little or no consequence. This is how we, as mere mortals, tend to view sin. But when we view sin as God sees it, we find that it is an affront to His holiness and a promotion of evil in a world that is engulfed in evil. And this important truth applies to *every member of the human race.*

The fact that this truth is universally applicable is especially evident when Paul reminded the Ephesians that he wasn't singling out the Gentiles among them, as if these principles of sin and systemic evil were true for them to the exclusion of himself or any converted Jews in their midst. Instead, Paul was quick to qualify the fact that he, along with his ministry companions, also marched *in this same solidarity with evil* when the Lord redeemed them: "Among them we too all formerly lived in the lusts of our flesh, indulging the desires of the flesh and of the mind, and were by nature children of wrath, even as the rest." (Ephesians 2:3). Paul's chief emphasis in all this was to herald the greatness of God's rich mercy and great love, but his crucial description of sin and systemic evil was the *necessary bridge to that lesson.* Without such a bridge, our understanding of the Gospel becomes deeply obscured, especially if any one of us imagines that we are exempt from *personal sin* or *systemic evil*; or that the problem of evil can be dealt with through the elimination of either Jews or Gentiles, or any other sector of society to the exclusion of others. The person who has been blinded to God's Word is an individual who cannot see the realities of this world and their need for the Savior.

To imagine that only those with a particular epidural tone are capable of evil is a bizarre and dangerous fantasy, and, as we have already reviewed, it is a view that replicates the ignorance and bigotry of those who *judged those with dark skin as being uniquely defective; worthy of derogation and subjugation.* The fact that this form of thought is being replicated in the modern day is, by itself, a reminder of the enduring and repeating nature of sin. It is also a reminder that Satan's tactics really don't change very much in his advancement of systemic evil throughout the world.

For example, the same promotion of evil that existed in the transatlantic slave trade among Europeans also existed in Africa as well. As stated at the beginning of this chapter, chattel slavery still thrives in the modern day; however, this isn't just a recent phenomenon. In fact, slavery did not immediately vanish from the world stage after the 19th century, but continued in countries outside of Britain and America. When the transatlantic slave trade ended in Britain (1807) and America (1808), this transition was predictably resisted by many European *as well as African slave traders.* For example, upon hearing the news of England's dissolution of the slave trade, King Awusa Halliday, monarch of Grand Bonny (Nigeria), said to Captain Hugh Crow in 1807: "We think that this trade must go on. That is the verdict of our oracle and the priests. They say that your country, however great, can never stop a trade ordained by God himself."[438] Additionally (as mentioned in the seventh chapter), Afonso I (King of Kongo) sternly protested the harsh reality of Africans

---

[438] Hugh Thomas, *The Slave Trade: The Story of the Atlantic Slave Trade* (Simon & Schuster), 572, Kindle.

kidnapping their fellow countrymen for sale; a fact of history that reveals a *co-belligerency of systemic evil*. Those who imagine that the transatlantic slave trade was a monolithic, European problem *only* are promoting a dangerous mythology. Without the cooperation of enslavers within Africa, the transatlantic slave trade could never have morphed into the vexatious monster that it became:

> This large labor force [of African slaves] would not have been available to the Europeans in the Americas without the cooperation of African kings, merchants, and noblemen. Those African leaders were, as a rule, neither bullied nor threatened into making these sales (for sales they were, even if the bills were settled in textiles, guns, brandy, cowrie shells, beads, horses, and so on). When, in 1842, the sultan of Morocco told the British consul that he thought that "the traffic in slaves is a matter on which all sects and nations have agreed from the time of the sons of Adam," he could have been speaking for all African rulers; or indeed all European ones fifty years before. There were few instances of Africans' opposing the nature of the traffic desired by the Europeans.[439]

This two-sided culpability regarding the practice of chattel slavery reveals a broader, *systemic evil*, both past and present, that especially persists in places where *the Gospel is known the least*. In his book, *How Christianity Changed the World*, Alvin Schmidt reminds us just how misinformed the modern era is regarding the past and present realities of slavery as well as the importance of the Gospel:

> Many do not know that the tragedy of slavery continued in a number of countries for more than a hundred years after it was outlawed in the United States in 1865. Ethiopia had slavery until 1942, Saudi Arabia until 1962, Peru until 1964, and India until 1976. Moreover, it still exists to this day in Sudan,[440]

---

[439] Ibid., 920.

[440] The discussion of modern-day slavery and human trafficking exceeds the focus of this book, but it is important to note that slavery persists in nations that

Africa's largest country. When people do not know—and many do not—that slavery is still present today in Sudan, their ignorance is largely the fault of the mass media's reluctance to report it. Politically correct media and school textbooks give the impression that slavery has primarily been a sin committed by white people who enslaved blacks. The fact that only about 25 percent of the Americans in the South had slaves before the Civil War is commonly not mentioned, nor is the fact that (according to the United States census of 1830), for example, 407 black Americans in Charleston, South Carolina, alone owned black slaves. Nor have the mass media made any effort to report that a Christian organization in Sudan known as Christian Solidarity International currently buys slaves, most of whom are black Christians, in order to set them free. In some instances this organization pays 50,000 Sudanese pounds per slave. Nor have the mass media reported that in the past several years more than three million Sudanese Christians and animists, mostly slaves, have been executed in recent years.[441]

---

have claimed to abolish it. When Schmidt wrote his work, there was a resurgence of slavery in Sudan during the Second Sudanese Civil War (1983-2005). Even though Sudan has changed some aspects of its laws regarding slavery, Sudanese enslavement in the region persists, requiring the continued ministry efforts of Christian Solidarity International (CSI). Several other Middle Eastern and African nations continue the plague of slavery such as in Mauritania, Niger, Congo, Ethiopia among several others. According to CSI, though they have helped to rescue as many as 100,000 people from enslavement, there are roughly 35,000 who remain as slaves in Sudan alone. It should also be mentioned that CSI's current method of securing the emancipation of slaves is as follows: "CSI does not exchange cash for slaves. Instead, we make cattle vaccine available to slave-owning cattle camps. When slaves are returned to Southern Sudan, they are documented by local community leaders and CSI staff. Tribal chiefs help locate the families of the liberated slaves." https://csi-usa.org/.

[441] Alvin J. Schmidt, *How Christianity Changed the World*, (Zondervan), 273, Kindle.

Simple facts such as these are nowhere to be found within SJI literature and are typically hidden in order to propagate the monolithic message of American "systemic white supremacy." However, those who dare to investigate matters objectively will find that SJI has little to no relationship with reality. Their philosophy of intersectionality has granted them a false sense of authority to judge the world in a manner that divides systemic evil into contrived classifications, resulting in significant division and racial bigotry.

SJI's fixation on America's historic participation with the slave trade has blighted the ability of many to see the real world around them. Among the most popular SJI books available to date, I have yet to read a single contributor to such work who has issued any serious protest against slavery in the modern day, and the hypocrisy of this procedure is breathtaking. BLM founder and admitted Marxist, Patrisse Khan-Cullors, may have time to binge-buy mansions in America, but she seems to have neither the time nor the resources to address the enslaved "black lives" in Africa *who need real help*. But Khan-Cullors is not alone regarding her remarkable double-standards. Just the sight of BLM protesters decrying injustice in America, while marching in the streets with shoes, clothing, and cell phones made by slave labor, transcends imagination. If black lives really did matter to these outspoken ideologues, then why do they offer so much silence on the subject of modern day slavery? Sometimes *facts* get in the way of our preconceptions and political agendas, and the danger of this trend continues to escape the notice of many.

2. The Reality of God's Sovereign Providence: Our examination of systemic evil would be too overbearing if it were not for the truth that God sovereignly prevails over all things. Though the "whole world lies in the power of the evil one" (1 John 5:19) we also know that the "the Son of God appeared for this purpose, that He might destroy the works of the Devil" (1 John 3:8). Such a destruction of evil was foreordained by the Lord Himself. By God's predetermined plan and foreknowledge, the Lord ordained that the Messiah would be nailed to a cross by the hands of godless men and die for the sins of many (Acts 2:23-24). As well, by His divine will He has appointed a day in which the world will be judged in righteousness by the risen and returning Son of God whereby all evil will be eternally condemned, and those who take refuge in Christ will reside in His kingdom forever (Acts 17:31). Until that day comes, the Lord continues to orchestrate the events of this world by His sovereign providence for the greater good of His people and for His ultimate glory (Romans 8:28-30).

Perhaps one of the best examples of God's sovereign rule over this world of evil is found in the life of Joseph, the son of Jacob, who was sold into slavery by his jealous brothers. We read in Genesis 37 that Midianite traders purchased Joseph and then sold him to Potiphar, the captain of Pharaoh's guard. Amidst the difficulty of his circumstances, Joseph remained focused on serving and honoring the Lord. By God's remarkable providence, Joseph rose to such a place of prominence in Egypt that he became second in command to Pharaoh himself. When famine struck the land, Joseph's brothers came to Egypt to purchase grain which led to a remarkable encounter between them. Because Joseph was responsible for the sale of grain, his brothers had to go to him in order to make the purchase. But rather than refusing them in their time of need, Joseph responded with profound grace and mercy with this message regarding God's sovereignty:

> Genesis 50:20–21: 20 "And as for you, you meant evil against me, but God meant it for good in order to bring about this present result, to preserve many people alive. 21 "So therefore, do not be afraid; I will provide for you and your little ones." So he comforted them and spoke kindly to them.

Though Joseph was gracious to his brothers he did not withhold the truth from them. What they did was in fact *evil.* Not just their *actions*, but the thoughts and intentions of their hearts were committed to evil: "you *meant* (*ḥāśăḇ*)[442] evil against me." In this statement he issues no excuses for their actions, but reminded them of God's sovereign kindness *despite them*: "you meant evil against me, but God *meant* (*ḥāśăḇ*) it for good in order to bring about this present result, to preserve many people alive." Joseph's repetition of the verb *meant* reminds us that though men *plan* evil, God's good and glorious *plan* prevails over all. However, the fact that an initial act of evil was used to accomplish a greater good *does not make the original act good*. It means that God Himself is good and sovereign over everything. And by this good and sovereign providence of the Almighty, the once rejected sibling, who was sold as a slave, became the provider and deliverer of the sons of Israel: "'...do not be afraid; I will provide for you and your little ones.' So he comforted them and spoke kindly to them." (Genesis 50:21).

Joseph's response to his brothers reveals the beauty of what God accomplishes in the heart of His people. As a child of God, Joseph understood that he was redeemed by God's kindness and grace, and, therefore, his gracious response to his brothers was an imitation of God Himself. As a lover of God, Joseph was able to extend mercy and love to the very brothers who sinfully betrayed him. How contrary is his response to what is advised by SJI counselors today! Joseph did not smolder with rage and hate openly bloviating about his "fantasies" of killing them and "burying their bod[ies]", walking away "relatively guiltless with a bounce" in his step.[443] As well, God's work of grace in Joseph's life was not a *"mere motif"* as argued by Emerson and Smith, such that there should be no effect in his life when dealing with his own family. Nor was Joseph's

---

[442] חָשַׁב (ḥāšab) think, plan, make a judgment, imagine, count. Leon J. Wood, "767 חָשַׁב," ed. R. Laird Harris, Gleason L. Archer Jr., and Bruce K. Waltke, *Theological Wordbook*, 329.

[443] Samuel Chamberlain, "NYC shrink who talked about shooting white people now says they are 'psychopathic,'" (New York Post, June 18 2021): https://nypost.com/2021/06/18/nyc-shrink-who-talked-about-shooting-white-people-now-says-they-are-psychopathic/.

previous experience of oppression an excuse to promote injustice as compensation for his past enslavement, as Neo-Marxist Ibram Kendi advises. Instead, we find a peace, trust, and contentment in the heart of Joseph that is not natural, but *supernatural*. This is so because his trust was in God's redemptive mercy and sovereign care.

The heart that is touched by God's grace looks beyond the straw, sticks, and the dust of this world and sees, with the eye of faith, Christ and His celestial crown. Such a transformation of grace could never be achieved by the faux-religion of SJI. All that is produced out of the troubled soil of this ideology is a root of bitterness, an unforgiving spirit, and a thirst for vengeance in the name of "justice."

Joseph's conduct is a model of behavior worth imitating. Despite the evil that surrounded him, he could trust in the goodness of God's providence. Only the Lord could orchestrate the affairs of men such that the evil of slavery, or the crucifixion of the sinless Messiah, could result in innumerable blessings. When Joseph was sold by his brothers, he had no capacity of knowing if he would survive the experience, or what would happen to him in the future. Like any one of us, our future remains a mystery to us all, but one thing we must remember is that the Lord holds our future in His good and sovereign hands.

The truth of God's sovereignty brings great peace to the heart of the child of God. The knowledge that one's life, circumstances, hopes, dreams, and future can be entirely entrusted to the Almighty resultantly removes the common fears that often beset anxious hearts. Without such trust in God and His sovereignty, all that we are left with are the devices of our own foolish speculations, fears, and even chronic ingratitude: "For even though they knew God, they did not honor Him as God, or give thanks; but they became futile in their speculations, and their foolish heart was darkened." (Romans 1:21). In this passage Paul describes the unbeliever's *ingratitude* towards God which reveals the great divide between those who trust in God and those who do not. Those who dishonor God and are filled with such ingratitude are given over to the *futility of their speculations* as those whose *hearts have been darkened.* However, the child of God seeks to trust the Lord and serve Him with genuine gratitude and trust, understanding that the Lord's care for His children is far greater than anything this world can supply. Such trust freed Joseph to serve God with a persevering faith.

Thankfully, there have been many other servants of Christ who walked in like manner, as in the case of those soldiers who advanced the Gospel and fought against the plague of slavery, *doing so with a determination to honor the Lord in everything.* Individuals like Anthony Benezet, Benjamin Rush, and James Oglethorpe[444] in America; Granville Sharp, William Wilberforce, John Newton, and Thomas Clarkson in Britain, all fought against slavery with remarkable intensity, and yet, *in the providence of God,* their efforts led to different results during their lifetimes. America's lagging progress was an unsettling and trying matter for many. In the case of Sharp, his forceful remonstrance to the colonies to "put away the accursed thing [slavery], that horrid oppression from among them, before they presume to implore the interposition of divine justice,"[445] did not yield the same results that he saw in England. In his disgust over this matter, he made a personal note in his journal suggesting that it would be "better for the nation [Britain] that their American dominions had never existed, or even that they had sunk in the sea, than that the kingdom of Great Britain should be loaded with the horrid guilt of tolerating such abominable wickedness.'"[446]

---

[444] James Oglethorpe was one of the founders of the colony of Georgia in 1733, but he later returned to England in 1743.

[445] Sharp, *A Declaration*, 28.

[446] "Granville Sharp adverting to the existing slave laws of the Colonies, says in his Journal...(18th Feb. 1772) 'If such laws are not absolutely necessary for the government of slaves, the law makers must unavoidably allow themselves to be the most cruel and abandoned tyrants upon earth, and perhaps, that ever were on earth. But, on the other hand, if it be said that it is impossible to govern slaves,

There were many others whose plans and efforts were similarly thwarted. James Oglethorpe, a British soldier, Member of Parliament, and staunch abolitionist wrote a letter to Sharp[447] in which he described his stalled efforts[448] to oppose slavery when the colony of Georgia was established:

"My friends and I settled the colony of Georgia, and by charter were established trustees, to make laws, &c. We determined not to suffer slavery

---

without such inhuman severity and detestable injustice, the same is an invincible argument against the least toleration of slavery among Christians; because temporal profits, cannot compensate the forfeiture of everlasting welfare—that the cries of these much injured people will certainly reach heaven—that the scriptures denounce a tremendous judgment against the man, who shall offend one little one—that it were better for the nation that their American dominions had never existed, or even that they had sunk in the sea, than that the kingdom, of Great Britain should be loaded with the horrid guilt of tolerating such abominable wickedness.'" Stuart, *A Memoir*, 178.

[447] Oglethorpe had been given a copy of GS's *Law of Retribution* which had so impressed him that he contacted its author in order to express his gratitude. This was the beginning of a longstanding friendship between the two: "Being at Wools ton Hall, Dr, Scott's house, he showed me your ' Law of Retribution.' I was greatly rejoiced to find that so laborious and learned a man had appeared as champion for the rights of mankind, against avarice, extortion, and inhumanity;—that you had, with an heroic courage, dared to press home, on an infidel, luxurious world, the dreadful threats of the Prophets." Hoare, *Memoirs*, 155-56.

[448] Oglethorpe repeatedly had to fend off efforts to reinstate slavery in Georgia. In a letter to the Georgia Trustees, he reminded them of the importance of their stand for liberty: "If we allow slaves we act against the very principles by which we associated together, which was to relieve the distresses. Whereas, now we should occasion the misery of thousands in Africa, by setting men upon using arts to buy and bring into perpetual slavery the poor people who now live there free." Thomas Wilson, *The Oglethorpe Plan: Enlightenment Design in Savannah and Beyond*, (University of Virginia Press, 12 February 2015), 128–133.

there; but the slave-merchants, and their adherents, occasioned us not only much trouble, but at last got the then government to favour them. We would not suffer slavery (which is against the Gospel as well as the fundamental law of England) to be authorised under our authority: we refused, as trustees, to make a law permitting such a horrid crime. The Government, finding the trustees resolved firmly not to concur with what they thought unjust, took away the charter by which no law could be passed without our consent.[449]

It was this same bad seed of chattel slavery that would later supply a roadblock to the Declaration's original anti-slavery clause, as we have already reviewed.[450] Sadly, the forces that opposed those early efforts of abolition within the colonies continued to persist. But it is this very contest that reminds us of the great battle for justice that continues within this world of systemic evil. It also reminds us of the principles of *human responsibility* and *God's sovereignty* as expressed in Proverbs 16:9: "The mind of man plans his way, But the LORD directs his steps." The diligent efforts of many to crush chattel slavery from the beginning *appeared* to supply nothing but failure, and yet we now know that those efforts would eventually yield the fruit of freedom.

As we have already observed, Sharp's two works, *An Extract from a Representation of the Injustice and Dangerous Tendency of Tolerating Slavery,* which was distributed by Benezet, and, *A Declaration of the People's Natural Rights to Share in the Legislature, in Support of the American Colonists,* which was distributed by Benjamin Franklin, may very well have made GS "an instrument in the great work of American Independence."[451]

Whether or not these materials had any influence on America's original Declaration of Independence remains a matter of speculation,

---

[449] Hoare, *Memoirs*, p. 157.

[450] "The clause...reprobating the enslaving the inhabitants of Africa, was struck out in complaisance to South Carolina and Georgia, who had never attempted to restrain the importation of slaves." Jefferson, *The Works of Thomas Jefferson*, 18.

[451] Hoare, *Memoirs*, 172.

especially since Jefferson's own description of the Declaration's original formulation leaves us with more questions than answers. As Jefferson indicated in his letter to James Madison, 30 August 1823: "...whether I had gathered my ideas from reading or reflection I do not know. I know only that I turned to neither book nor pamphlet while writing it. I did not consider it as any part of my charge to invent new ideas altogether & to offer no sentiment which had ever been expressed before." Ultimately, in God's kind providence, one such *un-invented* idea that remained in the final version of the Declaration was the assertion that *all men are created equal.* Like a small grain of salt, this important assertion became a *strong preservative* for the nation as time pressed on; however, it would take many years for the meaning and value of this statement to be appreciated and more fully applied.

On August 19 1791, Benjamin Banneker, an accomplished astronomer, surveyor, and mathematician, wrote a letter to Thomas Jefferson in which he expressed concern for those who remained under the oppression of slavery. In his correspondence, he rightly questioned Jefferson's inconsistency regarding his words and actions. What he wrote was gracious, respectful, but necessarily forthright:

Sir I freely and Chearfully acknowledge, that I am of the African race, and in that colour which is natural to them of the deepest dye,* and it is under a Sense of the most profound gratitude to the Supreme Ruler of the universe, that I now confess to you, that I am not under that State of tyrannical thraldom,[452] and inhuman captivity, to which too many of my brethren are doomed; but that I have abundantly tasted of the fruition of those blessings which proceed from that free and unequalled liberty with which you are favoured and which I hope you will willingly allow you have received from the immediate hand of that Being, from whom proceedeth every good and perfect gift. Sir, Suffer me to recall to your mind that time in which the Arms and tyranny of the British Crown were exerted with every powerful effort in order to reduce you to a

---

[452] "The state or condition of being a thrall; bondage, servitude; captivity" OED.

State of Servitude, look back I intreat you on the variety of dangers to which you were exposed, reflect on that time in which every human aid appeared unavailable, and in which even hope and fortitude wore the aspect of inability to the Conflict, and you cannot but be led to a Serious and grateful Sense of your miraculous and providential preservation; you cannot but acknowledge, that the present freedom and tranquility which you enjoy you have mercifully received, and that it is the peculiar blessing of Heaven. This Sir, was a time in which you clearly saw into the injustice of a State of Slavery, and in which you had just apprehensions of the horrors of its condition, it was now Sir, that your abhorrence thereof was so excited, that you publickly held forth this true and invaluable doctrine, which is worthy to be recorded and remember'd in all Succeeding ages. "We hold these truths to be Self evident, that all men are created equal, and that they are endowed by their creator with certain unalienable rights, that among these are life, liberty, and the pursuit of happyness." Here Sir, was a time in which your tender feelings for your selves had engaged you thus to declare, you were then impressed with proper ideas of the great valuation of liberty, and the free possession of those blessings to which you were entitled by nature; but Sir how pitiable is it to reflect, that altho you were so fully convinced of the benevolence of the Father of mankind, and of his equal and impartial distribution of those rights and privileges which he had conferred upon them, that you should at the same time counteract his mercies, in detaining by fraud and violence so numerous a part of my brethren under groaning captivity and cruel oppression, that you should at the same time be found guilty of that most criminal act, which you professedly detested in others, with respect to yourselves.

Banneker's appeal is simultaneously heartbreaking and encouraging. It is respectful and gracious, while getting to the heart of Jefferson's "pitiable" hypocrisy. This is especially accomplished when he quoted Jefferson's own words in the final version of the Declaration: *we hold these truths to be self-evident, that all men are created equal.*

Banneker was right when he called this expression a "true and invaluable doctrine." Not that it is *true and invaluable* as the words of mere mortals, but it is true because of the foundational reality of God's Word which repeatedly asserts that *all are the offspring of God* (γένος, *genos*: Acts 17:26, 29). Though Jefferson was the instrumental means by which the clause, *all men are created equal,* was written, we know that it was ultimately God's kind providence that led to this result. Thus, *despite Jefferson,* this *invaluable doctrine* remained as a corrective rudder that would eventually steer the nation to greater liberty.

Another test of this *invaluable doctrine* came in 1839 when a Spanish slave trade vessel called *La Amistad* was overtaken in a slave revolt. As the Amistad traveled from Cuba to the northern shore of the American east coast, a US vessel seized the ship and its crew. This produced a remarkable dilemma. The American seizure of a foreign vessel that contained enslaved Africans led to a unique legal contest. This legal contest eventually went to the US Supreme Court which ultimately ruled that those who were held as slaves on *La Amistad* were in fact *free men* who had been kidnapped and taken against their will. The majority opinion was delivered by Justice Joseph Story:

> It is also a most important consideration in the present case, which ought not to be lost sight of, that, supposing these African negroes not to be slaves, but kidnapped, and free negroes, the treaty with Spain cannot be obligatory upon them; and the United States are bound to respect their rights as much as those of Spanish subjects. The conflict of rights between the parties under such circumstances, becomes positive and inevitable, and must be decided upon the eternal principles of justice and international law. If the contest were about any goods on board of this ship, to which American citizens asserted a title, which was denied by the Spanish claimants, there could be no doubt of the right of such American citizens to litigate their claims before any competent American tribunal, notwithstanding the treaty with Spain. *A fortiori,* the doctrine must apply where human life and human liberty are in issue; and constitute the very essence of the controversy. The treaty with Spain never could have intended to take away the equal rights of all foreigners, who should contest their claims before any of our Courts, to equal justice; or to deprive such foreigners of the protection given them by other treaties, or by the general law of nations. Upon the merits of the case, then, there does not seem to us to be any ground for

doubt, that these negroes ought to be deemed free; and that the Spanish treaty interposes no obstacle to the just assertion of their rights...When the Amistad arrived she was in possession of the negroes, asserting their freedom; and in no sense could they possibly intend to import themselves here, as slaves, or for sale as slaves. In this view of the matter, that part of the decree of the District Court is unmaintainable, and must be reversed...Upon the whole, our opinion is, that the decree of the Circuit Court, affirming that of the District Court, ought to be affirmed, except so far as it directs the negroes to be delivered to the President, to be transported to Africa, in pursuance of the act of the 3d of March, 1819; and, as to this, it ought to be reversed: and that the said negroes be declared to be free, and be dismissed from the custody of the Court, and go without delay.

Throughout his opinion, Justice Story was careful to repeat the *invaluable doctrine* that *all men are created equal.* He rightly described the enslaved Africans as "kidnapped" men, thus referring to the principle of human life and liberty as *a fortiori.* He contrasted the "goods" (chattel) on the ship with those free men who could not have intended to "import themselves here, as slaves, or for sale as slaves." Story's argument is clearly rooted in the core truth regarding our shared humanity, not only as inferred by his judicial opinion, but also by what he wrote elsewhere on the subject of the slave trade:

American citizens are steeped up to their very mouths (I scarcely use too bold a figure) in this stream of iniquity. They throng to the coasts of Africa under the stained flags of Spain and Portugal, sometimes selling abroad "their cargoes of despair," and sometimes bringing them into some of our southern ports, and there, under the forms of the law, defeating the purposes of the law itself, and legalizing their inhuman but profitable adventures. I wish I could say that New England and New England men were free from this deep pollution. But there is some reason to believe, that they who drive a loathsome traffic, 'and buy the muscles and the bones of men,' are to be found here also. It is to be hoped the number is small; but our cheeks may well burn with shame while a solitary case is permitted to go unpunished. "And, gentlemen, how can we justify ourselves or apologize for an indifference to this subject? Our constitutions of government have declared, that all men are born free and equal, and have certain unalienable rights, among which are the right of enjoying their lives, liberties, and property, and of seeking and obtaining their own safety and happiness. May not the miserable[453] African ask, 'Am I not a man and a brother?' We boast of our noble struggle against the encroachments of tyranny, but do we forget that it assumed the mildest form in which authority ever assailed the rights of its subjects; and yet that there are men among us who think it no wrong to condemn the shivering negro to perpetual slavery?[454]

Former President John Quincy Adams had been called upon to defend the Africans in the *Amistad* case. During his presidency, he grew in his repulsion over slavery and became especially critical of Southern Democrats whose defense of the trade was strongest. In United States v. *La Amistad* he argued that the Africans were unjustly held against their will saying, "The moment you come to the Declaration of Independence, that every man has a right to life and liberty, an inalienable right, this case is decided."[455] In fact, Adams repeated this principle three times throughout the course of his defense and as a result of his labors, the court ruled in favor of the Africans' freedom on March 9th 1841.

United States v. *La Amistad* was a landmark decision that became a light of hope for many. As a legal precedent, it necessarily became another rebuke against the profound contradiction between the

---

[453] This term has changed somewhat in some modern connotations and is sometimes used to speak of the nature of a person. However, the historic denotation of this word speaks of someone who is in a state of misery or sorrow. Story employs this term in order in this latter sense to express compassion for those who were subjected to the torments of enslavement.

[454] William Wetmore Story, *Life and Letters of Joseph Story: Associate Justice of the Supreme Court of the United States, and Dane Professor of Law at Harvard University*, V. 1 (C.C. Little and J. Brown), 4899-4910, Kindle.

[455] John Quincy Adams, *Argument of John Quincy Adams Before the Supreme Court of the United States: The United States Vs. Amistad* (Lulu.com), 96, Kindle.

Declaration's creed and implementation. Twenty years later, that contradiction was confronted by the onslaught of the American Civil War. Along the way, many abolitionists sought to remain faithful in their defense of the Scriptures and of the integrity of all human life. Few of them saw the full fruit of their labors before passing from this life, but they remained faithful in their servitude to the Lord. When GS had received word regarding the passage of the Slave Trade Act 1807 "he is said to have immediately fallen on his knees, in devotion and gratitude to his Creator."[456] He passed away 6th of July 1813, twenty years before his ultimate goal was achieved: the Slavery Abolition Act 1833.

Wilberforce worked tirelessly towards these same objectives with the ultimate desire to end domestic slavery in Britain and America. In 1808, he penned a letter to Jefferson in an effort to increase the abolitionist cause in America, but with no effect. The constancy of his efforts met no small amount of resistance. In a letter to Lord Muncaster, he expressed his weariness in dealing with public affairs and individuals who had "no humiliation, no recognition of the providence of God."[457] He referred to all such human insolence as "practical atheism," inquiring if Muncaster didn't agree that "the slave trade . . . when estimated by the Scripture standard . . . may well strike terror into the heart of every serious man?"[458] Amidst his struggles and exhaustion, he penned these words in his journal on the 8th of March, 1818:

"Lay awake several hours in the night, and very languid this morning. My mind is very uneasy, and greatly distracted about the course to be pursued in the West Indian matters. It is hard to decide, especially where so many counsellors. This is clear, that in the Scriptures no national crime is condemned so frequently, and few so strongly, as oppression and cruelty, and the not using of

---

[456] Hoare, *Memoirs*, 428.

[457] Robert Isaac Wilberforce and Samuel Wilberforce, *The Life of William Wilberforce*, V. II (London: John Murray, Albemable St, 1838), 167.

[458] Ibid., 168.

our best endeavours to deliver our fellow-creatures from them (Jer. 6:6, Ezek. 16:49, Zeph 3:1; Amos 4:8 &c. I must therefore set to work, and, O Lord, direct, and support, and bless me. If it please Thee not to let me be the instrument of good to these poor degraded people, may I still be found working, like dear Stephen,[459] with vigour and simple obedience, remembering, 'It is well for thee that it was in thy heart.'"[460]

Unlike GS, Wilberforce was able to witness the passage of the Slavery Abolition Act in the House of Commons on 22 July 1833, one week before he died and one month before the act was formalized by Royal Assent.

All those who labored to this end did so not knowing what the outcome of their labors would be, but they *remained steadfast, unmovable, always abounding in the work of the Lord, knowing that their toil was not in vain in the Lord* (1 Corinthians 15:58). Only those with an eye of faith set upon the goodness of God and His sovereignty can labor faithfully in this manner.

Yet these are examples of those who labored for the cause of abolition as free citizens of their respective nations. What can be said of those saints who faced systemic evil under the oppressive hand of slavery during this same time? In the end, our earlier example of Joseph comes to mind when considering the life of Phillis Wheatley who was mentioned in the introduction. Wheatley was taken from her homeland of West Africa in 1761 and sold into slavery when she was only eight years old. A

---

[459] The story of Stephen is one of sacrificial servitude and is recorded in the book of Acts. Stephen had been ministering in the grace and power of God, preaching the Word of God to the people. When confronted by the members of the Sanhedrin, he preached the Gospel to them (Acts 7). The Council became enraged as a result of what Stephen said and began stoning him to death. Before he was crushed to death, he cried out with a loud voice, saying, "Lord, do not hold this sin against them!" (Acts 7:60).

[460] Robert I. Wilberforce, *The Life of William Wilberforce: In Five Volumes*, (Murray), 1178, Kindle.

remarkably gifted poet, Wheatley's poems made her uniquely popular around the globe, even capturing the attention of Thomas Paine, John Newton, George Washington, and Thomas Jefferson. In one of her poems, she recounts the torturous experience of her capture and separation from her parents:

> I, young in life, by seeming cruel fate
> Was snatch'd from Afric's fancy'd happy seat:
> What pangs excruciating must molest,
> What sorrows labour in my parent's breast?
> Steel'd was that soul and by no misery mov'd
> That from a father seiz'd his babe belov'd:
> Such, such my case. And can I then but pray
> Others may never feel tyrannic sway?

Despite the incomprehensible pain and oppression she endured, she was able to see the hand of divine providence which led her to saving faith:

> 'Twas mercy brought me from my Pagan land,
> Taught my benighted soul to understand
> That there's a God, that there's a Saviour too:
> Once I redemption neither sought nor knew.[461]

Though deprived of freedom, she understood that she had been released from the slavery of sin and that her emancipation in Christ was, in fact, true and eternal freedom. Rather than being overcome by a root of bitterness, she warned those who enjoyed the privileges of freedom not to live for this world, but to look with the eye of faith upon the crucified and risen Savior. In one particular poem she wrote to the students at the University of Cambridge with this Gospel appeal and warning:

---

[461] Phillis Wheatley, *The Poems of Phillis Wheatley: With Letters and a Memoir*, (Dover Publications), 3, Kindle.

WHILE an intrinsic ardor prompts to write,
The muses promise to assist my pen;
'Twas not long since I left my native shore
The land of errors, and Egyptian gloom:
Father of mercy, 'twas thy gracious hand
Brought me in safety from those dark abodes.

Students, to you 'tis giv'n to scan the heights
Above, to traverse the ethereal space,
And mark the systems of revolving worlds.
Still more, ye sons of science ye receive
The blissful news by messengers from heav'n,
How Jesus' blood for your redemption flows.
See him with hands out-stretcht upon the cross;
Immense compassion in his bosom glows;
He hears revilers, nor resents their scorn:
What matchless mercy in the Son of God!
When the whole human race by sin had fall'n,
He deign'd to die that they might rise again,
And share with him in the sublimest skies,
Life without death, and glory without end.

Improve your privileges while they stay,
Ye pupils, and each hour redeem, that bears
Or good or bad report of you to heav'n.
Let sin, that baneful evil to the soul,
By you be shunn'd, nor once remit your guard;
Suppress the deadly serpent in its egg.
Ye blooming plants of human race divine,
An Ethiop tells you 'tis your greatest foe;
Its transient sweetness turns to endless pain,
And in immense perdition sinks the soul.[462]

---

[462] Ibid., 4.

This poetic appeal is filled with the grace of the Gospel itself. Central to Wheatley's advisement of these young *blooming plants of the human race* is that they should gaze upon Christ with *hands out-stretched upon the cross* who *deign'd to die that they might rise again*. Only divine grace could produce a heart of care and concern for others in this manner: even for those whose earthly privileges were far greater than hers.

Thomas Clarkson referenced several samples of her exceptional poetry as a rebuke against those pro-slavery advocates who argued for the inferiority of blacks. In his work, *An Essay on the Slavery and Commerce of the Human Species, Particularly the African*, Clarkson pummeled the pro-slavery position with decisive force:

> Such is the poetry [of Wheatley] which I produce as a proof of my assertions. How far it has succeeded, the reader may by this time have determined in his own mind. I shall therefore only beg leave to accompany it with this observation, that if the authoress was designed for slavery, (as the argument must confess) the greater part of the inhabitants of Britain must lose their claim to freedom.[463]

Disturbingly, many colonists could not believe that an enslaved African could produce such excellent poetry. Because of this Wheatley had to defend the authenticity of her work in court in 1772 before an assembly of Boston luminaries: John Hancock, Thomas Hutchinson, Andrew Oliver, John Erving, and Charles Chauncey. They concluded that her writings were authentic, however, Thomas Jefferson weighed in on this question with his own morose judgment.

In a disturbing passage in which Jefferson revealed his views of blacks by means of a bizarre show of sophistry, he asserted that they were "in reason much inferior, as I think one could scarcely be found capable of

---

[463] Thomas Clarkson, *An Essay on the Slavery and Commerce of the Human Species, Particularly The African*, (London: Phillips 1788), 122.

tracing and comprehending the investigations of Euclid; and that in imagination they are dull, tasteless, and anomalous."[464] He then aimed his vacuous musings against Wheatley, saying "Religion, indeed, has produced a Phyllis Whately [sic]; but it could not produce a poet. The compositions published under her name are below the dignity of criticism."[465]

Jefferson was wrong for more reasons than we have paper and ink to record, but he especially erred when he said that religion "produced" Phillis Wheatley. Rather than *mere religion*, the Almighty God made her: not only as an image bearer and member of the human race, but as a member of His chosen race and family. No matter what others said about her, she knew she was a child of the King and would someday claim the celestial crown of Christ and have "Life without death, and glory without end." She clearly understood that, even if one could acquire all the *privileges* and *riches* of this world, it amounts to nothing for those who forfeit their soul (Matthew 16:26). For this reason she made her appeal to others to cling to the "matchless mercy in the Son of God!" Clearly, the reality of God's sovereignty wasn't a mere academic truth for Phillis Wheatley, it was the very foundation of her hope and joy whereby she knew that, as a child of the King of Righteousness, she would someday abide with her true Emancipator and Lord, forever.

Sadly and ironically, the joy, hope, and assurance that Wheatley possessed in Christ were entirely alien to Thomas Jefferson. The Jesus that he invented and embraced could never deliver a soul from the slavery of sin, nor could it find refuge from either the temporal or eternal wrath of God, and it appears that he had some sense of this fearful truth:

"The whole commerce between master and slave is a perpetual exercise of the most boisterous passions, the most unremitting despotism, on the one part,

---

[464] Jefferson, *Complete Works of Thomas Jefferson*, 186.
[465] Ibid.

and degrading submissions on the other.... I tremble for my country when I reflect that God is just; that his justice cannot sleep forever; that, considering numbers, nature, and natural means only, a revolution of the wheel of fortune, an exchange of situations, is among possible events; that it may become probable by supernatural interference! The Almighty has no attribute which can take side with us in such a contest."[466]

This somber reflection echoes Wilberforce's own thought that, slavery, "when estimated by the Scripture standard...should strike terror into the heart of every serious man."[467] But the words of these two men reveal a crucial difference. *By the standard of Scripture*, Wilberforce was driven by inviolable principles that would not allow him to rest until he fought slavery to the end. *Without the standard of Scripture*, Jefferson's thoughts and convictions had no anchor or stability, leaving him to the shifting machinations of his own mind. As well, though Jefferson was a man of great power, means, and influence he remained a spiritual pauper when compared to individuals like Phillis Wheatley, who possessed true wisdom from above along with all the eternal riches that are in Christ. *Such a contrast could not be more extreme.*

The very thought of a slave having a place of honor before God above a renowned founding father of the United States of America may cause some to stumble, *but it is a reality that should be carefully and seriously contemplated.*

---

[466] Ibid., 6398.

[467] Robert Isaac Wilberforce and Samuel Wilberforce, *The Life of William Wilberforce*, V. II, (London: Seeley, Burnside, and Seeley), 168.

JESUS'
JUSTICE

Psalm 2:4–5:
4 He who sits in the heavens laughs, The Lord scoffs at them.
5 Then He will speak to them in His anger
And terrify them in His fury:

CONCLUSION
HE WHO SITS
IN THE HEAVENS LAUGHS

Throughout the pages of this book we have repeatedly seen that human history is plagued with countless examples of those who sought to pull the levers of societal change apart from God's wisdom, resulting in incalculable harm to humanity. Not only has this pattern of behavior been seen in oppressive governments, false religions, and the barbarities of the transatlantic slave trade, but this contagion continues in the modern day.

As previously reviewed in the fourth chapter, Margaret Sanger sought to establish *racial hygiene* by means of birth control which, she insisted, "has been accepted by the most clear thinking and far seeing of the Eugenists themselves as the most constructive and necessary of the means to racial health."[468] It was Sanger who founded the American Birth Control League which later became the Planned Parenthood Federation of America. She also instigated the "Negro Project" which she believed would relieve the African American community of their "ignorance,

---

[468] Sanger, *The Pivot of Civilization*, 1539, Kindle.

superstitions, and doubts" about the "eugenic benefits" of abortion.[469] This leaves little doubt about Sanger's agenda and legacy, especially in light of the fact that "black women have been experiencing induced abortions at a rate nearly 4 times that of White women"[470] over the past few decades.

Though I am of the opinion that Sanger's beliefs were significantly corrupted by racial bigotry, I would suggest that her problems were much more rudimentary. For Sanger, charitable work within society was "evil"[471] because it enabled the further propagation of "feeble minded persons."[472] Thus it was her goal to make "sure that parenthood is absolutely prohibited to the feeble-minded,"[473] so that the "dead weight of human waste"[474] would be removed from society altogether.

Of all the problems that could be articulated about Sanger's corrupted thinking, one thing is for certain: she possessed the dangerous admixture of profound ignorance and arrogance. In her work, *A Plan for Peace,* Sanger indicated that world peace could be achieved if society controlled the population of "morons, mental defectives, epileptics"[475] while segregating all "illiterates, paupers, unemployables, criminals, prostitutes, dope-fiends"[476] on state-run concentration farms "on the basis

---

[469] Margaret Sanger, Letter to Dr. C. J. Gamble, 10 December 1939.

[470] US National Library of Medicine National Institutes of Health, "Perceiving and Addressing the Pervasive Racial Disparity in Abortion," (v.7; Jan-Dec 2020PMC7436774) https://www.ncbi.nlm.nih.gov/pmc/articles/PMC7436774/

[471] Sanger, *The Pivot of Civilization,*1183, Kindle.

[472] Ibid., 721.

[473] Ibid., 867.

[474] Ibid., 946.

[475] "The first step would thus be to control the intake and output of morons, mental defectives, epileptics." Margaret Sanger, *The Pivot of Civilization and a Plan for Peace* (Suzeteo Enterprises), 67, Kindle.

[476] "The second step would be to take an inventory of the secondary group such as illiterates, paupers, unemployables, criminals, prostitutes, dope-fiends; classify

of health instead of punishment."[477] In what amounted to an early form of medical-tyranny, she argued that "certain dysgenic groups in our population [would be given] their choice of segregation or sterilization."[478] She, like other eugenicists of her day, claimed a license to judge certain members of the human race as meriting either subjugation (sterilization) or even elimination (abortion) for the greater good of society and for the cause of racial health.

In this sense, she bore an ideological likeness to the pagan philosophers of yesteryear who justified their own version of *racial health* via infanticide, as described by the 1st century Roman philosopher Seneca:

> We knock mad dogs on the head, we slaughter fierce and savage bulls, and we doom scabby sheep to the knife, lest they should infect our flocks: we destroy monstrous births, and we also drown our children if they are born weakly or unnaturally formed; to separate what is useless from what is sound is an act, not of anger, but of reason.[479]

Clearly, there really is nothing new under the sun (Ecclesiastes 1:9). Whatever else that can be said about Sanger's legacy, her bankrupt ideology resulted in the deaths of 62 million unborn children in America since 1973, or approximately ten Jewish Holocausts; and this human

---

them in special departments under government medical protection, and segregate them on farms and open spaces as long as necessary for the strengthening and development of moral conduct. Having corralled this enormous part of our population and placed it on a basis of health instead of punishment, it is safe to say that fifteen or twenty millions of our population would then be organized into soldiers of defense—defending the unborn against their own disabilities." Ibid.

[477] Ibid.

[478] Ibid., 253.

[479] Lucius Annaeus Seneca, *Complete Works of Seneca the Younger (Illustrated)* (Delphi Ancient Classics Book 27), 16227, Kindle.

slaughter continues in the present day with the enthusiastic support of most SJI ideologues. Humanity's notions about justice are no match for God's true justice, and this is why history reveals that whenever human life is assessed by *human reason*, remarkable cruelties are the predictable result.

This is why we began our study with a brief examination of Psalm 2 which reveals what I have called the *longest war in human history*. This longstanding contest consists of those who *devise vain things* and *take counsel together* in their open rebellion against *the Lord and His Anointed King* (Psalm 2:2, 6). Amidst this boisterous fanfare, the Lord *sits in the heavens* and *laughs* at their impotent verbal assaults while promising a coming day of judgment in which the Son of God will shatter His enemies *with a rod of iron* and crush them all *like earthenware* (Psalm 2:4-9).

However, amidst these stark declarations of coming judgment is the promise of the Son's kind and gracious provision of mercy: "Do homage to the Son, lest He become angry, and you perish in the way, For His wrath may soon be kindled. *How blessed are all who take refuge in Him!*" (Psalm 2:12). This remarkable psalm heralds God's kind and merciful message *to all humanity,* that those who *take refuge in the Son* will not *perish in His wrath* but will be forever *blessed, as Jesus Himself said: "God so loved the world, that He gave His only begotten Son, that whoever believes in Him should not perish, but have eternal life"* (John 3:16).

It is a remarkable matter to consider that the Lord extends His mercy and love, through the Gospel, to those who are open rebels within His creation. It is also a remarkable matter to consider that despite the Lord's provision of mercy, many continue to devise vain things and take counsel together in their open rebellion against Him. In their profound arrogance, as we have observed, *they refuse the Almighty's wisdom and justice, doing so out of the vain presumption that their own sense of wisdom and justice is better than His (1 Corinthians 1:18-25).*

In view of this, our focus has been set upon the multiple *vain things* that have been devised by humanity, but with a special focus on the contemporary machinations of SJI. Thus, *the preceding nine chapters* have supplied warnings to the reader concerning the dangers of this ideology and how it opposes Jesus' justice by *heralding the wisdom of man above God (chapter 1); by seeking to remedy past injustices with present day injustices (chapter 2); by seeing oppression (whether real or perceived) as establishing personal merit and innocence (chapter 3); by promoting faulty views of God's creation of the human race and therefore advancing an abundance of ignorance and racial bigotry (chapter 4); by advancing its own doctrinal creed and religious system of atonement that supplies no real solutions or true hope (chapter 5); by promoting a false Gospel which consistently generates bigotry, hatred, and resentment against others on the basis of their epidermis (chapter 6); by focusing on the past to such an extent that the triumphs of the Gospel, both past and present, are seriously obscured (chapter 7); by failing to distinguish the true church versus the false church when evaluating the past and present (chapter 8); and by falling short of any comprehensive understanding of systemic evil and God's sovereign providence over all (chapter 9).*

Because of these significant problems, SJI promotes a worldview and epistemology that is entirely incompatible with the Christian faith and produces a hostile ingratitude within its followers. And though so much more could be said about the societal chaos that it brings, its greatest injustices consist of its substitute authority, promised deliverance, and claims of efficacy in solving the problems of this world. Because of this it repeatedly stands as an affront to the majesty, dignity, and power of Jesus Christ. Our consideration of this last point has only been briefly reviewed thus far and therefore deserves further attention before we conclude this book:

1. Jesus' Majesty: The subject of Jesus' majesty is of paramount importance because it affirms His unmatched authority over all of creation. This Anointed

King (Psalm 2), who is seated at the right hand of Majesty on high (Psalm 110:1, Hebrews 1:3), is thrice affirmed as the "King of kings and Lord of lords" (1 Timothy 6:15; Revelation 17:14, 19:16).

As the sovereign and just King of the Universe, any challenge to His supreme authority is an act of personal rebellion *against Him*. In view of this, those who presume to craft versions of justice that are contrary to Jesus' justice are simply *devising a vain thing* and are thus advancing further enmity against Him. For this reason, we repeatedly compared the standards of SJI to that of Jesus' justice in order to discern just how dangerous this contemporary ideology is.

In the end, we have no license or authority to instruct this King of *justice and righteousness* (Isaiah 9:-7) regarding what justice is. Those who dare to oppose this Holy Monarch in this manner will someday face Him in the day of *His wrath*.

2. Jesus' Dignity: When we speak of Jesus' dignity we are affirming His *essential and moral supremacy* in view of His *excellence, nobility, and worthiness to be honored*.[480] Though the eternal Son of God entered the human race and became a man, He did not succumb to the temptations of this world, but instead lived a life of perfect obedience and sinlessness (John 8:29). In light of the perfection of His dignity, He died on the cross as the sinner's *unblemished and spotless* substitute.

It is for this reason that He is called *Jesus Christ the Righteous* (1 John 2:1-2) because His perfection of obedience, in life and death, establishes a righteous merit for the one who believes in Him (Psalm 2:12, Romans 5:1). Apart from His merit, there is no Gospel. But in view of the perfection of His *dignity*, there are no substitutes for the salvation that He alone offers as the priestly *King of Righteousness* (Psalm 110:4).

Therefore, any and all man-made religions, which offer alternate systems of deliverance and forgiveness, are an affront to Him who said: "I, even I, am the Lord; and there is no savior besides Me." (Isaiah 43:11).

---

[480] "The quality of being worthy or honourable; worthiness, worth, nobleness, excellence." OED.

3. Jesus' Power: Because the Son of God shares the same essence of deity with the Father, and in view of His exaltation through His death, burial, and resurrection, Jesus possesses *all rule and authority and power and dominion* over everything (Ephesians 1:21). For this reason, He is called the Despot (δεσπότην, *despotēn*) and Lord (κύριον, *kurion*) over all (Jude 4).

In contemporary settings, whenever we speak of a despotic leader, we typically have in mind a ruler who uses his power in order to abuse his subjects.[481] In view of humanity's fallen nature it is the case that whenever mere mortals attain unchecked power, they gravitate towards a despotism that is fraught with countless forms of injustice. But when we consider Jesus' power it is necessary that we keep in mind the essence of His dignity and justice. Such a consideration reminds us that He exercises His power in holiness, justice, righteousness, faithfulness, mercy, and love. Moreover, every exercise of His power is in keeping with *all* of His divine attributes. This is why His eternal kingdom is a place of matchless beauty, dignity, and glory such that it is pleasing to know that *there will be no end to the increase of His government or of peace* (Isaiah 9:7).

Unlike the cruel despots of this world, Jesus' reign consists of infinite goodness and true peace for He alone has the power to save, forgive, and transform sinners into conformity with his holiness. Such is the matchless Omnipotence of the King of Righteousness. Neither SJI, nor any other philosophy or system of government, can augment or substitute the work of King Jesus.

Taken together, we are warned about the great dangers of any ideology which stands as an affront to the matchless authority of Christ. Because SJI presents itself as a religion replete with its alternate authority, mechanisms of reconciliation and forgiveness, and faux power to transform society, it is, in its entirety, *a blasphemous affront to the majesty, dignity, and power of Jesus Christ.* Its Neo-Marxism places it

---

[481] Of, pertaining to, or of the nature of a despot, or despotism; arbitrary, tyrannical. OED.

within the same dangerous and secular pathway of those who, like Spencer and Marx, produced nothing but misery, oppression, and death.

All these troubling considerations make it especially disturbing that many in the modern church are embracing SJI as if it were a new and useful tool to be used as an aid to, or a substitute for, the Gospel. Yet, the fact that there are those within the professing church who are being lured by this dangerous ideology is not at all new since this isn't the first ideological Trojan horse to be presented at her doors, as Spurgeon rightly reminds us:

> No lover of the gospel can conceal from himself the fact that the days are evil. We are willing to make a large discount from our apprehensions on the score of natural timidity, the caution of age, and the weakness produced by pain; but yet our solemn conviction is that things are much worse in many churches than they seem to be, and are rapidly tending downward. Read those newspapers which represent the Broad School of Dissent, and ask yourself, How much farther could they go? What doctrine remains to be abandoned? What other truth to be the object of contempt? A new religion has been initiated, which is no more Christianity than chalk is cheese; and this religion, being destitute of moral honesty, palms itself off as the old faith with slight improvements, and on this plea usurps pulpits which were erected for gospel preaching.[482]

When secularism flourishes within this fallen world, there should be little surprise. However, when the church opens her doors to such godless thinking, this is an unspeakable disgrace. The encroaching influences of the world must never be allowed to enter the ranks of Christ's people and those who allow them to creep in unnoticed[483] are nothing more than

---

[482] Charles H. Spurgeon, *The Downgrade Controversy 1887*, (Prisbrary Publishing, C. H. Spurgeon Collection Book 12), 385, Kindle.

[483] Jude 4: For certain persons have crept in unnoticed, those who were long beforehand marked out for this condemnation, ungodly persons who turn the

ravenous wolves in sheep's clothing;[484] hirelings who flee at the sight of the enemy.[485]

By this means, SJI's Neo-Marxism continues to make its advance by infusing secularism into the confessional standards of the church, all beneath the cloak of religion. Sadly, the ubiquitous influence of this movement continues to increase while the professing church loses her resolve to resist this contagion.

If this continues, there is a chance that we could re-enter another dark phase in which another pseudo-religion is given the power and authority to exercise tyranny over the people and persecute the true church of Christ. Should this happen *again*, we are comforted with the knowledge of Christ's sovereignty and power to preserve His church: "...I will build My church; and the gates of Hades shall not overpower it." (Matthew 16:18). Whenever Christ's church has faced challenging times, the Lord has providentially preserved her Gospel witness within this fallen world.

Previously, we considered the hostile treatment Spurgeon received for his abolitionist views. Despite the hostility and opposition he received from the American South, God accomplished a remarkable work of providence amidst it all:

Southern Baptists ranked among Spurgeon's chief antagonists. The Mississippi Baptist hoped "no Southern Baptist will now purchase any of that incendiary's books." The Baptist colporteurs of Virginia were forced to return all copies of

---

grace of our God into licentiousness and deny our only Master and Lord, Jesus Christ.

[484] Matthew 7:15: "Beware of the false prophets, who come to you in sheep's clothing, but inwardly are ravenous wolves.

[485] John 10:12: "He who is a hireling, and not a shepherd, who is not the owner of the sheep, beholds the wolf coming, and leaves the sheep, and flees, and the wolf snatches them, and scatters them.

his sermons to the publisher. The Alabama Baptist and Mississippi Baptist "gave the Londoner 4,000 miles of an awful raking" and "took the hide off him." The Southwestern Baptist and other denominational newspapers took the "spoiled child to task and administered due castigation." In the midst of this mayhem, Spurgeon attempted to publish several notebooks of sermons from his earliest ministry. His promise to his readers in 1857 would not be fulfilled, however, due to difficult life circumstances in London. How poetic, then, that 157 years after The Nashville Patriot slandered Spurgeon for his "meddlesome spirit," a publishing house from Nashville would complete the task he failed to accomplish. How symmetrical that Spurgeon's early sermons would be published not by Passmore & Alabaster in London but by Americans. And not only Americans, but Southern Americans. And not only Southern Americans, but Southern Baptist Americans with all the baggage of their bespeckled beginnings.[486]

Though human history is filled with the ebb and flow of great darkness and spiritual awakenings, one thing is for certain: God is accomplishing His sovereign will for His ultimate glory. This is wonderful, mysterious, and tremendously comforting truth. It should remind us that those who take refuge in the Son *are blessed* no matter what happens in this life. And it was this comforting message of the Son of God's sovereignty over all that was given to the hurting and oppressed souls to whom the author of Hebrews wrote:

Hebrews 1:1–3: 1 GOD, after He spoke long ago to the fathers in the prophets in many portions and in many ways, 2 in these last days has spoken to us in His Son, whom He appointed heir of all things, through whom also He made the world. 3 And He is the radiance of His glory and the exact representation of His nature, and upholds all things by the word of His power. When He had made purification of sins, He sat down at the right hand of the Majesty on high.

---

[486] George, *The Lost Sermons of C. H. Spurgeon*, 1.

Thankfully, these truths regarding the Son of God continue to this day because *Jesus Christ is the same yesterday and today, yes and forever (Hebrews 13:8)*. Such words were given to a uniquely oppressed and afflicted people who were losing hope and the only balm that could heal their wounds would come by *fixing their eyes on Jesus*[487] who is the exalted Son of God, the King of kings, the Savior, the Creator, and sustainer of all who *upholds all things by the word of His power.* By the power of His Omnipotent love, those who take refuge in Him are forever blessed. This tremendously beautiful, reverential, and hopeful vision of Christ was supplied as medicine for their hurting souls and it remains as the hope of every generation of God's people.

With all of this in view, we conclude this work with some final words of hope, warning, encouragement, and exhortation in light of all that we have considered regarding Jesus' justice:

1. Beware of *novel* doctrines: How should we respond to the continued avalanche of materials promoting SJI/CRT? We must hold to the priority of God's authoritative Word while remembering that there really is nothing new under the sun. J.C. Ryle warned his readers about the dangers of an "Athenian[488] love of novelty,"[489] which is a clear reference to those Athenian philosophers who "used to spend their time in nothing other than telling or hearing something new." (Acts 17:21). Yet, such a tendency is not constrained to the Athenians alone.

There is within human nature this proclivity of being enticed by things that appear to be new and innovative, but such a love of novelty is quite dangerous. Though the Athenians believed that they were embracing new

---

[487] Hebrews 12:2.

[488] Ryle's mention of *Athenian love of novelty* refers to Acts 17:21: (Now all the Athenians and the strangers visiting there used to spend their time in nothing other than telling or hearing something new.).

[489] J.C. Ryle, *Holiness: Its Nature, Hindrances, Difficulties, & Roots,* (Charles Nolan Publishers, Moscow Idaho, 2001), XXIX.

ideas, they instead were merely rehashing the ancient idolatry of self-worship and racial bigotry.

When we remember that *there really is nothing new under the sun* (Ecclesiastes 1:9), we become better guardians against those who proffer "new" and "novel" doctrines. In reality, the appearance of novelty is merely a guise for what is really being sold: ancient error.

Many today seem to imagine that SJI presents a new way of thinking about the world in which we live, when in reality it is advancing some very old and destructive philosophies. Rather than being new and helpful, it is nothing more than a dangerous distraction from God's ancient wisdom.

2. Our great need for *wisdom and love*: How should we respond to those individuals who are promoting SJI? It is important to remember that the preponderance of SJI in the world today is an opportunity for us to stand up for the truth of God. It is crucial that we listen carefully to those who are promoting this philosophy in view of the fact that some will know little of the subject, while others may be deeply entrenched in the tenets of SJI.

In all cases, we need to speak the truth in love with the goal of heralding the supremacy of Jesus' justice and the message of the Gospel overall. It is often helpful to begin with an inductive approach which calls on the other person to explain their position and define their terms. Only then will we be able to discern the nature of the conversation that is needed, the points of discussion that will be most helpful, and whether or not we need to begin with the basics of the Gospel or enter into more advanced discussions of theology.

In the end, the centerpiece of everything is that we convey the majesty, dignity, and power of King Jesus, doing so with wisdom and love.

3. Beware of *celebritism and the fear of man*: How should we respond when prominent Evangelicals are found promoting SJI? It is my conviction that the modern church has become dangerously distracted from her high calling to *adore* and *reverence* Christ alone. What lures her from this precious priority is that forbidden fruit whereby the homage that is due to the Creator is instead directed towards the creature.[490] Whenever the church is overcome with the

---

[490] Romans 1:25.

fear of man or *celebritism*, she is drawn away from her much needed focus on Christ. *Concerning fear*, SJI effectively plagues the church today because so many dread the charge of "racism" more than they reverence the Almighty. Those who market and promote SJI know full well that by perpetuating the philosophy of "white guilt" they can shame individuals into compliance. But this often results in the many catastrophic errors already reviewed in this book. There is also the problem of *celebritism*, in which the *popularity* of various individuals serves to sway the masses. American culture is addicted to such celebritism, and this dangerous opiate has entered the church as well.

Today's fawning masses will often receive the instructions of popular pastors, enthusiastically embracing their false directives with little to no critical thought or examination. This is a massively dangerous tendency and the fact that many popular pastors are now promoting the contagion of SJI poses a serious threat to Christ's bride (for more on this subject, see appendix II).

4. Seeking Jesus' justice in the *local church*: What should an individual do if their leadership begins to promote SJI within the church? Sadly, this is becoming a common question, especially as more churches fall prey to the influences of SJI.

As with any question about doctrinal matters, ask to meet with one of the elders of the church and be prepared to ask questions with a genuine spirit of inquiry. Your first goal must be to discern if the church is in fact moving in a troubling direction or if you simply have a false perception of things. If it seems clear that your church's leadership is falling to the influence of SJI, humbly express your concerns by means of Scripture in the love of Christ. One never knows what seeds of influence may be planted in simple conversations like these.

However, if there is no further evidence of a change of trajectory for the better, then it is best to leave such an assembly, doing so with a clear description of your choice recorded in a letter and given to the leadership, dispatched with the prayer that they will take your expressed concerns to heart.

Choices such as these must never be made rashly or with a disregard to the souls who will be affected by such a decision.

5. Beware of *romanticism or negativism*: How should we respond to the good, the bad, and the ugly realities of history? As mere mortals we all run the risk of seeing the world around us, whether past or present, with romantic or negative biases. There is always the danger of responding to history like a pendulum, swinging too hard in one direction or the other, and our failure to recognize this will make us slaves of our own subjective biases.

Our examination of Thomas Jefferson revealed this tendency when we focused on those who have romanticized his memory, especially in the area of his views regarding Christianity and slavery. By examining Jefferson's own words, we learned that he isn't the stellar role model that some would have us to believe.

On the other hand, we have examined much of the negativism found within SJI's summary of history, in American society and in the church. Anyone who consumes such literature may become convinced that this nation is the greatest haven of evil on the planet, or that "the church" is a breeding ground for cross burning members of the KKK.

Both extremes blind us to reality, corrupting our ability to be helpful stewards within society and the church. As believers, we have an important responsibility to be fair and objective in our analysis of the past or present because falsified histories help no-one.

6. Beware of *presumption*: How should we relate to highly politicized court cases? Related to the previous point, it is necessary for us to reserve judgment on matters for which we have little or no knowledge. The modern media has nearly perfected the art and science of promoting societal presumption on a massive scale when it comes to covering controversial legal cases. The list of examples seems endless: Tawana Brawley, O.J. Simpson, the Duke lacrosse case, Richard Jewell, the Covington Catholic students, George Zimmerman, Michael Brown, and George Floyd just to name a few. Though these cases had differing contexts and outcomes, the media has learned that heightened attention to controversial cases is big business for them, and they have no hesitation to try such cases in the court of public opinion long before any evidence is confirmed or legal judgments are made.

The great danger that we face in our society comes whenever we feel tempted to join such presumptuous madness and thereby pass premature judgments ourselves. Not only is this toxic influence growing in society at large, but its influence is growing within the church. While it may be understandable to see this problem in the former context, it surely has no place in the latter.

As believers, we must refrain from prejudging cases before facts can be known lest we join this world's systemic evil of slander and gossip.

7. How should we respond to *privilege and poverty?*: Those who consume a regular diet of SJI writings will often express a sense of shame over the blessings and privileges that they enjoy here in America. Along with this, many of these same individuals also express guilt over the presence of poverty in America and around the globe.

First, as we consider one's blessings and privileges, we are reminded of the importance of God's providence, especially when we consider that no one can determine their nation of birth. Because of this there is no inherent reason for an individual to feel guilty for the privileges they enjoy in their native land. What actually matters is how one stewards those blessings and privileges; whether they are used for the flesh or for the glory of God.

This is why we looked at the lives of Granville Sharp and William Wilberforce. The very blessings and privileges that were availed to these men were stewarded for the advancement of the Gospel and for the greater good of mankind. By using the sum total of their lives, training, social connections, and means of communication, they became tremendous instruments for the cause of abolition throughout England, America, and even the whole world.

Second, as we consider the presence of poverty in America and around the globe, we are reminded of the Marxist and Neo-Marxists strains of thought within SJI literature. Whatever equalization that is achieved in Socialism comes at the expense of a loss of personal liberty.

Yet even the Utopian equality and freedom from poverty that is promised in Socialist states is clearly a ruse. Countries that actually practice Socialism have economic classes with profound disparities between the ruling class and the people; with a great number of Socialist states being uniquely impoverished. There is a reason why Jesus said, "the poor you have with you always" (Matthew 26:11).

None of this is mentioned in order to promote indifference towards poverty. As we discussed in chapter 3, the foremost commandment of love prohibits us from having an indifference towards the needs of others. When we have opportunity, we are to do good to all men, especially to those who are of the household of the faith (Galatians 6:10); we must avoid the trap of laziness such that we become a burden to others (1 Thessalonians 4:12, 2 Thessalonians 3:10); we therefore are to labor with our own hands in order that we may have something to share with those who have need (Ephesians 4:28, Luke 3:11).

Moreover, it is crucial to remember James' warnings against being a hearer of the Word rather than a doer of the Word (James 1:22) when he said: "This is pure and undefiled religion in the sight of our God and Father, to visit orphans and widows in their distress, and to keep oneself unstained by the world." (James 1:27).

Here in America, more than 80 percent of the elderly who live alone are women; "two out of three—67 percent—are widows...often in poverty or near poverty."[491] Not only was this a pressing need in the 1st century church (Acts 6:1), but it continues *en masse* in the present day.

On a personal note, this has been a matter of discovery for our own family over the years. Just the privilege of receiving neighbors into our home, many of whom were widows having various needs, has been a tremendous blessing to us and a profound discovery of the lesson of James 1:27. It is a reminder to me that there are a great number of needs that are sometimes just a few steps from one's front door. Rather than marching in the streets to protest poverty, all one has to do is meet one's neighbors and discover that there are a great number of lonely, impoverished, and often infirmed individuals who could benefit from some simple hospitality in Christ (Luke 14:12-14).

8. How do we live in a world of *systemic evil?*: Writing to the church at Corinth, the Apostle Paul expressed his concern that the Devil had led them

---

[491] Don Colburn "Woes of Widows" (The Washington Post, 28 April, 1987). https://www.washingtonpost.com/archive/lifestyle/wellness/1987/04/28/the-woes-of-widows-in-america/c617cb51-77a3-4158-b190-3b7414101339/.

astray "from the simplicity and purity of devotion to Christ"[492] According to Paul, this church had been drawn away from the purity of the Gospel because they openly received false apostles and deceitful workers who preached "another Jesus."[493] When one stops and contemplates this tragedy, we are given a very sobering warning. Corinth had its beginnings, in part, through the faithful ministry of the Apostle Paul (Acts 18), and yet this same church had degraded over time to such an extent that it was flirting with apostasy. By this we are left to wonder how such an assembly could experience this dangerous and traumatic reversal.

Paul explains this matter quite clearly when he described the Devil's predictable scheme: "for even Satan disguises himself as an angel of light. Therefore it is not surprising if his servants also disguise themselves as servants of righteousness; whose end shall be according to their deeds." (2 Corinthians 11:14–15). Paul's brief tutorial on Satan's schemes is far too often ignored or forgotten.

It is important to remember that the Devil isn't in the habit of breaking down the church's doors, identifying himself, and confessing his intention as he attempts to lead others astray. Even a dull fool could sniff out such attempted treachery. Instead, Paul describes for us the well-planned and well-disguised co-belligerence between Satan and his servants. We are not specifically told who these servants were and yet we should remember that both fallen men and the demons serve Satan's agenda, as we have previously reviewed. In view of this, it is likely that he is raising, once again, the full spectrum of systemic evil as consisting of the Devil, his demons, *as well as the sons of disobedience.*

Clearly, Satan seeks to deceive others by investing all of his tactical energies in this matter of *disguising himself as an angel of light;* that is, he

---

[492] 2 Corinthians 11:2–3: 2 For I am jealous for you with a godly jealousy; for I betrothed you to one husband, that to Christ I might present you as a pure virgin.3 But I am afraid, lest as the serpent deceived Eve by his craftiness, your minds should be led astray from the simplicity and purity of devotion to Christ.

[493] 2 Corinthians 11:4: 4 For if one comes and preaches another Jesus whom we have not preached, or you receive a different spirit which you have not received, or a different gospel which you have not accepted, you bear this beautifully.

endeavors to give the appearance of being a servant of God who teaches the truth. And the disguise that is required for this tactical deception is one that is fraught with religious garb and religious language.

Yet, despite this sophistic cover, all that is presented is *another Jesus*: a false savior that can save no-one at all. This is one of the chief reasons why we took the time to uncover the religious nature of SJI. Its religious garb and language may give it a better appearance to some, but in the end it is one of a thousand false gospels created throughout history in order to lead others astray.

However, the chief remedy to this demonic treachery consists of one simple strategy for all of Christ's body. We must remain focused on the simplicity and purity of devotion to Christ. All who hear the voice of the Chief Shepherd and follow Him will never be led astray.

The principles stated within this conclusion are not new at all. God's people have always been called upon to be vigilant, discerning, and cautious in life: "be careful how you walk, not as unwise men, but as wise, making the most of your time, because the days are evil." (Ephesians 5:15-16). Since its inception, the church has needed to "contend earnestly for the faith" (Jude 3) because "certain persons have crept in unnoticed...ungodly persons who turn the grace of God into licentiousness and deny our only Master and Lord, Jesus Christ." (Jude 4).

Such realities heighten the believers' understanding of the importance of *contending earnestly for the faith,* understanding that the Christian life is a spiritual battle against the forces of evil and require a powerful weaponry consisting of the full armor of Almighty God (Ephesians 6:10-18).

Finally, throughout my labors on this book I have on many occasions wondered who might end up reading its content. It has been my hope and prayer that both believers and unbelievers alike will receive this book's message. And so I say to you, dear reader, consider carefully what you have read especially as it relates to your own soul. As Spurgeon has rightly said concerning King Jesus:

"If His first coming does not give you eternal life, His second coming will not. If you do not hide in his wounds when He comes as your Saviour, there will be no hiding place for you when He comes as your Judge."[494]

Dear reader, if you have not yet placed your faith and trust in Christ, my urgent plea is that you would remember and heed the same appeal that has been repeated throughout this book: take refuge in the Son! How blessed are all who take refuge in Him! Psalm 2:12.

---

[494] Charles Haddon Spurgeon, "He Cometh with Clouds," Metropolitan Tabernacle Pulpit Volume 33, October 27, 1887 (Revelation 1:7).

JESUS' JUSTICE

APPENDIX I

PSALM 110
JESUS, THE KING OF RIGHTEOUSNESS

The beauty, depth, and importance of Psalm 110 could very easily justify an entire book, and for this reason I readily admit to the reader that our treatment of this frequently quoted text has been tremendously brief. Moreover, there are a great number of eschatological discussions that typically arise from this important psalm, however, such matters have not been the focus of our study. What has been emphasized is the manner in which Psalm 110 is utilized in several New Testament books in order to convey several core truths about the Messiah's own *nature* and *work*:

1. He is exaltated as YHWH's coregent and equal (Psalm 110:1): THE LORD says to my Lord: "Sit at My right hand, Until I make Thine enemies a footstool for Thy feet."

2. He is the exalted king of the nations (Psalm 110:2): The LORD will stretch forth Thy strong scepter from Zion, saying, "Rule in the midst of Thine enemies."

3. He commands an army of willing servants (Psalm 110:3): Thy people will volunteer freely in the day of Thy power; In holy array, from the womb of the dawn, Thy youth are to Thee as the dew.

4. He is the priestly King of Righteousness (Psalm 110:4): The LORD has sworn and will not change His mind, "Thou art a priest forever According to the order of Melchizedek."

5. As YHWH's coregent He will judge His enemies (Psalm 110:5-6): Psalm 110:5-6: 5 The Lord[495] is at Thy right hand; He will shatter kings in the day of

---

[495] There has been much debate concerning the Messiah's participation in judgment in Psalm 110, especially with respect to verse five. Some argue, in deference to the Masoretic text, that the word "Lord" in verse five refers to YHWH. This would then see the Messiah as an instrument of judgment rather than its source. However, I share the view of those who consider the reference to "Lord" in the fifth verse (אדני, 'ḏny – without the diacritic additions of the later, Masoretic text) as referring to the same "Lord" in verse one: the Messiah. This view sees the Messiah as the subject of the sentence in verse five ("The Lord is at Thy right hand") which conceptually parallels the decree of verse one. Interpretive distinctions such as these are certainly important, however, we must keep in mind the manner in which the Scriptures repeatedly uphold the important message of *coregency* between YHWH and the Messiah within this and other Messianic texts. For example, in Psalm 2, YHWH is the one who actively installs the Messiah as King and gives Him sovereign dominion over the nations, however, it is by the *Son's coming wrath* (Psalm 2:12) that the *nations will be shattered like earthenware* (Psalm 2:9). We see this same manifestation of *coregency* in the text of Revelation 6 when the "kings of the earth and the great men and the commanders and the rich and the strong and every slave and free man, hid themselves in the caves and among the rocks...and they said to the mountains and to the rocks, 'fall on us and hide us from the presence of Him who sits on the throne, and from the wrath of the Lamb; for the great day of *their wrath* (ὀργῆς αὐτῶν) has come; and who is able to stand?" (Revelation 6:16-17). Though the wrath of the Father and the Son are *distinguished* in these passages, we find that their judgment is delivered with *indivisible* unity, justice, omnipotence, and divine authority (see also Acts 17:31 and John 5:22). In the end, caution must be observed against stressing too much of a distinction regarding the coregency of YHWH and His Messiah, particularly in passages where eschatological judgment is in view.

His wrath. 6 He will judge among the nations, He will fill them with corpses, He will shatter the chief men over a broad country.

6. He will ultimately triumph as the undefeated conqueror (Psalm 110:7): He will drink from the brook by the wayside; Therefore He will lift up His head.

This abundantly rich psalm is filled with tremendous solemnity and joy. There is great joy because of the Messiah's eternal redemption and triumph; and there is deep solemnity in view of the nations that are justly crushed because of their rebellion against this sovereign King. Of the many rich truths that are contained in this psalm, its most repeated portion comes from the first verse in which we find the divine declaration (נְאֻם > *neûm*)[496] concerning the Messiah's exalted position at YHWH's "right hand." This crucial revelation affirms the Messiah's coregency[497] with YHWH since "session (being seated) at the right hand of God means joint rule. It thus implies divine dignity, as does the very fact of sitting[498] in God's presence."[499]

---

[496] This root is used exclusively of divine speaking. Hence, its appearance calls special attention to the origin and authority of what is said. Leonard J. Coppes, "1272 נָאַם," ed. R. Laird Harris, Gleason L. Archer Jr., and Bruce K. Waltke, Theological Wordbook of the Old Testament (Chicago: Moody Press, 1999), 541.

[497] Roy B. Zuck, A Biblical Theology of the New Testament, electronic ed. (Chicago: Moody Press, 1994), 96.

[498] The fact that divine dignity was conveyed through the act of sitting (rather than standing) in God's presence is evident in some Jewish traditions relating to angels. As was mentioned in the third chapter, some embraced the heretical belief that the angel Metatron was God's equal because he was given permission to sit in the presence of God. Errors such as these remind us why the author of Hebrews invested so much time demonstrating the supremacy of Christ over the angels: "Of the apostate Archer it is related that when he ascended to Paradise, he saw Metraton, to whom permission was given to remain seated while he

We should also note the parallels between Psalms 2 and 110. In both texts YHWH reveals the Messiah's Kingly authority and coregency (Psalm 110:1; 2:6-8), and this is followed by a promise of divine wrath for all those who fail to bow in submission to His majestic authority (Psalm 110:5-6; 2:9-12). There is also the parallel of redemptive hope for those who take refuge in the Messiah (Psalm 2:12) who is the surety and hope (Psalm 110:4) of all who serve Him (Psalm 110:3). These themes of the Messiah's *exaltation, deliverance,* and *divine judgment* supply a crucial foundation for many New Testament books, especially with respect to the subject of the Messiah's *just and righteous nature.*

Though Christ's work as redeemer and judge yields diametrically opposing results for humanity (heaven and hell, Matthew 25:46), *in either outcome* the righteousness/justice of His own glorious nature is fully revealed. This is why both Psalms 2 and 110 are repeatedly featured in this book. Their disclosure of Jesus' Justice have supplied a firm foundation for our examination of justice. In addition to these important texts, the Gospels repeatedly herald the beauty and glory of Jesus' justice with the promise that He will bring *justice to the nations* (Matthew 12:18)[500] and lead *justice to victory* (Matthew 12:20).

As we observed in the introduction, the Hebrew OT supplies several terms that represent the semantic domain of justice: צֶדֶק, (*ṣeḏeq,* righteous/justice), יָשָׁר (*yāšār,* straight), שָׁלֵם (*šālēm,* perfect) and מִשְׁפָּט (*mišpāṭ,* judgment). Wilson lists *ṣeḏeq* as the most common Hebrew

---

recorded the merits of Israel. Archer said, 'It has been taught that in heaven there is no sitting, contention, back, or weariness. Are there then two Powers!' (Chag. 15a)." Cohen, *Everyman's Talmud,* 102.

[499] Gerhard Kittel ed., *The Theological Dictionary of the New Testament,* (Michigan: Eerdmans Publishing, 1991), III:1089.

[500] Isaiah 42:1: 1 "BEHOLD, My Servant, whom I uphold; My chosen one in whom My soul delights. I have put My Spirit upon Him; He will bring forth justice (מִשְׁפָּט, *mišpāṭ*) to the nations.

term used for the English word justice.[501] Lexically speaking, *ṣedeq* speaks of a *canonical standard or a measuring rule.*[502] Implicit within this thought is the idea of something that is straight[503] (i.e., a *reliable* measuring rod). Therefore, it is no surprise that the word is often used to speak of "the act of doing what is required according to *a standard.*"[504] Even in the English language, the historic use of the word righteous[505] (Old English: *rihtwis*) is self-descriptive in that the transitive-verbal use of *righteous* denoted the thought of "to set right; to justify; to do justice to; to make righteous."[506] As well, the ethical connotation of *rihtwis* described the man who walks in *right wisdom* according to God's standard, rather than the *crooked standard* of this world. In many respects, the semantic domain of our own English word is illustrative of the idea of *ṣedeq* (G. *dikaios*) in its historic form and use. At the core of it all is the notion of God's infallible standard, whether by itself or as imitated by men.

By contrast we should consider this: the mutable standards of men are no match for the unalterable standard of God Himself. As one

---

[501] Within the semantic domain of the English word justice, Wilson presents צֶדֶק, *ṣedeq* as the primary term in addition to יָשָׁר (straight), שָׁלֵם (perfect) and מִשְׁפָּט (judgment). Wilson, *Old Testament Word Studies*, 235-36.

[502] Louw & Nida, *Greek-English Lexicon*, 743.

[503] *ṣādăq* - to be right, straight, i.q. *yāśăr* as of a straight way (see *ṣedeq* Ps. 23:3). Gesenius, W., & Tregelles, S. P. (2003). Gesenius' Hebrew and Chaldee lexicon to the Old Testament Scriptures. Translation of the author's Lexicon manuale Hebraicum et Chaldaicum in Veteris Testamenti libros, a Latin version of the work first published in 1810-1812 under title: Hebräisch-deutsches Handwörterbuch des Alten Testaments.; Includes index. (702). Bellingham, WA: Logos Research Systems, Inc.

[504] Louw & Nida, *Greek-English Lexicon*, 743.

[505] The OED lists righteous as being used, historically, as an adjective, an adverb, a noun and as a verb. Though this last use is now obsolete, it is clear that it contained thought of distributive righteousness/justice.

[506] Ibid.

whose background is in physics, I can't help but to think of the illustration found in the SI system of units.[507]   From 1791 to 1983, the French Academy of Sciences attempted to achieve an unfailing standard of measurement found in what is called a meter. Their search for such a standard definition began with a fraction (1/10,000,000[th]) of the Earth's meridian (from the equator to the North Pole), to the path-length of light as it travels in a vacuum in the time interval of $1/299,792,458^{second}$. The progression of these standards marks great improvements in defining the unit of measurement known as the meter, and yet despite all these improvements over the years, there will always be an associated element of error within this "standard."

All this leads us to a remarkable point of consideration: with all of the refinements that can be introduced into the methods of establishing an absolute standard, there will always be an associated uncertainty simply because of the involvement of fallible men in what is a fallen and mutable world. I offer this to you as a contrasting illustration to the concept of God's righteousness/justice. The *denotative* reality of *ṣedeq* is that God's righteous/just standard is *immutable, holy, and perfect.* There is no associated uncertainty with His standard – because He is the *sine qua non* of all that might ever be called *righteous and just.* In view of this, it must be understood that God's righteousness/justice is infallible, perfect, and completely devoid of impurity.[508] This is why it was essential for us to consult Psalm 110 which clearly identifies Jesus, *by antitype,*[509] as Melchizedek (*mălkiy-ṣeḏeq*) the eternal King of Righteousness/Justice.

---

[507] SI: F. Le Système international d'unités.

[508] Isaiah 64:6 For all of us have become like one who is unclean, And all our righteous deeds are like a filthy garment; And all of us wither like a leaf, And our iniquities, like the wind, take us away.

[509] Christ's identity as the King of Righteousness is established, *by antitype,* through the *witness* (μαρτυρεῖται > *martureitai*) of Psalm 110:4 (Hebrews 7). Thus, the historic Melchizedek (Genesis 14:18-20) serves as the *type* for the *Antitype,* Jesus Christ.

Those who rage in their rebellion against this King of Righteousness will experience nothing but His eternal judgment, but those who take refuge in the Son behold His beauty as their Priest King who forever makes intercession on their behalf, as Spurgeon explains:

> Psalm 110 Verse 4. We have now reached the heart of the psalm, which is also the very centre and soul of our faith. Our Lord Jesus is a Priest King by the ancient oath of Jehovah: "he glorified not himself to be made an high priest, "but was ordained there unto from of old, and was called of God an high priest after the order of Melchizedek. It must be a solemn and a sure matter which leads the Eternal to swear, and with him an oath fixes and settles the decree for ever; but in this case, as if to make assurance a thousand times sure, it is added, "and will not repent." It is done, and done for ever and ever; Jesus is sworn in to be the priest of his people, and he must abide so even to the end, because his commission is sealed by the unchanging oath of the immutable Jehovah. If his priesthood could be revoked, and his authority removed, it would be the end of all]lope and life for the people whom he loves; but this sure rock is the basis of our security—the oath of God establishes our glorious Lord both in his priesthood and in his throne. It is the Lord who has constituted him a priest for ever, he has done it by oath, that oath is without repentance, is taking effect now, and will stand throughout all ages: hence our security in him is placed beyond all question.[510]

This is why Christ's citation of Psalm 110 during Passion Week is so striking. It is filled with redemptive hope as well as the terrors of judgment against the Messiah's enemies. His first quotation of Psalm 110, which left his hearers in a state of silent bewilderment (Matthew 22:46, Mark 12:34, Luke 20:40), revealed a prophetic preview of His coming judgment, especially as He issued a series of stern rebukes and prophetic "woes" against the Scribes and the Pharisees. Then, just prior to His

---

[510] Charles Spurgeon, *The Treasury of David: The Complete Seven Volumes*, 64912-64921, Kindle.

crucifixion, Jesus repeated this royal and messianic psalm as He was being tried before the Council of the Sanhedrin. When the high priest demanded that Jesus answer this question: "tell us whether You are the Christ the Son of God" Jesus first answered in the affirmative, saying, "I am," and then quoted Psalm 110:1 in addition to Daniel 7 "...and you shall see THE SON OF MAN SITTING AT THE RIGHT HAND OF POWER, and COMING WITH THE CLOUDS OF HEAVEN." There was nothing ambiguous about this response of His. Jesus' overall answer affirmed that He was *the* Son of God who would bring justice to the nations (Psalm 110:1) and whose everlasting dominion would *never to be destroyed*.[511] Upon hearing this, the high priest tore his robe and said to the Council, "what further need to we have of witnesses? You have heard *the blasphemy*" (Mark 14:53-65, italics mine). This horrific charge of blasphemy against the Son of God reminds us of the great concerns expressed in the book of Hebrews. Those Jews who rejected Jesus as the Messiah saw Christianity as a blasphemous religion with a false Christ at its center, and many 1st century Christians had to face these accusations on a regular basis. Thus, when the author of Hebrews wrote his letter he was addressing Jewish-believers who regularly faced the onslaught of such accusations, even from those of their own tribal communities. For this reason, the entire book of Hebrews is filled with words of encouragement as well as words of warning to those who would drift from the message of the Gospel of Christ:

Hebrews 2:1–3: 1 FOR this reason we must pay much closer attention to what we have heard, lest we drift away from it. 2 For if the word spoken through

---

[511] Daniel 7:13–14: 13 "I kept looking in the night visions, And behold, with the clouds of heaven One like a Son of Man was coming, And He came up to the Ancient of Days and was presented before Him. 14 "And to Him was given dominion, Glory and a kingdom, that all the peoples, nations, and men of every language Might serve Him. His dominion is an everlasting dominion which will not pass away; and His kingdom is one which will not be destroyed."

angels proved unalterable, and every transgression and disobedience received a just recompense, 3 how shall we escape if we neglect so great a salvation?

In the third chapter of this book we contemplated the solemn nature of these verses. Those who had heard the truth, but were *drifting away in unbelief,* needed to contemplate a very serious question: *how will they escape if they neglect so great a salvation?* This idea of escaping from an imminent danger would make little sense without a serious apprehension of Psalm 110. Within the first chapter of Hebrews, this psalm was used to reveal the Messiah's offices of *redeemer and king*:

1. The Exalted Redeemer: Hebrews 1:3:...When He had made purification of sins, *He sat down at the right hand of the Majesty on high* (Psalm 110:1a, 4)

2. The Reigning King: Hebrews 1:13: But to which of the angels has He ever said, "SIT AT MY RIGHT HAND, UNTIL I MAKE THINE ENEMIES A FOOTSTOOL FOR THY FEET"? (Psalm 110:1b)

As to His latter office, Christ's monarchial rule will result in judgment against all those who oppose Him (Psalm 110:5-6; 2:8-12). This preview of the twofold offices of Jesus Christ is then followed, not only with the warnings of Hebrews 2:1-3, but with a series of repeated warnings against the perils of unbelief (Hebrews 3:12-18, 4:7-13, 5:11-14, 6:1-8). He then proceeds to expand on the supremacy of Christ's priesthood (in the order of Melchizedek) from chapters 7 through 9 and returns to his former summary of Christ's dual role as the exalted redeemer and reigning king *via* Psalm 110:

1. The Exalted Redeemer: Hebrews 10:11–12: 11 And every priest stands daily ministering and offering time after time the same sacrifices, which can never take away sins; 12 but He, having offered one sacrifice for sins for all time, SAT DOWN AT THE RIGHT HAND OF GOD (Psalm 110:1a)

2. The Reigning King: Hebrews 10:13: 13 waiting from that time onward UNTIL HIS ENEMIES BE MADE A FOOTSTOOL FOR HIS FEET. (Psalm 110:1b)

By repeatedly revealing the glory of Christ as the exalted redeemer and returning judge, we find that the author of Hebrews gives us the Apostolic pattern of Gospel exhortation by: *1. Disclosing the majesty, dignity, power, and glory of Christ's work on the cross and 2. Warning those who heard this message but were wandering away from the truth.* Overall, the book of Hebrews is filled with Gospel pleadings based upon the text of Psalm 110:

1. The Exalted Redeemer (Psalm 110:1a):

Hebrews 1:3: And He is the radiance of His glory and the exact representation of His nature, and upholds all things by the word of His power. When He had made purification of sins, *He sat down at the right hand of the Majesty on high*;

Hebrews 8:1: NOW the main point in what has been said is this: we have such a high priest, *who has taken His seat at the right hand of the throne of the Majesty in the heavens*

Hebrews 10:12: but He, having offered one sacrifice for sins for all time, *SAT DOWN AT THE RIGHT HAND OF GOD*,

Hebrews 12:2: fixing our eyes on Jesus, the author and perfecter of faith, who for the joy set before Him endured the cross, despising the shame, and has *sat down at the right hand of the throne of God*.

2. The Reigning King (Psalm 110:1b):

Hebrews 1:13: But to which of the angels has He ever said, "SIT AT MY RIGHT HAND, *UNTIL I MAKE THINE ENEMIES A FOOTSTOOL FOR THY FEET*"?

Hebrews 10:13: waiting from that time onward *UNTIL HIS ENEMIES BE MADE A FOOTSTOOL FOR HIS FEET*.

3. The Priestly King of Righteousness (Psalm 110:4):

Hebrews 5:6: just as He says also in another passage, *"THOU ART A PRIEST FOREVER ACCORDING TO THE ORDER OF MELCHIZEDEK."*

Hebrews 6:20: where Jesus has entered as a forerunner for us, having become *a high priest forever according to the order of Melchizedek.*

Hebrews 7:17–21: 17 For it is witnessed of Him, *"THOU ART A PRIEST FOREVER ACCORDING TO THE ORDER OF MELCHIZEDEK."* 18 For, on the one hand, there is a setting aside of a former commandment because of its weakness and uselessness 19 (for the Law made nothing perfect), and on the other hand there is a bringing in of a better hope, through which we draw near to God. 20 And inasmuch as it was not without an oath 21 (for they indeed became priests without an oath, but He with an oath through the One who said to Him, *"THE LORD HAS SWORN AND WILL NOT CHANGE HIS MIND, 'THOU ART A PRIEST FOREVER'");*

In Matthew Henry's commentary on Psalm 110 he begins with these words: "This psalm is pure gospel"[512] and he is right. The entire structure and argument of the book of Hebrews rests principally on Psalm 110, especially in view of its repeated reminders of the Messiah's twofold offices as redeemer and king. As such, it issues many appeals to the Gospel as our only hope, but remains faithful to underscore the consequences that remain for those forsake Jesus:

Hebrews 10:12: but He, having offered one sacrifice for sins for all time, SAT DOWN AT THE RIGHT HAND OF GOD...

Hebrews 10:26–31: 26 For if we go on sinning willfully after receiving the knowledge of the truth, there no longer remains a sacrifice for sins, 27 but a certain terrifying expectation of judgment, and THE FURY OF A FIRE

---

[512] Henry, *Matthew Henry's Commentary*, 903.

293

WHICH WILL CONSUME THE ADVERSARIES.28 Anyone who has set aside the Law of Moses dies without mercy on the testimony of two or three witnesses. 29 How much severer punishment do you think he will deserve who has trampled under foot the Son of God, and has regarded as unclean the blood of the covenant by which he was sanctified, and has insulted the Spirit of grace? 30 For we know Him who said, "VENGEANCE IS MINE, I WILL REPAY." And again, "THE LORD WILL JUDGE HIS PEOPLE." 31 It is a terrifying thing to fall into the hands of the living God.

This sobering warning, in context, reveals that nothing else but a *terrifying expectation of judgment* will remain for *all* who sinfully reject the *knowledge of the truth* regarding God's provision of *a sacrifice for sins* (Hebrews 10:1-25).[513] The sacrifice for sin that is so desperately needed has been supplied in the person and work of the Son of God (Hebrews 1:3; 10:1-18).

As we observed in the third chapter of this book, the author of Hebrews never suggests that his audience's extensive oppression and suffering could offer salvific efficacy. Instead, the only suffering that was efficacious for their salvation was the suffering that Jesus endured in the sacrifice of Himself, dying as our substitute as the sinless *King of Righteousness (Melchizedek).* Unlike the Old Testament priests who repeatedly offered temporary, ineffectual, and *imperfect* sacrifices with blood not their own, the Son of God was manifested in the flesh to put away sin by the righteous sacrifice of Himself, not offering the blood of goats and calves,[514] but offering the sacrifice of His own blood, thereby

---

[513] "After the receiving" (accusative case of the articular infinitive second aorist active of λαμβανω [lambanō] after μετα [meta]). Knowledge (ἐπιγνωσιν [epignōsin]). "Full knowledge," as in 6:4f. There remaineth no more (οὐκετι ἀπολειπεται [ouketi apoleipetai]). "No longer is there left behind" (present passive indicative as in 4:9), for one has renounced the one and only sacrifice for sin that does or can remove sin (10:1–18). A.T. Robertson, *Word Pictures*, Heb 10:26.

[514] Hebrews 9:23-26.

obtaining eternal redemption for His people.[515] Whereas some rabbinic teachers of the day would have taught that the oppression of Roman rule would establish sufficient merit to deliver one's soul, the author of Hebrews pointed his readers to only one hope: the Lord Jesus Christ and His *righteous sacrifice*. Only His suffering and sacrifice for sins can deliver the sinner from the coming day of wrath: a wrath that is *justly due to all* because *all have sinned and fall short of the glory of God (Romans 3:23)*. Thus, when this priestly King of Righteousness died on the cross, He did so as the sinner's *just* substitute, so that God may be *just* and the *justifier* of the one who has faith in Jesus (Romans 3:26). Without this sacrifice for sin, all that is left is the *terrifying expectation of judgment* (Hebrews 10:27). Why? Because apart from Jesus' holy and just sacrifice, *it is a terrifying thing to fall into the hands of the living God (Hebrews 10:31)*.

May it never be inferred that these warnings in the book of Hebrews were designed in order to coerce or cajole its readers in some twisted sense of psychological manipulation. Many who complain about the warnings in Scripture frequently issue this charge. To be sure, there will always be some preachers who will speak of the fires of hell apart from the soothing waters of the Gospel. Yet this entirely contradicts the apostolic preaching of the Gospel which presents the *promises* of the Gospel as well as the *penalties* that come to those who reject the Savior. No sinner enters into saving faith by the manipulations of men, but by the sovereign drawing of the Holy Spirit. Though Psalm 110 is filled with grave warnings of coming judgment, it also supplies the sweet and tender doctrine of His gracious work of salvation and sanctification, as Spurgeon well summarizes:

Psalm 110 Verse 3. Thy people shall be willing in the day of thy power, in the beauties of holiness from the womb of the morning: thou hast the dew of thy youth. In consequence of the sending forth of the rod of strength, namely, the

---

[515] Hebrews 9:11-14.

power of the gospel, out of Zion, converts will come forward in great numbers to enlist under the banner of the Priest King. Given to him of old, they are his people, and when his power is revealed, these hasten with cheerfulness to own his sway, appearing at the gospel call as it were spontaneously, even as the dew comes forth in the morning. This metaphor is further enlarged upon, for as the dew has a sparkling beauty, so these willing armies of converts have a holy excellence and charm about them; and as the dew is the lively emblem of freshness, so are these converts full of vivacity and youthful vigour, and the church is refreshed by them and made to flourish exceedingly. Let but the gospel be preached with divine unction, and the chosen of the Lord respond to it like troops in the day of the mustering of armies; they come arrayed by grace in shining uniforms of holiness, and for number, freshness, beauty, and purity, they are as the dewdrops which come mysteriously from the tooming's womb. Some refer this passage to the resurrection, but even if it be so, the work of grace in regeneration is equally well described by it, for it is a spiritual resurrection. Even as the holy dead rise gladly into the lovely image of their Lord, so do quickened souls put on the glorious righteousness of Christ, and stand forth to behold their Lord and serve him. How truly beautiful is holiness! God himself admires it. How wonderful also is the eternal youth of the mystical body of Christ! As the dew is new every morning, so is there a constant succession of converts to give to the church perpetual juvenility.[516]

For those who forsake the Lord's gracious salvation, they are left with nothing more than this solemn warning: "The Lord is at Thy right hand; He will shatter kings in the day of His wrath. He will judge among the nations, He will fill them with corpses, He will shatter the chief men over a broad country." (Psalm 110:5–6). Again, Spurgeon helps us to consider the beauty and terror of these verses:

The last verses of this psalm we understand to refer to the future victories of the Priest King. He shall not forever sit in waiting posture, but shall come into the fight to end the weary war by his own victorious presence. He will lead the final charge in person; his own right hand and his holy arm shall get unto him

---

[516] Spurgeon, *The Treasury of David*, 64893-64906, Kindle.

the victory. ... In the last days all the kingdoms of the earth shall be overcome by the kingdom of heaven, and those who dare oppose shall meet with swift and overwhelming ruin. What are kings when they dare oppose the Son of God? A single stroke shall suffice for their destruction.[517]

In the spirit of Psalm 110 and the book of Hebrews, this work has sought to present the blessed promises of the Gospel while issuing the requisite warnings that remain for those who have heard the truth, but are *drifting away* from its core tenets (Hebrews 2:1); and SJI is clearly leading many away from the core tenets of the Gospel. Because the teachings and propositions of SJI are a blasphemous affront to Jesus Christ, the exalted and returning King of Righteousness, it must be made clear that those who proffer its core tenets do so as the enemies of the Gospel. The nations have raged against the Lord and His Anointed King throughout human history, but we must remember that the Lord delights in extending His mercy to all who call out to Him in faith (Ezekiel 33:11). Because of this precious truth, we can say with the Apostle Paul: "...we also urge you not to receive the grace of God in vain— for He says, "AT THE ACCEPTABLE TIME I LISTENED TO YOU, AND ON THE DAY OF SALVATION I HELPED YOU"; behold, now is "THE ACCEPTABLE TIME," behold, now is "THE DAY OF SALVATION" (2 Corinthians 6:1–2).

---

[517] Ibid., 64942-64948.

JESUS' JUSTICE

APPENDIX II

THE FEAR OF MAN VS.
THE FEAR OF ALMIGHTY GOD

In the fifth chapter of this book we examined the remarkable power that the fear of man can have over the life of an individual. Those who feared public humiliation and purgatorial punishment eagerly threw their coins into Tetzel's coffers, falsely hoping for redemption. In the modern day, many throw their coins into the coffers of various SJI pedagogues for fear of being branded as a "racist" and being shunned by society. This fear of being labelled as a racist is quite strong and has proven to be a powerful tool of manipulation against those who are prone to fearing man rather than fearing Almighty God.

To those reading this book, who are followers of Christ, let me simply state that such conduct is sin. As those who have been bought with a price, we are to glorify God and reverentially serve Him with the sum total of our being (1 Corinthians 6:20). Such reverence is a tender and loving work of grace which draws God's children closer to Him, "...I will put the fear of Me in their hearts so that they will not turn away from Me" (Jeremiah 32:40). This godly fear is a cure for our spiritual double-mindedness: "Teach me Thy way, O LORD; I will walk in Thy truth. Unite my heart to fear Your name" (Psalm 86:11) and it is central to genuine wisdom, for without it we become utter fools, for "the fear of the Lord is the beginning of wisdom" (Psalm 111:10). Such fear gives us a holy hatred for evil, "The fear of the Lord is to hate evil" (Proverbs 8:13) and it helps us to see that God's forgiveness of the sinner is truly *awesome*,[518] "...there is forgiveness with Thee, that Thou mayest be feared" (Psalm 130:4). Without godly reverence we fall short of the heavenly standard of true worship, "...Give praise to our God, all you His bond-servants, *you who fear Him*, the small and the great." (Revelation 19:5, italics mine). Overall, as stated earlier, those who fear God as He deserves are entrusted with His banner of truth, "Thou hast given a banner to those who fear Thee, that it may be displayed because of the truth. [Selah]" (Psalm 60:4). Many will flock to a deity that is portrayed as having a universal love, mercy, and grace for all without exception, but fewer still will bow the knee to the One who is worthy of the creature's unmitigated awe, reverence, and obedience. Any other priority leads to a treacherous pathway. One of the great models of such reverential worship was clearly established by the early church in Jerusalem, as recorded in Acts chapter two:

> Acts 2:41–47: 41 So then, those who had received his word were baptized; and there were added that day about three thousand souls. 42 And they were continually devoting themselves to the apostles' teaching and to fellowship, to the breaking of bread and to prayer. 43 And everyone kept feeling a sense of awe [*phobos* - fear]; and many wonders and signs were taking place through the apostles. 44 And all those who had believed were together, and had all things in common; 45 and they began selling their property and possessions, and were sharing them with all, as anyone might have need. 46 And day by day continuing with one mind in the temple, and breaking bread from house to house, they were taking their meals together with gladness *àgalliasei* – extreme joy] and sincerity of heart [*apheloteti* - humility, simplicity], 47 praising [*ainountes*] God, and having favor with all the people. And the Lord was adding to their number day by day those who were being saved.

---

[518] Our modern culture has sadly degraded the word *awesome* to a slang equivalent of the term "cool," however, in this book this biblical word is used in its historic, denotative sense of that which inspires *awe* or *fear* in an individual.

This simple section of Scripture reveals the very *simplicity and purity of devotion to Christ* that Paul called for in 2 Corinthians 11:3. In describing these brethren, Luke tells us nothing about musical styles or church programs; instead, he reveals some specific attitudes which characterized their worship: *fear, extreme joy, and sincerity of heart.* How *unsurprising* it is that the Holy Spirit would yield such affections for Christ in addition to what we already gleaned from our examination of Psalm 2: "Worship the LORD with reverence, and rejoice with trembling." (Psalm 2:11). This call of joyful and reverential worship is the privilege of all God's children throughout the generations.

In Acts, Luke mentions that these early believers had a humility, or sincerity of heart (*aphelotēti*), which clearly indicates that they were no longer the prisoners of their own pride and hedonistic selfishness, but with gladness of heart, they shared their possessions with those in need as servants of Christ. As for their fear and extreme joy, such affections are evident in their continual devotion (*proskarterountes*)[519] to Christ's authoritative instructions for the church: *And they were continually devoting themselves to the apostles' teaching and to fellowship, to the breaking of bread and to prayer* (Acts 2:42). These beautiful signs of genuine life in the Jerusalem church are deeply encouraging, for they direct us to the path and trajectory which honors Christ. Alternately, the church at Jerusalem was the very antithesis of the church at Sardis (Revelation 3:1-6) which had a reputation for being alive, even though it was dead. In the current day, we must wonder if modern Evangelicalism will move in a trajectory which leans towards the church at Jerusalem, or towards the church at Sardis. Only time will tell, but in the meantime we must take heed unto ourselves and guard against the irreverence and shallowness of heart which leads to the graveyard of Sardis. We are all

---

[519] Luke's use of the present active participle of *proskartereō* reveals the perpetual nature of their devotion to Christ's authority and prescribed activities of the church.

imperfect members of our respective flocks, and we must take care to grow in Christ and thereby become better contributors to our respective assemblies.

Church leaders must be careful to uphold nothing else but the standards of God's word, rather than becoming engrossed with what the contemporary culture is doing. If our churches are growing in devotion to Christ and His word (*Solus Christus* and *Sola Scriptura*), as seen in the simplicity of worship at Jerusalem, then we should thank God for this and pray for His increase in such a direction. Churches that are able to grow in such a simplicity and purity of devotion to Christ represent the same kind of church piety, fellowship, and mission described by Bunyan in *The Pilgrim's Progress.* In his allegory, Bunyan called such an ideal church *The Palace Beautiful* which offers important reminders regarding the true church's mission, conflict, and opposition in this world. As soon as Christian saw the palace he proceeded towards it, but was momentarily hindered by the sight of two lions on either side of the road. He then recalled meeting two men earlier, Mistrust and Timorous, who were traveling to the city of Zion until they saw the lions and ran away in fear. Christian, also fearful for his life, proceeded with great trepidation until the Porter of the palace (i.e., a doorkeeper – pastor: John 10:3) called upon him to press on firmly in faith:

> "But the Porter at the lodge, whose name is Watchful, perceiving that Christian made a halt, as if he would go back, cried unto him, saying, 'Is thy strength so small?' Mark 4:40. 'Fear not the lions, for they are chained, and are placed there for trial of faith where it is, and for discovery of those that have none: keep in the midst of the path, and no hurt shall come unto thee.'"

Bunyan helps us to see several important principles in this portion of his allegory. *First,* he shows us the great danger of fearing anything or anyone but God alone. Christian had become paralyzed with fear until the Porter exhorted him to cease from such fear and proceed on his journey. Only then was he able to make progress in the right direction. *Second,* once

Christian came to the palace, he asked the Porter about whose house it was. The Porter's answer was this: "This house was built by the Lord of the hill, and he built it for the *relief* and *security* of pilgrims." Bunyan's use of the words *relief* and *security* remind us of what the church must supply for Christ's sheep. Genuine *relief* comes to the believer's heart through a trust in Christ and the heralding of His authoritative word; however, beneath the banner of faux religion, the people will become distressed and dispirited as sheep without a shepherd (Matthew 9:36). The church is also to be a place of spiritual *security* for Christ's sheep rather than a place of danger. We are reminded of Jude's prophetic rebukes of those wolves who had *crept in unnoticed* within the walls of the church, seeking to ravage the sheep with their false teachings. Shepherds who allow such carnage are not shepherds at all because the church must be a haven of safety. *Third*, Christian was greeted by Piety, Prudence, and Charity who reviewed and discussed his testimony of faith and his progress of life. In this lengthy portion of the narrative, Bunyan shows us just how important it is for the church to receive into its membership only those who have genuine faith in Christ. And so as he described The Palace Beautiful, we find that those who had genuine faith were eagerly received and with great joy they feasted on their conversation about the Savior and His redeeming love:

> The table was furnished with "the best of meats and the finest of wines."13 All their conversation at the table was about the Lord of the Hill: such as what He had done, why He did what He did, and why He had built that house. From what they said, I perceived that He had been a great warrior and had fought with and slain the one who had the power of death,14 but that He hadn't done it without great danger to himself, and this made me love Him all the more."[520]

---

[520] John Bunyan, John; Hazelbaker, L. Edward, *The Modern English Edition of Pilgrim's Progress* (Bridge-Logos), 1688-1692, Kindle.

The richness of their godly dialogue was then followed by an important step for Christian, which depicts the goal and priority of every Christian within the church:

"The next day, they took Christian and led him into the Armory where they showed him all kinds of equipment that their Lord had provided for Pilgrims. This equipment included the Sword, Shield, Helmet, Breastplate, Prayers, and Shoes that will not wear out.28 There was enough of all this there to equip for the service of their Lord as many people as there are stars in the sky for multitude."[521]

It is in this crucial station (the armory) that Christian was equipped with the full armor of God and thereby readied for the remainder of his journey to his heavenly home. As for the bounty of supplies found within the armory, Bunyan reminds us that *there was enough of this to harness out as many men for the service of their Lord as there be stars in the heaven for multitude.* Within this small section of *The Pilgrim's Progress* we have a simple yet beautiful picture of what Christ's church is designed to do: to equip Christ's sheep amidst a world of great, Satanic hostility:

Ephesians 6:11–13: 11 Put on the full armor of God, that you may be able to stand firm against the schemes of the devil. 12 For our struggle is not against flesh and blood, but against the rulers, against the powers, against the world forces of this darkness, against the spiritual forces of wickedness in the heavenly places. 13 Therefore, take up the full armor of God, that you may be able to resist in the evil day, and having done everything, to stand firm.

Bunyan's allegory illustrates the profound truth of Scripture which teaches that all of the power and authority of this dark world of systemic evil is impotent against Christ and His church. As we have already considered, the whole world lies in the power of the evil one (1 John 5:19) and the world forces of darkness and wickedness rage on a daily basis,

---

[521] Ibid, 1733-1736.

issuing deceptions and temptations to the church without end. However, when we see Satan's lions, we must remember that they are chained and restrained by our sovereign Lord who alone has the keys of death and Hades.[522] Our place of safety is in the pathway of *His truth* and the building of *His making,* rather than in this world which is passing away.

May it be that our estimation of the importance and value of Christ's church would increase to the end that we would labor more for its unity, up-building, and outreach to the lost. And the voice of affirmation that we should seek the most comes not from the praise and accolades of men, but from that gracious expression given from the One who will one day say, *well done, good and faithful servant.*[523] In the end, we must be most invested in Christ's view of us above all.

Our calling as believers is to uphold the priorities of *Solus Christus* and *Sola Scriptura* as individuals and as Christ's body. We must therefore serve one another by subjecting ourselves to one another in the fear of Christ (Ephesians 5:21), magnifying His supremacy while guarding against any competitors to His office, whatever their popularity may be. As Christ's body we are to unfurl the banner of truth which He has entrusted to those who fear Him (Psalm 60:4), heralding a salvation that is by grace alone (*Sola Gratia*), through faith alone (*Sola Fide*) in Christ alone (*Solus Christus*), all for the glory of God alone (*Soli Deo Gloria*). In order to pursue this central mission of the church, we must seek to decrease so that Christ may increase in our individual lives (John 3:30), in our homes, in His church, and in this fallen world that needs Him so desperately.

Dear brethren, let us serve one another in the *love, joy, and fear of our blessed Lord and Savior, Jesus Christ (Ephesians 5:21).*

---

[522] Revelation 1:17-20.
[523] Matthew 25:21.

JESUS' JUSTICE

APPENDIX III

THE HONOUR
OF THE HOLY SCRIPTURES

As far back as 2012 I felt the necessity to write this book and yet I only began constructing its first sentences in the early weeks of 2021. Clearly, in God's providence, I needed those intervening years of study and preparation before coming to this place. As well, after completing most of its manuscript, I came to discover that I still wasn't prepared to write this book's final pages. This is because of my latent discovery of Mr. Granville Sharp. When I say latent, I mean that I discovered his voluminous labors as an abolitionist only recently, even though I have known his name since my days in seminary. Every pastor who has studied Greek grammar knows of Sharp in light of the grammatical rule that bears his name, known as *the Granville Sharp rule,* which applies to TSKS Greek constructions (<u>T</u>he + <u>S</u>ubstantive + *kai* + <u>S</u>ubstantive).[524] Yet despite

---

[524] "The following rule by Granville Sharp of a century back still proves to be true: `When the copulative KAI connects two nouns of the same case, if the article HO or any of its cases precedes the first of the said nouns or participles, and is not repeated before the second noun or participle, the latter always relates to the same person that is expressed or described by the first noun or participle; i.e., it denotes a further description of the first-named person.'" H. E. Dana, ThD. And Julius R. Mantey, ThD., D.D., *A Manual Grammar of the Greek New Testament* (New York: Macmillan Publishing Co., 1994), 147.

such universal knowledge of his rule, Sharp is little known for much of anything else. When I began reading Sharp's works I was deeply struck by what a fierce champion of the Gospel he was. My initial interest in his work began when I came across this passage of his (cited in the seventh chapter):

> But it is not enough, that the Laws of England exclude Slavery merely from this island, whilst the grand Enemy of mankind triumphs in a toleration, throughout our Colonies, of the most monstrous oppression to which human nature can be subjected! And yet this abominable wickedness has not wanted advocates, who, in a variety of late publications, have attempted to palliate the guilt, and have even ventured to appeal to Scripture for the support of their uncharitable pretensions; so that I am laid under a double obligation to answer them, because it is not the cause of Liberty alone for which I now contend, but for that which I have still much more at heart, the honour of the holy Scriptures, the principles of which are entirely opposite to the selfish and uncharitable pretentions of our American Slaveholders and African Traders.[525]

Among the many important elements within this passage is GS's heart-felt desire to contend for *the honor of the holy Scriptures*. The fact that this was his chief goal speaks volumes about his priorities. Though he wrote as many as 61 books and pamphlets throughout his lifetime, I chose to focus on his works dealing with slavery and relied most heavily on other sources like Prince Hoare's *Memoirs of Granville Sharp*, which stands above any other work about his life. But in addition to Hoare, I also relied on Charles Stuart's, *A Memoir of Granville Sharp*, and also came to discover contributions by Daniel B. Wallace, author of *Greek Grammar Beyond the Basics*,[526] as well as James Walvin, author of *The Zong*. I

---

[525] Sharp, *Extract...of Tolerating Slavery*, 2-3.

[526] Though Wallace offers some commentary about GS when describing the grammatical rule that bears his name, his online article, *"Granville Sharp: A Model of Evangelical Scholarship and Social Activism,"* (Bible.org, June 30 2004)

mention all this for the benefit of those who desire further information about Sharp beyond what is supplied in this short appendix.

Granville Sharp was born on 10 November 1735, in Durham England, to Judith Wheler and Thomas Sharp. In his early years he served as an apprentice for several linen-factory owners who represented a wide variety of beliefs. These early experiences, as GS has noted, "taught me to make a proper distinction between the opinions of men and their persons."[527] In two such experiences, GS was challenged by a Jew regarding biblical prophecies, and by a Socinian concerning the Trinity and the atonement of Christ. As a result of these early debates, GS set forth to study the Greek and Hebrew languages in order to become more learned in the Scriptures.[528] GS was 22 years old when his mother passed away in 1757, and his father died the following year. During this same time he began work as a clerk in the Ordnance Office at the Tower of London, but continued his biblical studies in full force. In 1765 GS began his defense of Jonathan Strong, which launched our summary of his anti-slavery work in the seventh chapter. As we learned, his continued involvement in the abolitionist cause would eventually include his strenuous efforts to lead the Colonies to this important understanding: if liberty was to be established *for one* then liberty must be established *for all* on the scriptural basis of a shared humanity.[529] Yet, despite his best efforts, this principle was not upheld at the time of America's declared independence. But GS was not in the habit of surrendering important causes, nor could he, in good conscience, resign from the priority of warning those who perpetuated slavery outside of England.

---

will supply the reader with a much more thorough summary of the life and achievements of GS:

https://bible.org/article/granville-sharp-model-evangelical-scholarship-and-social-activism.

[527] Hoare, *Memoirs*, 28.

[528] Ibid., 29.

[529] Sharp, *A Declaration*, 28.

On January 23rd 1807 representatives from the West India Planters introduced a petition before the House of Lords in an effort to kill the proposed *Act for the Abolition of the Slave Trade*. This event stirred GS into action whereby he wrote, *The System of Colonial Law Compared with the Eternal Laws of God,*[530] in 1807. In this work, GS noted that the opposing petition contained thirteen lengthy paragraphs, but had one small section that fatally corrupted the whole of their argument. Within this eighth and smallest paragraph, it was stated that the Abolition of the Slave Trade bill was problematic because it conflicted with the laws of the colonies. But this was the Achilles Heel of their position because, as GS pointed out, since Colonial law was in violation of the Law of God in view of its continued "toleration of slavery and oppression."[531]

---

[530] The complete title is: *The System of Colonial Law Compared with the Eternal Laws of God and with the Indispensable Principles of the English Constitution.*

[531] "It is therefore my duty, most humbly to suggest, that the examination of one single paragraph out of the thirteen...will afford just and legal grounds for a full and incontrovertible determination *against every other assertion contained in the whole petition*, which will save, to their Lordships, much valuable time. For the petitioners have declared, (not only *unjustly*, but also *imprudently* for their own cause) in their 8th paragraph, 'that the operation of the Bill, if it shall pass into a Law, will be to violate the system of Colonial Law *relative to* property, &c.' This assertion naturally prompts a prior consideration, on the opposite side of the question, before it can be deemed worthy of any, even the least, attention, viz, Whether, on, the contrary, 'the System of Colonial law,' doth not itself violate the whole System of English Law, nay the very foundation of Law, Justice, and Righteousness...all must agree, (I mean all that are learned in the Law, and duly acquainted with the principles declared by the most ancient and approved writers on the English constitution,) that '*the System of Colonial Law,*' which tolerates slavery and oppression, is absolutely contrary to the Laws of God, national and revealed, and, of course, is contrary to the English Constitution, to which all our Kings are sworn; and therefore contrary also to the King's Crown and Dignity, because every human being, in any part of the King's dominions, at

This recalls to mind the disparate treatment of slaves in England and the Colonies. In the seventh chapter we reviewed the case of Somerset v. Stewart in which Sharp argued that there was no "positive law" supporting slavery in England. This argument became the foundational reasoning by which James Somerset was declared a free man. Without a positive law protecting slavery, there was no sense in which Somerset could be retained as a slave. While this legal maneuver didn't abolish slavery, it did create a juridical standard in England that was different than what was upheld in the colonies. Thus, GS exposed this contradiction by the standard of English law, but then revealed *the ultimate authority of his argument*:

> These are the grounds of my confidence, that *"the System of Colonial Law,"* cannot possibly *be favoured* by any Peer that is *learned in the Law;* but I have still *more sure grounds of confidence* in the decided determination of the HOLY SCRIPTURES on this particular point; and I have, therefore, added at the end of this paper the Extract of a letter (dated 3rd Oct. 1806 [*Extract on the Extreme Wickedness, and total Illegality of Tolerating Slavery in any Part of the British Dominions*]).[532]

In this *Extract on the Extreme Wickedness and total Illegality of Tolerating Slavery,* GS quoted several OT prophets, to include Jeremiah (chapter 22:13), just as William Wilberforce would do 16 years later in his *Appeal to the Religion, Justice, and Humanity of the Inhabitants of the British Empire in behalf of the Negro Slaves in the West Indies*: "Woe to him who builds his house without righteousness and his upper rooms without justice, who uses his neighbor's services without pay and does not give him his wages." (Jeremiah 22:13). Any student of Sharp's works will know that his principal appeal was always to the authority of holy

---

home or abroad, not only natives, but also strangers, while they reside therein, are certainly entitled to the full protection of the King's Courts, without *respect of persons.* Sharp, *The System of Colonial Law,* 9-10.

[532] Ibid.

Scripture, and he even anticipated the complaints of those who likely disdained such a priority, as he stated in his classic work, *The Law of Retribution; or A Serious Warning to Great Britain and her Colonies, founded on unquestionable Examples of God's Temporal Vengeance against Tyrants, Slave-holders, and Oppressors*:

> I am well aware, indeed, how very unfashionable it is, now-a-days, to quote *Scripture*, when matters of *Law, Politics,* or *Trade* are called in question; yet I flatter myself that the following examples, drawn from thence, are perfectly suitable for my present point, and consequently must have weight to convince all persons, who sincerely acknowledge the *Truth of the Scriptures*, that we have the greatest reason to apprehend the infliction of some heavy Judgment from Almighty God upon these Kingdoms, on account of the monstrous load of Guilt which the British Subjects, *on each side of the Atlantic*, have incurred by the *Oppressions* above-mentioned.[533]

In all his contests against slavery, he remained concerned over the great potential of losing ground in this battle through various compromises. He knew that there would always be those who would seek to preserve slavery, and the representatives of the West India Planters who sought to appeal the Abolition of the Slave Trade bill were further evidence of such a problem. This is why he wasted no time in opposing their appeal. There was also the problem of those who sought to overturn slavery with a piecemeal approach, beginning with the dissolution of the slave trade and then concluding with the abolition of slavery itself. Sharp always opposed this reasoning because of the compromise of justice it represented. Thus, he added this qualification to *The System of Colonial Law Compared with the Eternal Laws of God and with the Indispensable Principles of the English Constitution*:

---

[533] Granville Sharp, *The Law of Retribution; or A Serious Warning to Great Britain and her Colonies, founded on unquestionable Examples of God's Temporal Vengeance against Tyrants, Slave-holders, and Oppressors*, (London: W Richardson, 1776), 3-4.

The worthy promoters of the Bill for the *Abolition of the Slave-Trade,* have generally conceived (with exception to myself) that there was no necessity to bring forward the farther question respecting the illegality of SLAVERY in the Colonies, because they wished for a *gradual Abolition* of the Colonial oppression, hoping that, if *the Trade was abolished,* some prudent regulations would of course be soon adopted to supersede the other. But the PLANTERS and MERCHANTS themselves have brought forward the necessity of this *additional* measure by their imprudent charge against the Bill, urging that it would *"violate the System of Colonial Law"* – a charge which certainly demands an immediate declaration that the whole *"System of Colonial Law"* is totally ILLEGAL, and inconsistent with every just principle of English Law.[534]

Those who had petitioned against the abolition of the slave trade expressed their concerns over a possible slave revolt, similar to what had taken place in Haiti (Hayti) in 1804. Their concern was that the prospect of freedom may instigate the rise of a "black power" that would lead to a violent revolt, endangering the slaveholders in the process. In response to this, Sharp reminded these petitioners that they needed to be concerned about a much more dangerous "Black Power," that is, the Devil who had enslaved these enslavers of men:

The Petitioners have ample reason, indeed, to "shrink with horror"..."from a contemplation of these scenes which that country has frightfully exhibited,"- but when it is manifest that this pretended HORROR has no other source but a self-interested jealousy that Parliament will "violate" (as they say) their "System of Colonial Law," (thus proving that they really feel no compunction for their enormous guilt in having so long, and so obstinately, persisted in that gross perversion of all the indispensable principles of Natural Justice and Righteousness,) it is high time to warn them of the actual "existence of a BLACK POWER" which is infinitely more dangerous to their most important interests than the Freed Men of Hayti[535] can possibly be-For the Power of Darkness,-

---

[534] Sharp, *The System of Colonial Law*, 9-10.
[535] This is an archaic spelling of Haiti.

"the Prince of this World" hath unhappily inveloped[536] (as it seems) their faculties of discernment, on this particular subject, in so black a cloud of mercenary prejudices,-in such a "mist of darkness" (the most dangerous "BLACK POWER!") that even the Petitioners themselves seem entangled in the toils of this Kidnapper, so as to be in manifest danger of being led away as the SLAVES and PROPERTY of this cruel DEALER in the SOULS OF MEN, if they do not, by a timely repentance, revolt from him and break his fetters, that they may recover their natural powers of distinction in morality, to discern GOOD from EVIL, RIGHT from WRONG, JUSTICE from INJUSTICE...[537]

At the conclusion of his work, *The System of Colonial Law Compared with the Eternal Laws of God,* GS included his *Extract of a Letter on the Extreme Wickedness and total Illegality of Tolerating Slavery in any Part of the British Dominions,* in which he issued severe warnings in view of the "righteous judgment of God" against those who would seek to preserve the slave trade, and slavery with it. In all of this, it seems impossible to imagine the enormity of what Sharp and others like him faced in their opposition against slavery. Much of the globe remained engulfed in this historic practice and for this reason the abolitionist cause was, at times, a very lonely one.

The majority of what I have cited from GS has focused on his strong warnings against slavery. In view of the weight of his abolitionist efforts, this is to be expected, however, we would fail to gain a balanced perspective of him if we ignored his exhortations to believers to walk in love in view of the foremost commandment. In his work, *The Law of Liberty,* he exposited the text of James 2:12 with an emphasis on the law of love as cited in James 2:8 "You shall love your neighbor as yourself":

..."if we love one another" (says *the beloved* Apostle) "*God dwelleth in us, and his Love is 'perfected in us'*" (1 John iv. 12) So that the two great Commandments appear to be reciprocally included and blended together in

---

[536] Obsolete form of envelop.

[537] Sharp, *The System of Colonial Law,* 9-10.

their consequences; by which we may more readily perceive the propriety of our Lord's declaration, that the *second great Commandment is like unto the first*; and this reciprocal connexion between them enables us also to comprehend the reason why *the second* is given *alone* (when both are undoubtedly necessary) as the grand test of Christian obedience, and as the sum and essence of the whole Law of God; *"For all the Law is fulfilled"* (says the Apostle Paul) *"in one word, (even) in this, Thou shalt love thy Neighbour as thyself."* (Gal. v. 14)... *"So speak ye, and so do,"* says the Apostle James) *"as they that shall be "judged by* the LAW OF LIBERTY." (James ii.12.) This title properly belongs, indeed, to the *whole Law*, or Gospel of Christ, and seems to be so applied by the same Apostle in the preceding chapter (25th verse) wherein he speaks of *"the perfect* LAW OF LIBERTY"[538]

Of course, his exposition on the foremost commandment of love in, *The Law of Liberty*, was presented as a corrective to slavery (which is entirely antithetical to Dabney's exposition of the same text), yet the above passage reveals GS's desire to see the Gospel of Christ heralded above all. His overall appeal was not only given to unbelievers, but to believers who had entered into error.[539] In the end, he wasn't merely an abolitionist *alone*, but he was a herald of Christ and His Gospel above all. As before stated, if the reader wishes to learn more about GS I would ask that you consult the more voluminous works noted at the beginning of this section.

I should remind the reader, once again, that the point of this section is not to exalt a mere mortal in an act of celebritism, as I condemned in the prior appendix. Instead, as stipulated in the seventh chapter, it is my goal to exalt the One who emancipated this man's soul and used him as an imperfect vessel of God's grace. The fact that he had a

---

[538] Granville Sharp, *The Law of Liberty, or Royal Law by which All Mankind will Certainly be Judged! Earnestly Recommended to the Serious Consideration of all Slaveholders and Slavedealers*, (London, 1776) 30.
[539] Ibid.

desire to magnify the Lord by means of honoring the holy Scriptures is a testament to the Lord's amazing grace in saving *any sinner*.

Finally, while few today know the name of Granville Sharp, I would rather suspect that this is how GS would have preferred it. Having taken the time to read his memoirs and research his life and work, I have come to the conclusion that the lack of knowledge of GS in the current day is a testament to his humility. He was a man who was solely focused on his duties and cared not for the praise of men. Though he was called upon to serve as the chairman of the Society for Effecting the Abolition of the Slave Trade whereby "he regularly attended every meeting of the Society, and signed as Chairman every paper that was handed to him, [but] he was never once seated in the chair during the long continuance of twenty years"[540] in which he served the Society. Thomas Clarkson

---

[540] The merits of Mr. Sharp's preparatory labours were justly appreciated by the Society. From the first hour that the Committee was formed, he was, by a general sentiment of the members, regarded as their Chairman, and was addressed as such on every occasion of their meeting. But he would never consent to take the chair, although repeatedly pressed to do so. It appeared, therefore, to the Committee, to be suitable to the dignity of their cause, and to their sense of his exalted character, that they should, by a public expression of their wishes, overrule this singularity of feeling; and, accordingly, in one of the following meetings, they drew up a Resolution, by which Granville Sharp was appointed Chairman of the Committee, as "father of the cause in England." But no external action could at any time make him swerve from a rule of conduct which he had once laid down for himself as right to be pursued. He felt warmly the honour of such a mark of respect, but he was no hypocrite in his wish to decline it. Although he felt that the office being assigned to him, he was bound by the resolution of the Committee to consider it as an object of his duty; and although, in consequence, he regularly (when in town) attended every meeting of the Society, and signed as Chairman every paper that was handed to him, he was never once seated in the chair during the long continuance of twenty years. Prince Hoare, *Memoirs of Granville Sharp: With Observations on Mr. Sharp's*

mentions that GS would even refrain "from coming into the room till after he knew it (the Chairman's seat) to be taken."[541] In the end, he simply wanted to be known as nothing more than a co-laborer with the other members of the Society, rather than be seen as someone who was ranked above them. There are other examples of such humility, but I share the above sample with the reader in order to herald and showcase the beauty of Christ's work of grace in a child of God. GS never married, but used his gifts and training with profound stewardship until the day of his passing on July 6th, 1813.

After his passing, many memorials were dedicated to his memory, including one from the African Institution which was founded in 1807. After a lengthy description of his lifelong achievements,[542] an interesting

---

biblical Criticisms by the r. r. the lord bishop of St. David's (Colburn), 7872-7891, Kindle.

[541] "...the modesty of Mr. Sharp was such that, though repeatedly pressed, he would never consent to take the chair; and he generally refrained from coming into the room till after he knew it to be taken. Nor could he be prevailed upon, even after this resolution, to alter his conduct: for though he continued to sign the papers, which were handed to him by virtue of holding this office, he never was once seated as the chairman, during the twenty years in which he attended at these meetings. I thought it not improper to mention this trait in his character. Conscious that he engaged in the cause of his fellow-creatures, solely upon the sense of his duty as a Christian, he seems to have supposed either that he had done nothing extraordinary to merit such a distinction, or to have been fearful lest the acceptance of it should bring a stain upon the motive, on which alone he undertook it. Clarkson, *The History of the Abolition of African Slave*, 144.

[542] "Sacred to the memory of Granville Sharp, ninth son of Dr. Thomas Sharp, Prebendary of the cathedrals and collegiate churches of York, Durham, and South Well, and grandson of Dr. John Sharp, Archbishop of York. Born and educated in the bosom of the church of England, he ever cherished for her institutions the most unshaken regard, while his whole soul was in harmony with the sacred strain, "glory to God in the highest, on earth peace and good will toward men," on which his life presented one beautiful comment of glowing piety

qualification was included in order to remind the reader that the eulogy they were reading was not an exaggeration in any measure:

> In his private relations he was equally exemplary; and having exhibited through life a model of disinterested virtue, he resigned his pious spirit into the hands of his Creator, in the exercise of charity, and faith, and hope, on the sixth day of July, A.D. MDCCCXIII., in the seventy eighth year of his age. Reader, if, on perusing this tribute to a private individual, though shouldest be disposed to suspect it as partial, or to censure it as diffuse know that it is not panegyric, but history. Erected by the African Institution of London, A.D. 1816.[543]

As already stated (on several occasions now), GS was nothing more than a vessel of God's grace; a mere mortal who needed Christ's redeeming love and emancipating power just like anyone else. Because of this, the value of examining the life of such an individual is that we would herald the majesty, dignity, and power of the Lord Jesus Christ above all; that we would know that everyone who is His by faith can say with the Apostle Paul, "For by grace you have been saved through faith; and that not of yourselves, it is the gift of God; not as a result of works, that no one should boast. For we are His workmanship, created in Christ Jesus for

---

and unwearied beneficence. Freed by competence from the necessity, and by content from the desire, of lucrative occupation, he was incessant in his labors to improve the condition of mankind, founding public happiness on public virtue. He aimed to rescue his native country from the guilt and inconsistency of employing the arm of freedom to rivet the fetters of bondage, and established for the Negro race, in the person of Somerset, the long-disputed rights of human nature. Having in this glorious cause triumphed over the combined resistance of interest, prejudice, and pride, he took his post among the foremost of the honourable band associated to deliver Africa from the rapacity of Europe, by the abolition of the slave trade. Nor was death permitted to interrupt his career of usefulness, till he had witnessed that act of the British Parliament by which the abolition was decreed." Hoare, *Memoirs*, 473.

[543] Ibid., 473.

good works, which God prepared beforehand, that we should walk in them." (Ephesians 2:8–10). Therefore, no matter what station of life we are in, we can serve the Lord in the strength of *His might* (Ephesians 6:10) and stand firm against the schemes of the devil (Ephesians 6:11) and resist him in the day of evil (Ephesians 6:13) as the spiritually armed soldiers of Christ (Ephesians 6:13-18) who live and serve for His ultimate glory.

Soli Deo Gloria

J E S U S'
J U S T I C E

APPENDIX IV
INTERPRETING THE
WHITE SPACES OF THE HISTORICAL RECORD

With all that we have reviewed concerning slavery, it is quite obvious that far more could be said about this important subject. And yet this book is not about the history of slavery, per se, but it has instead focused on the profound contrast between Jesus' justice and SJI. However, having surveyed aspects of the transatlantic slave trade, it seems necessary to add a word of caution about the interpretation of this period of history, especially when we try to discern the lives, beliefs, and actions of individuals. In the end, *we must avoid interpreting the white spaces of the historical record.* Clearly, there are many things that we don't know concerning the motives and intentions of those who were involved in 19th slavery, whether as participants or as abolitionists. This is largely due to our incomplete historical record from this period. Some individuals owned slaves without ever relenting of their choice, while others, like John Adams, refused to own any slaves throughout their lives. Some individuals resolved to free their slaves during their lifetime, while others did so posthumously. There are also the remarkable stories like that of Francis Barber, the slave of Samuel Johnson who has been called "the most distinguished man of letters in English history."[544] Barber became much more of a family member to Johnson, and through their bond of friendship the former slave became the trusted heir. Additionally, George Washington changed his views on slavery[545] towards the end of his life and therefore sought to free his slaves in his written will. Yet despite his wishes, those slaves whom Martha Washington inherited through a prior marriage could not be released by law. This is because, prior to the passage of the 13th Amendment in 1865, state laws varied on the question of emancipation. Because of this, emancipated slaves ran the risk of re-enslavement after their release. For example, the freed slaves from the Amistad had a difficult road before them not long after they were declared free by the US Supreme Court (1841). *First,* a group of individuals threatened to re-enslave and even kill the Amistad Africans before they would have a chance to return to their homeland.[546] *Second,* efforts to return the Amistad Africans were thwarted because of the ongoing tribal wars within their homeland that would have threatened their safety.[547] In the modern day, organizations like Christian Solidarity

---

[544] Rogers, Pat (2006), "Johnson, Samuel (1709–1784)", Oxford Dictionary of National Biography, Oxford Dictionary of National Biography (online ed.), Oxford University Press.

[545] "Throughout the 1780s and 1790s, Washington stated privately that he no longer wanted to be a slaveowner, that he did not want to buy and sell slaves or separate enslaved families, and that he supported a plan for gradual abolition in the United States." Mount Vernon, "Washington's Changing Views on Slavery" https://www.mountvernon.org/george-washington/slavery/washingtons-changing-views-on-slavery/.

[546] Marcus Rediker, *The Amistad Rebellion* (Penguin Publishing Group), 194, Kindle.

[547] "When news arrived from people knowledgeable about the Gallinas Coast that warfare might make it difficult for the "Mendi People" to find their way to their inland homes, the effect was demoralizing: "Nearly all of the Mendians became sad & became indifferent as to work or study," recalled A. F. Williams, who was helping to oversee their time in Farmington." Ibid., 212.

International (CSI) *buy slaves in order to secure their freedom.* In a world where most nations have outlawed slavery, this is a feasible task. However, in the 19th century world, which was transitioning from legalized slavery to abolition, the life of a released slave was often fraught with much uncertainty and potential danger.

I mention all of this in order to point out the need for restraint when seeking to adjudicate the circumstances and choices of those who lived through this era. In the modern day, we hear more and more debates about who owned slaves, who didn't, and how we should think about such facts of history. My particular choice of critiquing Thomas Jefferson and RL Dabney was rooted in the fact that their corrupted views of Africans were well documented and worthy of refutation. However, beyond such particular cases, there are many other historic situations in which we have little information. Based upon my readings, I have also wondered if the ethical choices of some were more along the lines of CSI: purchasing a slave, *not to own a slave,* but to secure the safety and security of a fellow human. While we can debate the ethics and veracity of such a choice (and such debate is certainly reasonable and welcomed), no one in their right mind can pretend that the choices of the modern American in any way compares with the complexities that existed during this tumultuous period. And for this reason, we must be careful not to exceed what is revealed in the written record *while refraining from interpreting the white spaces of history.*

JESUS′ JUSTICE

INDEX

www.ingramcontent.com/pod-product-compliance
Lightning Source LLC
Chambersburg PA
CBHW031944090426

42739CB00006B/75